Collective Rationality and Coll

Collective reasoning plays an important role in rational cooperation. This book examines that role, focusing on cooperation among people who have conflicting moral commitments. The first half shows how the two main aspects of cooperation within a group – the choice of a particular cooperative scheme to be implemented and the decision by each member to contribute to it – can be understood as guided by reason. The second half considers how reasoning itself can take a cooperative form and how, when it does, it can facilitate cooperation to achieve further goals. The book also sheds light on a number of related topics, including the place of deliberation in democratic decision making and the negotiation of the proper understanding of contested concepts.

Presenting a detailed analysis of the relation between rational cooperation and collective reasoning, this book will be of particular interest to philosophers of the social sciences and to students in political science, sociology, and economics concerned with contemporary debates in social and political theory.

". . . written in a beautifully lucid and economical style . . . tightly argued without being overly complicated by unnecessary detail. The organization of the material is excellent, enabling McMahon's systematic and comprehensive account of some very complex matters to emerge in a most natural and compelling fashion." E. J. Lowe, University of Durham

Christopher McMahon is Professor of Philosophy at the University of California, Santa Barbara.

Collective Rationality and Collective Reasoning

CHRISTOPHER MCMAHON

University of California, Santa Barbara

CAMBRIDGE
UNIVERSITY PRESS

PUBLISHED BY THE PRESS SYNDICATE OF THE UNIVERSITY OF CAMBRIDGE
The Pitt Building, Trumpington Street, Cambridge, United Kingdom

CAMBRIDGE UNIVERSITY PRESS
The Edinburgh Building, Cambridge CB2 2RU, UK
40 West 20th Street, New York, NY 10011-4211, USA
10 Stamford Road, Oakleigh, VIC 3166, Australia
Ruiz de Alarcón 13, 28014 Madrid, Spain
Dock House, The Waterfront, Cape Town 8001, South Africa

http://www.cambridge.org

First published 2001

Printed in the United States of America

Typeface Palatino 10/12 pt.   *System* DeskTopPro$_{/UX}$ [BV]

A catalog record for this book is available from the British Library.

Library of Congress Cataloging in Publication Data
McMahon, Christopher, 1945–
Collective rationality and collective reasoning / Christopher McMahon.
p. cm.
Includes bibliographical references and index.
ISBN 0-521-80462-0 – ISBN 0-521-01178-7 (pbk.)
1. Cooperativeness – Moral and ethical aspects. 2. Cooperation. 3. Reasoning. I. Title.
BJ1533.C74M39   2001
171'.2 – dc21

00-065986

ISBN 0 521 80462 0 hardback
ISBN 0 521 01178 7 paperback

For Kevin, Elizabeth, Ian, and Cory

Contents

Contents

Preface

In writing this book, I have tried to make the main text reasonably accessible to nonspecialist readers. Thus for the most part, the necessary positioning of the argument with respect to the work of other authors is relegated to the endnotes. Some of the notes, however, contain further elaborations of points made in the text that could be of interest to nonspecialists. A good strategy for such readers might be to check the discursive material in the notes for each chapter after finishing it.

I would like to thank two anonymous referees for their comments on the manuscript and my colleague Tony Brueckner for discussion of some points in Chapter 5. Parts of Chapter 1 are taken from my paper, "Collective Rationality" (*Philosophical Studies*, 98 [2000] 321–344, copyright 2000 Kluwer Academic Publishers), with kind permission from Kluwer Academic Publishers. Work on this book was supported by a sabbatical quarter from the University of California, Santa Barbara.

Introduction

This book examines a set of interrelated issues connected with rational cooperation, especially cooperation among people who have conflicting moral commitments. I begin by considering how cooperation can be guided by reason. Then I explore how the activity of reasoning itself can take a cooperative form.

As I view rational cooperation, it has two parts. There are two respects in which cooperation can be, or fail to be, guided by reason. One concerns whether an individual has sufficient reason to contribute voluntarily to a cooperative enterprise; the other, whether the members of a group of cooperatively disposed people can regard the choice of a particular cooperative scheme – which assigns contributions – as adequately justified. The first half of the book provides a general account of these two aspects of rational cooperation and explores their political interpretation.

The second half of the book focuses on collective reasoning. Collective reasoning is treated as a form of mutually beneficial cooperation. Thus it, too, presents issues relating to the reason to contribute and the choice of cooperative schemes. The examination of these issues is, however, postponed until the final chapter. The bulk of the discussion of collective reasoning is concerned with how the cooperative product should be understood. That is, if collective reasoning is a form of mutually beneficial cooperation, what exactly do individuals engaged in it produce, and how do they benefit from what they have produced? Philosophically, these are the most interesting questions that arise in connection with the phenomenon of collective reasoning, and the first three chapters of the second half of the book are devoted to answering them.

The book begins in Chapter 1 with an account of the reason to contribute. I do not attempt to show that free riders are irrational. Rather, I assume that individual agents sometimes have sufficient reason to participate in cooperative enterprises, and focus on how this reason is best formulated. I conclude that it should not be understood as grounded in a substantive moral principle, such as the so-called principle of fairness. When agents have self-interested reasons for defecting from a cooperative scheme, a moral reason for contributing, like that provided by the principle of fairness, can almost always prevail. But this approach is less satisfactory when agents have moral reasons for defecting. In such cases, any moral reason justifying contribution must compete with other moral reasons that support a different course, and we cannot assume that the conflict will usually be resolved in favor of cooperation. I argue that this problem can be avoided if we understand the requirement to contribute to cooperative schemes differently. Instead of grounding it in a particular substantive moral reason, we should view it as based on a formal principle that I call the *Principle of Collective Rationality* (PCR). The fundamental idea is that agents should treat prisoner's dilemma situations as if they presented ordinary coordination problems.

The issues addressed in Chapter 1 have been studied by game theorists, but the treatment I offer is nontechnical. Basically, it explores "moral" solutions to the problem of securing cooperation when individuals could better promote their values by acting as free riders. Such solutions do not rely on the threat of punishment to secure compliance. Rather, they posit certain reasons for action acceptance of which, by the members of a group, will lead to cooperative behavior. I criticize the most widely discussed solution of this sort, provided by the principle of fairness, and propose an alternative.

Chapter 2 explores a number of phenomena connected with the second aspect of rational cooperation, the choice of a cooperative scheme. The PCR creates a framework within which the choice of a cooperative scheme can take place. Usually several different schemes will be jointly feasible for the members of a cooperatively disposed group, in the sense that the PCR would give each a reason to make his assigned contribution to any of them. Cooperation cannot proceed until one of these is chosen to serve as its basis. On the view I present, the substantive or procedural values held by the members of a group determine whether they can regard the choice of a scheme as appropriate. A group of cooperatively disposed people that has made the choice of a cooperative scheme, or of a procedure for selecting schemes, is a collective agent. The phenomenon of independent contribution, in which cooperatively disposed people separately decide what their contributions to a cooperative undertaking will be, is also examined. The remainder of the chapter provides accounts of collective responsibility, collective intention, authority, and promising.

Chapters 3 and 4 consider the political dimension of the two aspects of rational cooperation identified in the initial chapters. Chapter 3 explores some issues in political philosophy concerning when an individual has sufficient reason to contribute to a cooperative scheme – basically, issues connected with the requirement to obey the law. Chapter 4 discusses democracy as a particular mechanism by which a group can choose among cooperative schemes. Special attention is paid to the role of deliberation in democratic decision making. This provides a transition to the topic of collective reasoning.

An important theme throughout the book is the way moral commitments can be distorted in cooperative contexts – or alternatively, can undermine rational cooperation if they are not distorted. I argue that the PCR prevents problems of this sort from arising in connection with the first aspect of rational cooperation (contribution to a cooperative scheme). But if, as I suggest, procedural or substantive values provide the basis on which the members of a group can regard the choice of a scheme as guided by reason, the distortion of commitments constitutes a serious problem for the second aspect of rational cooperation. The principal moral virtue of a cooperative scheme is fairness. It is primarily because a scheme fairly resolves competing claims, or has been chosen by a fair procedure, that the members of a group can regard it as appropriately chosen. But in adjudicating competing claims, the value of fairness demotes them to interests, to considerations the satisfaction of which is important primarily as satisfying those advancing them. And if this is resisted on the ground that evaluative commitments are to be sharply distinguished from interests, it may not be possible to regard the choice of a cooperative scheme as guided by reason. These problems arise with special force in political contexts.

The discussion of collective reasoning in the second half of the book focuses primarily on the practical case. Of course, reasoning collectively about matters of fact is widespread, but collective reasoning about practical matters is especially germane to rational cooperation. It opens up the possibility that a group of cooperatively disposed people could reason their way to the choice of a cooperative scheme.

The first issue that I discuss concerning collective reasoning is not, however, restricted to the practical case. In Chapter 5, I consider in a general way how, if collective reasoning is viewed as a form of cooperation, the cooperative product should be understood. I argue against taking it to be a collective judgment concerning what the relevant reasons support. Rather, the cooperative product should be understood as a common pool of reasons and arguments on the basis of which each participant can make up his or her own mind about the question being addressed. That is, collective reasoning involves cooperation to create a common resource on which each can draw, as seems appropriate, to form an *individual* judgment. This means that the members of a group can benefit from collective reasoning even if they do not reach agreement, although in some cases agreement will be necessary if a further cooperative goal is to be attained. The final section of the chapter considers how the phenomenon of the "negotiation" of the proper use of concepts, especially newly introduced concepts, is to be understood. I argue that it is best seen as a form of collective reasoning (in contrast to a struggle between people or groups possessing varying amounts of social power).

Collective reasoning is typically prompted by disagreement, but at least in the practical case, disagreement within a group is open to two different interpretations. One possibility is that it indicates that someone is malfunctioning in assessing the force of a particular set of reasons germane to the question being considered. In this case, collective reasoning can be understood as a way of eliminating, or at least reducing, the malfunction. This alternative is examined in Chapter 6. Among the topics discussed is whether collective reasoning of this sort might play a role in the characterization of the true requirements of morality. The moral theories of Jürgen Habermas and T. M. Scanlon are explored in detail.

The other possibility is that the initial disagreement does not reflect cognitive malfunction, because the parties legitimately hold different values. In such a case, they might simply agree to disagree. But they will not find this posture satisfactory if they are in a situation where they could realize some further benefit by cooperating, but must first decide upon a cooperative scheme. This raises the question whether a group that disagrees without malfunction could generate the choice of a cooperative scheme by a process of collective reasoning – whether there is a process of reasoning that could take the members from their initially disparate starting points to agreement on a scheme. I explore this issue in Chapter 7, focusing on the capacity of collective reasoning to combine different conceptual perspectives, including those posited by postmodern theories, and on its capacity to transform the reasons it works with, thereby reducing conflicts among them.

Having discussed in these three chapters how the members of a group can benefit from collective reasoning – how collective reasoning can produce something that benefits each member of a group – I conclude in Chapter 8 by considering the place in collective reasoning of the two aspects of rational cooperation distinguished in the earlier chapters. This case presents some unusual features. First, the explicit choice of a cooperative scheme has reduced importance because it is not possible to assign contributions to each member. What each contributes will depend on the thoughts provoked as collective reasoning unfolds. Nevertheless, I suggest that a group engaged in collective reasoning can be seen as facing a choice among different ways of proceeding. The second unusual feature of collective reasoning, viewed as a form of mutually beneficial cooperation, is that people often do not regard contributing to a process of collective reasoning as a burden. They are eager to contribute. Moreover, those who do not contribute are not usually labeled as free riders – as getting the benefits without doing any work. Indeed, the principal vice of collective reasoning is hogging the discussion. I explore, and attempt to explain, this peculiarity.

One final point should be mentioned. This book undertakes to treat together, in a relatively short space, the topics of collective rationality and collective reasoning. One of its principal objectives is to reveal the connections between them – to show how collective reasoning can play a role in rational cooperation and how it can, in turn, be regarded as a form of rational cooperation. To this end, the argument of the book traces the implications of a few principal themes concerning collective rationality and collective reasoning for a variety of issues in moral, social, and political philosophy. Much more could be said about many of these issues, and indeed about the topics of collective rationality and collective reasoning, than I say here. But I believe that the relatively economical approach I have taken is justified as keeping the larger themes in focus.

Chapter 1

The Reason to Contribute

Cooperation is central to the flourishing of groups, communities, and societies – that is, to the flourishing of socially situated human beings. When we think about how our actions or omissions contribute to the attainment of what we value, we cannot restrict ourselves to their effects considered as individual events. We also need to take into account the effects of combinations of actions or omissions. We must not, however, lose sight of the fact that such combinations are aggregates of individual actions. Thus, whatever reason there may be for a group to produce a combination of actions must ultimately be reduced to a reason for the individual members of the group to perform the component actions. Let us call a combination of actions that each of the members of a group can regard as effecting an improvement in the realization of his or her values a *cooperative scheme* (within that group). In this chapter, I formulate and defend a principle that determines when individuals have sufficient reason to contribute to a cooperative scheme.

I. RATIONALITY

I call this principle the *Principle of Collective Rationality (PCR)*. My intention is to contrast collective rationality with individual rationality. The difference between them lies in how a conclusion about what to do is derived from the substantive values that a given agent accepts. What I mean by this should become clear as the exposition proceeds, but a few general remarks about practical rationality may help to set the stage.

Although rationality admits of a privative construal, on which it means the mere absence of irrationality, here I understand it positively, as doing what there is the best reason for one to do.[1] I offer an account of what there is the best reason for an individual to do in cooperative contexts. It treats agents as choosing among candidate actions on the basis of the outcomes with which they are correlated. This device also plays a role in utility theory, which views rationality as the maximization of expected utility. That theory can be understood either descriptively, as generating predictions concerning how agents will behave, or normatively, as formulating an ideal by reference to which the behavior or reasoning of agents can be criticized.[2] Utility theory presents certain problems, however. It imposes conditions on the preferences of agents, such as transitivity, that are often not satisfied when the content of preferences is read straightforwardly. And although satisfaction of these conditions can be achieved by reinterpreting preferences, this raises questions about the explanatory and justificatory adequacy of the theory.[3] The account that I offer of what there is the best reason for an agent to do in cooperative contexts avoids these problems. It shares with utility theory only the idea that what there is the best reason to do is determined by the value (from the agent's point of view) of the outcomes correlated with the available actions. The key to my account is a distinction between two different ways of correlating actions with outcomes.

The first of these is associated with a principle that I call the *Principle of Individual Rationality* (PIR). This correlates each action with the outcome it will produce, where production is understood to encompass any way an action can make a difference to the world. Thus, the appearance of an action in the world is a part of its outcome. But the value of an outcome for an agent is not determined by her preferences. Agents are regarded as holding *principles of value* that establish the desirability of the available outcomes. That is, value is determined by principles that constitute certain features of outcomes as *reasons* for producing them (or in the case of negative values, avoiding them). Since an action is part of its outcome, this approach is capable of accommodating both consequentialist and deontological moral theories. The PIR directs an agent to perform the action that will produce the most desirable outcome, given her principles of value. Utility theory presupposes a ranking of possible outcomes that is complete and transitive, but I do not assume that an individual's principles of value generate a ranking that satisfies these conditions. Thus, my account is compatible with evaluative incommensurabilities.

The PIR is adequate for most purposes, but it has unwelcome consequences in cooperative contexts, where an agent must choose whether to contribute to a cooperative scheme. In an important class of cases, the PIR dictates declining to contribute. So when all or most of the agents in cases of this sort act as the PIR directs, they lose the benefits of cooperation.

The PCR is designed to avoid this result. Like the PIR, it presupposes a set of possible outcomes and directs an agent to perform the action correlated with the outcome that has the greatest value (given his principles of value). But it correlates actions with outcomes in a different way. When an agent faces a choice whether to contribute to a cooperative scheme, the PIR directs him to compare the value of the outcomes produced by two different actions, contributing and declining to contribute, considered as individual events. The PCR, by contrast, directs him to compare the value of the outcomes produced by two different *combinations* of actions, of which contributing and declining to contribute constitute parts.

It should be stressed that the PCR does not give agents a reason to cooperate by giving them a new principle of value in light of which the act of contributing to a cooperative scheme can be seen as producing a more valuable outcome than the act of declining to contribute (defecting). Outcomes are evaluated using the same principles of value that are employed in conjunction with the PIR. The fact that the PCR operates on a given set of substantive values, rather than itself identifying a substantive value, is one reason that I term it a principle of rationality.

In speaking this way, however, I do not mean to suggest that the PCR should be regarded as displacing the standard utility maximizing conception of practical rationality. Acceptance of the PCR can be modeled within standard utility theory, as the possession of a certain sort of complex preference. Also, I do not claim that agents who fail to acknowledge the reason to contribute to cooperative schemes that is formulated by the PCR are irrational in some absolute sense. Rather, the PCR is offered as the best way of characterizing the dispositions of people who are, as a matter of fact, prepared to behave cooperatively. I elaborate on these points in Sections III and VI.

In the remainder of this chapter I describe the problem that the PCR is meant to address and defend this principle as the best solution to it. Initially, I shall assume the commensurability of an agent's substantive values. Incommensurability will be discussed in Section VII. Also, in developing the distinction between individual an collective rationality, I shall assume that the outcomes of individual actions, and of combinations of actions, are certain. Risk or uncertainty can be accommodated by supposing that each action, or combination, is correlated with a set of possible outcomes, and that there is some basis, subjective or objective, on which agents can assign probabilities to the members of these sets.

II. TWO KINDS OF COOPERATION

Elementary game theory provides some models of cooperation that can be used to introduce the problem the PCR is meant to solve. The first is a coordination problem. Perhaps the simplest example is that in which two individuals want to meet and do not care where they meet. Let us suppose there are two possible meeting places, the courthouse and the pier. If both go to either the courthouse or the pier, each will regard the outcome as more desirable than the outcome that would have obtained had one of them gone to the courthouse and the other to the pier. The following matrix illustrates this situation. The numbers indicate the value that each attaches to the outcomes of the four possible combinations.[4] A's payoffs are on the left, B's on the right.

		B	
		Courthouse	Pier
A	Courthouse	1,1	0,0
	Pier	0,0	1,1

Figure 1.1 Coordination Problem.

In a coordination problem, each of the cooperative combinations is a *Nash equilibrium*. A Nash equilibrium is a combination such that no party wishes she had acted differently given how the others have acted.[5] The cooperative combinations are also *coordination equilibria*, in that they have the additional feature that no one wishes anyone *else* had acted differently, given how she has acted. But for our purposes, it is enough that each of the cooperative combinations is a Nash equilibrium. This has the consequence that when the members of a group face a coordination problem, cooperation is supported by the PIR. The PIR does not justify defection from any of the cooperative outcomes, once achieved. And it justifies each in doing her part to create a cooperative outcome, if she has sufficient reason to believe that the other party will do likewise.

As the last point reveals, achieving cooperation in a situation displaying a coordination problem is not automatic for agents who accept the PIR. One of the equilibria must be such that each has sufficient reason to suppose that the other will do her part in realizing it. This means that cooperation presupposes the solution of an *assurance problem*. Another kind of coordination problem, known as an assurance game, provides a further illustration of this point.[6]

		B	
		Courthouse	Pier
A	Courthouse	4,4	−1,1
	Pier	1,−1	2,2

Figure 1.2 Assurance Game.

This matrix can be interpreted as follows. The parties prefer to meet at the courthouse, because it is closer to their places of work. But the courthouse is an ugly building, while the pier is beautiful. So if there is going to be a failure of coordination – if each is going to be waiting in vain for the other – each wants to be the one who goes to the pier. The important point, however, is that while both prefer one of the cooperative combinations to the other, an assurance problem must still be solved if they are to realize it. And given that each prefers not to wait alone at the most convenient meeting place, the requisite assurances may have to be relatively strong.

The second model of rational cooperation that we need to consider is the well-known prisoner's dilemma. It is illustrated by the following matrix.

		B	
		Cooperate	Defect
A	Cooperate	7,7	$^{-}$5,9
	Defect	9,$^{-}$5	0,0

Figure 1.3 Prisoner's Dilemma.

Here, two of the possible combinations have the feature that for one of the parties, the outcome is the best possible, while for the other it is the worst. Of the remaining two, one is preferred by both to the other. This jointly preferred combination is the one that, intuitively, counts as cooperative. The combination that each places third in desirability is worse for both, and in the remaining two combinations, one of the parties would prefer any of the other three possibilities.

In prisoner's dilemma situations, agents guided by the PIR cannot achieve cooperation, even when each has good reason to believe that the other will behave cooperatively. If A has reason to believe that B will do his part in realizing the cooperative combination – that he will make what we may call a "cooperative move" – the rational course for her is to behave uncooperatively (to defect). In prisoner's dilemma situations, the cooperative combination is not a Nash equilibrium. And if A has good reason to believe that B will *not* do his part, once again the rational course for her is to behave uncooperatively. Thus, whatever assumption each of the parties makes about the behavior of the other, the result of adherence by both to the dictates of the PIR will be the realization of the combination that each ranks third – which means failure to achieve the benefits of cooperation.

Two further points should be noted here. First, this result is robust. It does not matter what probability each assigns to a cooperative move by the other. For any hypothesis that each forms about the likelihood of cooperation by the other, the rational course will be noncooperation. In the language of game theory, behaving uncooperatively in a prisoner's dilemma game is a *dominant* strategy, and the result of the adoption of this strategy by both parties is a *dominant strategy equilibrium*. Second, the outcome that results from rational action by each is such that there is another outcome that both would judge to be better. That is, there is an outcome that is strongly Pareto superior to it.[7]

In prisoner's dilemma situations, action in accordance with the PIR results in each getting less of what he values than he could get if both behaved "irrationally" – if each failed to do what, according to the PIR, he has most reason to do. This result has an air of paradox since intuitively, the rational action in a situation is that which will bring an agent the most of what he values. But in prisoner's dilemma situations, where what each party gets is affected not only by what he does but also by what the other does, rational action, as understood by the PIR, seems to lack this feature.

We should also consider a third kind of two-person game, which in certain respects stands between a coordination game and the prisoner's dilemma. This is the game of chicken.[8] A chicken game resembles the prisoner's dilemma in that each ranks highest the outcome in which he defects while the other makes a cooperative move, and ranks general cooperation second. The difference is that each prefers the outcome in which he alone makes a cooperative move to general noncooperation. This reflects the fact that each regards what he can accomplish by performing a cooperative move alone as desirable enough to outweigh the cost. The result is that each will "chicken out" and bear the costs of cooperation if he believes the other is not going to make a cooperative move. Each party ranks general cooperation higher than unilaterally making a cooperative move because when there is general cooperation, a greater benefit results, or costs to each are reduced, or both. But it remains the case that the net gain to each is highest if the other performs a cooperative move alone. In a chicken game, action in accordance with the PIR can lead to the production of at least a certain amount of the cooperative benefit. But it can also lead to the noncooperative outcome, since it is rational in light of the PIR to precommit to noncooperation, thereby shifting the burden to the other party, and if both do this, the least desirable outcome of general defection will result. It should also be noted that adherence to the PIR will lead to the second-ranked outcome of general cooperation only if each supposes falsely that the other will not contribute. The following matrix illustrates a chicken game.

		B	
		Cooperate	Defect
A	Cooperate	7,7	5,9
	Defect	9,5	0,0

Figure 1.4 Chicken Game.

In real life, two-person games are uncommon. But there are multi-person cases displaying the same structure as the prisoner's dilemma, and there are also multiperson cases having the form of coordination problems and chicken games.[9] Many of these cases involve the production of public goods – goods that display the features of indivisibility and nonexcludability.[10] Nonexcludability makes it possible to be a free rider, to receive the benefits of the cooperative efforts of others without contributing oneself, and the PIR often supports this. But if many behave in this way, the result will be suboptimal.

It is useful in discussing multiperson cases to distinguish two kinds of cooperatively producible goods that might be brought about by a combination of actions.[11] The first are *incremental goods*. An incremental good has the feature that each contribution to its production increases its value for every group member by a small amount. For the production of such goods, the key question is how this incremental gain relates to the cost of contribution. If the incremental increase in the value of the good that an act of contribution will produce is greater than the cost to the contributor, making the contribution will be rational under the PIR. The task of producing the good within the group will lack the paradoxical features of the prisoner's dilemma. But in the usual case, the cost of contribution exceeds the incremental increase in value that will result. Suppose, for example, that cars in the Los Angeles basin are not equipped with pollution-control devices, and the good at issue is the reduction of air pollution. And suppose further that each car owner's installation of such equipment would cost $200. The incremental reduction in pollution that each act of installation would produce, and thus the benefit that each owner would receive as a direct result of her action, would be so small as to be undetectable – and would thus be exceeded by the cost of contribution.

In cases of this sort, contribution is not dictated by the PIR. Rather, it is rational to act as a free rider on the contributions of others. Yet if all act this way, the result will be the loss of a benefit that each might judge to be worth the cost of her contribution. It is plausible that most residents of Los Angeles would judge the reduction in pollution resulting from the general installation of pollution-control equipment to be worth the expenditure of $200 (amortized over several years). For the normal case in which, over the whole progression from zero to full participation, the cost to each contributor of making a contribution exceeds the incremental benefit produced, this situation resembles the prisoner's dilemma. If each performs a certain "irrational" act, each will be better off than if none do.

The multiperson analogue of a coordination problem, by contrast, involves the production of *step goods*. Here the good in question does not grow incrementally with each contribution. Contributions have no effect until a certain threshold number of them have been made, at which point the good in question comes into existence. An example of a step good is a bridge. The efforts to construct it produce none of the good of facilitating movement in an area until the last piece has been put in place.

The simplest case of producing a step good is a strict multiperson coordination problem. All the members of a large group must coordinate their actions in a certain way to produce something that each regards as valuable. If any fail to do so, no one gets any of the benefit at issue. An illustration is provided by a hunting expedition that works by surrounding and converging on an animal. If any member fails to do his part, there will be a breach in the perimeter and the animal will escape.[12] Of course, here we are assuming that the benefit each will derive from the production of the cooperative outcome exceeds the cost to him of his contribution.

The most common cases of this sort, however, are not so simple. The crossing of the threshold requires that some but not all of the members of the group display cooperative behavior. Jean Hampton has provided an ingenious analysis of such cases that reveals that, in principle at least, the PIR can underwrite the requisite cooperation.[13] If the conditions Hampton specifies can always be satisfied, it is only in connection with the production of incremental goods that compliance with the PIR will create difficulties. It is worth noting, however, that Hampton's solution for step goods is rather complicated and may seldom be realizable in practice.

Finally, multiperson chicken games are also a possibility. These can be understood as multiperson cases where it is rational to precommit to noncontribution, yet there is a danger that if too many do this, the result will be suboptimal.[14] Step goods that can be produced by a proper subset of all potential contributors may display this structure.

III. THE PROBLEM

We can now formulate the problem we will be addressing. The PIR seems to direct defection from mutually beneficial cooperative schemes designed to produce incremental goods. Further, while there may, in theory, be a way that agents who accept the PIR can produce step goods, the procedure will probably be impractical in many cases. And if the members of a group treat the production of a step good as a chicken game, there is a significant risk of an outcome that is Pareto inferior to general cooperation.

Many people have been dissatisfied with these results, and have attempted to provide arguments that justify contributing in such cases. It seems likely, however, that we are here confronted with a typical skeptical problem. Such problems arise when we have some belief that virtually everyone is unwilling to give up and also a compelling argument that acceptance of that belief is unjustified. The characteristic response is an attempt to rebut the argument. But these responses are rarely completely successful, and thus we are left with a set of more or less permanently beguiling philosophical problems. Familiar examples include skepticism regarding knowledge of the external world or, closer to our concerns here, the egoistic skepticism about morality that finds expression in the question, "Why be moral?" Skepticism about the rationality of contributing to a mutually beneficial cooperative scheme when one could better promote one's values by acting as a free rider should, I think, be added to this list. None of the existing attempts to rebut the skeptical challenge has gained general acceptance, and it is doubtful that any ever will.[15]

One these attempts in particular deserves discussion. Cooperation displaying the structure of the prisoner's dilemma often takes place in contexts where those who could benefit from it will be in the same situation again. This means that people who act uncooperatively at a given point can be punished by being denied the benefits of cooperation in the future. If cooperation is "open-ended" – if there is no definite point of termination – and the parties do not discount the future too sharply, it will no longer be the case that the PIR dictates defection. What is gained by defecting at a given point is outweighed by what is lost through the denial of future cooperative benefits.

It is not, however, realistic to suppose that defection can always be punished by exclusion from future benefits. In the first place, while they may not be typical, there can be "one shot" cooperative enterprises that each potential participant understands will not be repeated. Second, in the real world, one can often defect without being detected. In large cooperative endeavors that produce incremental public goods from relatively private contributions, there may be no way to determine whether a given individual has contributed or not. And finally, even when defection can be detected, the remaining cooperators may find carrying out the threat to punish defection too costly. This is especially likely when they would have to suspend cooperation – thus denying themselves its benefits – in order to punish a defector by denying her its benefits.[16]

Pointing to the repetitious nature of many cooperative enterprises is not, then, enough to solve our problem, and it is unlikely that any other strategy that operates within the framework of the PIR will be completely successful either. But comparison with the other branches of philosophy suggests that progress can be made even without an argument that defeats the skeptical challenge. Normative moral theory provides the best example. This enterprise sets the question "Why be moral?" to one side and concentrates on how the requirements of morality, which it assumes to have a legitimate place in our lives, are best understood. Its method is the method of reflective equilibrium. As characterized by Norman Daniels, the "wide" form of this method involves identifying at least two kinds of justificatory elements: considered judgments in which we have a high degree of confidence and general theoretical considerations that are germane to the issue being decided.[17] We then attempt to determine which moral principles these elements, taken as a whole, require. Daniels argues that if the theoretical considerations are independent of the considered judgments, the method of wide reflective equilibrium is not simply descriptive, but possesses normative force. For those who accept its "premises," it identifies genuine moral requirements.

An example from Daniels shows that the method of wide reflective equilibrium need not employ the Rawlsian device of choice in the Original Position.[18] He suggests that we could use this method to decide between classical and nonclassical logics for a given region of discourse. In this case, we have considered judgments of the validity of various inferences and general theoretical considerations, pertaining (as in the work of Michael Dummett, whose view Daniels discusses) to such matters as the possibility of learning a language. Since the decision concerning which principles to accept is constrained independently from two directions, the method accomplishes something more than a mere codification of intuitions.

We can take a similar approach to mutually beneficial cooperation. Many people contribute to cooperative schemes even when they could do better as free riders, and presumably they feel confident that contributing is, in some way or other, in accordance with reason. For these people, the important question is not whether they should contribute, but exactly how the requirement to contribute is to be understood. We can use the method of wide reflective equilibrium to answer this question.

The main contemporary proposals regarding the requirement to contribute to a mutually beneficial cooperative scheme invoke principles that identify substantive moral considerations supporting this action. The most familiar is the principle of fairness. I believe, however, that cooperative dispositions are not best modeled in this fashion. Rather, as I have said, they should be seen as grounded in a formal principle that connects actions with valued outcomes in a way different from the way the PIR connects them.

It should be emphasized, as was mentioned earlier, that the argument that follows does not attempt to show that free riders are irrational. We are *assuming* that there is sometimes sufficient reason to contribute to cooperative schemes even when one could benefit as a free rider, and considering how this reason is best formulated.

IV. RATIONAL COOPERATION AND FAIRNESS

The skeptical challenge to mutually beneficial cooperation arises because the PIR often directs agents not to contribute to cooperative schemes. In particular, it does this in situations having the form of a multiperson prisoner's dilemma. In such situations, making one's assigned contribution typically produces only a tiny increase in the value of the world from one's own standpoint, and one can do better by using the resources in question in some other way.

Most people who are prepared to contribute to mutually beneficial cooperative schemes probably take themselves to be acting on reasons of fairness. They think that failing to behave cooperatively would be unfair. This fact is reflected in the most widely accepted account of the reason to contribute, the principle of fairness. This states that if one has voluntarily accepted the benefits of a fair cooperative scheme, one has a prima facie moral obligation to make one's assigned contribution.[19]

The principle of fairness is what I have called a principle of value. It identifies a substantive moral value that supports contributing to mutually beneficial cooperative schemes. Other principles sometimes invoked for this purpose include the natural duty of justice and the principle of consent or promising. Approaches to the justification of cooperation that employ substantive moral principles operate within the framework of *individual* rationality. From the standpoint of the PIR, one decides whether to contribute to a cooperative scheme by comparing the difference that one can make to the value of the world (as one understands this) by doing so with the difference that one can make by using in some other way the resources at issue. Substantive moral principles that justify cooperation work by assigning negative moral value to noncontribution, in the expectation that this will tip the balance against it.

I do not dispute that the moral value of fairness plays a central role in our thinking about cooperation. But I believe that the requirement (which we are assuming to exist) to participate in at least some cooperative schemes when one could benefit by riding free is not best understood as a requirement to promote the value of fairness as the PIR directs.

I have suggested that we employ the method of wide reflective equilibrium to identify the practical requirement underlying the dispositions of cooperatively disposed people. This method involves, in part, bringing to bear general theoretical considerations that seem relevant. In the present context, the main such consideration involves the notion of Pareto optimality. An outcome is Pareto optimal within a particular group if and only if there is no alternative outcome in which at least one member is better off (the sense of finding her values more fully realized) and none is worse off. The inadequacy of the PIR as a basis for cooperative action consists primarily in the fact that general compliance with its dictates often results in a suboptimal outcome. This yields a condition that must be satisfied by any purported formulation of the requirement to contribute to cooperative schemes. General acceptance of this requirement by the members of a group should not threaten their achievement of Pareto optimal outcomes. I shall argue that promoting the value of fairness in accordance with the PIR can run afoul of this condition.

Promoting the value of fairness in accordance with the PIR is normally sufficient to secure contribution when the reasons for declining to contribute are nonmoral. For example, an agent whose reason for declining is that contributing would be personally costly to her will usually find that the value of fairness trumps such self-regarding concerns. But an agent may also have *moral* reasons for declining to contribute to a cooperative scheme. The moral gains (in light of her values) that she could realize by using in some other way the resources she is called upon to contribute may outweigh the resulting incremental loss in whatever moral benefit she regards the scheme as producing. When this happens, any special moral reason, such as the obligation of fairness, that supports contributing must compete with other moral reasons that support the opposite course, and it may be defeated by them. That is, an individual may judge that there is sufficient moral reason for her to act as a free rider on some cooperative scheme because the moral good that she could do by using in another way the resources she is called upon to contribute outweighs not only the incremental moral loss that her defection from the scheme will produce, but also the obligation of fairness to contribute.

This is especially plausible if we suppose that the strength of the obligation of fairness is a function of the actual unfairness that would be brought into the world by noncontribution. The unfairness that results when one (additional) individual defects from a cooperative scheme in a large group is not, as unfairness goes, very great. Consider the unfairness displayed by an urban resident who saves money by disconnecting the pollution-control equipment on his car, thus acting as a free rider on the pollution-controlling efforts of other car owners (numbering several million). And compare this with the unfairness displayed by parents who decide to fund higher education for their sons but not their daughters.[20]

17

It may be useful to express these points in a formula. Let C be the incremental gain in moral value (from an agent's point of view) that results from his contribution to a cooperative scheme. Let D be the gain in moral value (again, from his own point of view) that he could produce by defecting, and let U be the incremental increase in the unfairness of the world associated with that defection. An agent guided by the PIR has sufficient reason to contribute if $C > (D-U)$, and sufficient reason to defect if $C < (D-U)$. But C will usually be tiny. So if $(D-U)$ is positive – as it could easily be, especially if, as I have suggested, U is not very great – the PIR will often dictate defection even though the agent accepts the principle of fairness.

This has the consequence, however, that general adherence to the principle of fairness will not always be able to prevent suboptimal outcomes, where optimality is now understood by reference to the moral values held by the members of the group. That is, an outcome is suboptimal within a group if there is at least one feasible alternative that some group member would judge to be *morally* preferable and none would judge to be *morally* worse (and it is "strongly" suboptimal if there is an alternative that all would judge to be preferable). If enough members of a group that has adopted a cooperative scheme find the moral case for defection stronger than the case for contributing – find that $C < (D-U)$ – and act accordingly, the result could be a state of affairs that each judges to be worse, from the standpoint of her moral values, than the state of affairs that would have obtained had all made their assigned contributions. Each defector may deem the reduction, resulting from the aggregate defections, in the moral value brought into the world by the cooperative scheme to outweigh the gain these defections produce. The likelihood of this is increased to the extent that the members hold different principles of value (other than the principle of fairness), or give them different weight, so that each regards the others as accomplishing little by defecting. In a situation of this sort, there will be an alternative pattern of actions that makes some better off, in light of their moral values, without making others worse off – indeed, a pattern that makes all better off – namely, that in which the defectors all contribute.

I do not claim that the problem I have described would be widespread. When the contributions required by a given cooperative scheme are modest, or the scheme is of short duration, it is unlikely that defection for moral reasons will pose a serious problem. But the case is different when we consider the political cooperation required to maintain a state. This involves obeying the law, and many people will have moral reasons for disobeying certain laws. The argument I have given suggests, then, that if political cooperation has a rational basis, it cannot be provided by a substantive moral value like fairness or justice. I discuss the political case further in Chapter 3. For present purposes, it is enough that there is a theoretical problem concerning the principle of fairness. There can be circumstances in which the theory of cooperative rationality that we get by combining considerations of fairness with the PIR would fail to underwrite cooperative behavior that is, intuitively, required. If we assume moral pluralism – if we suppose that people hold different moral values, or give them different weights – we can imagine situations in which the members of a group will confront the same kinds of collective-action problems that are found when agents are guided solely by self-regarding considerations. And introducing fairness just throws an additional moral value into the mix; it does not change the fundamental structure of the situation.

It has been suggested to me that the solution to this difficulty is straightforward. We wish to describe the requirement underlying the dispositions of cooperatively disposed people, which include a disposition to cooperate even when they have moral reasons for defecting. We can do this, without abandoning the principle of fairness, by simply supposing that the sense of fairness of cooperatively disposed people is such that they always judge defecting to have whatever degree of unfairness would be required to outweigh any moral reasons that might support it.

But this proposal is clearly inadequate. We cannot just stipulate that considerations of fairness are always strong enough to prevail. Unfairness supervenes on other features of situations, and any change in the degree of unfairness displayed by actions of a certain kind must be appropriately correlated with changes in these features. One relevant feature is the size of the cooperating group. Other things being equal, defection seems to bring less unfairness into the world the larger the group of cooperators, perhaps because it inflicts a smaller loss on each of the cooperators. But the strength of any moral reasons for defecting will be independent of the size of the cooperating group. In particular, members of large groups could have strong moral reasons for defecting. It might be replied that the unfairness of defection is also determined by the gain, in terms of the realization of her values, that an agent achieves by defecting – so that the stronger the moral reason for defecting, the stronger the reason of fairness against it. But the unfairness of defection does not work this way. We must distinguish between what an agent denies to others and what she gains for herself. What makes defecting unfair is that the agent who does it gets the benefit of the contributions of others without giving them the benefit of her contribution. The gain that she realizes, in terms of her values, by using in some other way the resources she was expected to contribute is immaterial. The others are treated unfairly to the same degree by her defection whether she accomplishes a lot (from her point of view) or only a little.

It should also be mentioned that there may be another, potentially much more devastating, problem for fairness-based approaches to cooperation when the cooperators have moral concerns. The notion of fairness applies to the distribution of benefits and burdens in a group. But it may be doubted whether it is appropriate to think of the promotion of morally desirable outcomes as a matter of distributing benefits to individuals, even in a pluralistic society.

To be sure, in such a society some may find their moral concerns, excluding fairness, more fully realized, while others find theirs less fully realized. But it is unclear whether this should be seen as unfair. Those whose concerns are frustrated will regard the world as getting morally worse (by their lights), and they will be justified in doing what they can to prevent this, but not, it seems, because the deterioration is unfair to them personally. Similarly, while those who find the world improving would have something to be grateful for, it can be doubted whether they should be viewed as gaining at the expense of others.[21] If, however, the notion of unfairness is out of place in characterizing differences between people in the realization of their moral concerns, someone who defects for moral reasons from a cooperative venture that secures moral gains cannot properly be said to be bringing unfairness into the world. Yet if enough others do likewise, with the result that the benefits of cooperation are lost, it seems clear that we can regard the defectors as acting contrary to reason in some way. So to account for the reason to contribute, we must look beyond the value of fairness.

Two final points concerning the argument of this section should be mentioned. First, the principle of fairness is what I have called a principle of value. In discussing it, I have been assuming that the value it identifies as providing a reason to contribute to cooperative schemes is precisely the value of fairness. Failure to contribute, under the conditions specified by the principle, would be unfair. But the argument I have given does not depend on this. We can suppose that the principle of fairness identifies a moral reason that is sui generis. The important point is that it is a particular substantive moral reason among many others, with which it can come into conflict and by which it may be defeated.

Second, there is a possible response to the difficulty described in this section that preserves a place for the value of fairness in providing a reason to refrain from free riding. Fairness plays its characteristic role in resolving conflicts of interest. Thus, cooperative behavior on the part of individuals with moral concerns can be grounded in fairness if they are prepared to demote these concerns to interests. This means viewing their moral values not as identifying inherently desirable features of the world, but as considerations the satisfaction of which is important primarily as satisfying them – as giving them what they want. This issue, concerning the extent to which moral concerns can legitimately be regarded as normatively akin to interests, so that their realization is appropriately governed by the notion of fairness, will arise repeatedly in subsequent chapters. But clearly it would be desirable if, at each juncture where the expedient presents itself, we could avoid it.

V. THE PRINCIPLE OF COLLECTIVE RATIONALITY

I shall now introduce an alternative way of understanding the reason to contribute to a cooperative scheme. The basic idea is very simple. We should interpret the disposition to behave cooperatively as a disposition to treat prisoner's dilemma situations – and any other situations in which general compliance with the dictates of the PIR would threaten suboptimality – as if they were ordinary coordination problems. We can put this idea more precisely by saying that to be cooperatively disposed is to assign the same payoff to defection that one assigns to the noncooperative outcome. As the matrices below reveal, this has the effect of turning the prisoner's dilemma into a kind of assurance game. The cooperative outcome becomes a Nash equilibrium.

		B					B	
		C	D				C	D
A	C	7,7	$-5,9$		A	C	7,7	$-5,0$
	D	9,-5	0,0			D	0,-5	0,0

Figure 1.5a (left) and Figure 1.5b (right).

We could say that having effected this transformation, cooperatively disposed agents consult the PIR to determine what they should do. But an alternative, which I shall adopt, is to incorporate the transformation of payoffs characteristic of cooperatively disposed people into a new principle of rationality that states a practical requirement governing action in situations where general conformity to the dictates of the PIR would threaten suboptimality. Cooperatively disposed people can then be understood as people who accept this principle. This, of course, is the Principle of Collective Rationality (PCR). Formulated to apply to the multiperson as well as the two-person case, it reads as follows:

(PCR) One has sufficient reason to contribute as provided to a cooperative scheme that produces something that one regards as good if the value to one of the outcome of the scheme, when one's contribution is added to the others that will actually be made, exceeds the value to one of the noncooperative outcome. Conversely, one has sufficient reason to defect from a cooperative scheme if the value to one of the noncooperative outcome exceeds the value to one of the outcome of the scheme (when one's contribution is added to the others that will actually be made).[22]

It should be borne in mind that we are employing the method of reflective equilibrium. Thus, the claim that I make on behalf of the PCR is that it provides a way of formulating the reason for action accepted by cooperatively disposed people that is preferable to viewing this reason as grounded in a substantive moral value that operates in conjunction with the PIR.

The PCR provides sufficient reason to contribute to a cooperative scheme only if enough others will contribute so that when one's contribution is added to theirs, the value (from one's own point of view) of the cooperative outcome exceeds that of the noncooperative outcome. This means that in a given case, an agent who accepts the PCR must consider whether there is good reason to believe that enough other contributions will be forthcoming. That is, the PCR will direct an agent to contribute to a cooperative scheme only if the assurance problem is solved.[23]

The PCR speaks of contributing "as provided." It thus presupposes that a definite scheme has somehow been designated as the one on the basis of which cooperation is to proceed. As I have characterized cooperatively disposed people, this need not always be the case. They may face a situation in which there are several different cooperative schemes on the basis of which they could contribute, several different combinations of actions that constitute Nash equilibria (given their cooperative dispositions). In such a case, the PCR will not provide a reason for action until one of the feasible cooperative schemes has somehow been selected, and the assurance problem solved. The choice of a cooperative scheme will be discussed in Chapter 2. For the time being, let us suppose that we are dealing with a case in which a particular scheme is conventionally established in a group – that is, has been in effect for some time. The convention assigns certain behaviors to each, and these constitute his or her contribution to the scheme. In this case, the assurance problem is solved by virtue of the fact that the members of the group have acquired, through socialization, a habit of behaving as the convention prescribes, and this is common knowledge.[24] The question they consult the PCR to answer is whether to continue contributing (or instead to break the habit).

Cooperatively disposed people, as I have characterized them, will also be able to achieve general cooperation in chicken games. The transformation effected by assigning defection the same payoff as the noncooperative outcome is illustrated as follows:

		B				B	
		C	D			C	D
A	C	7,7	5,9	A	C	7,7	5,0
	D	9,5	0,0		D	0,5	0,0

Figure 1.6a (left) and Figure 1.6b (right).

As can be seen, in a two-person chicken game, cooperatively disposed people will actually regard contributing as a dominant strategy. In the multiperson case, however, it will be necessary to consider whether enough others will contribute so that when one's contribution is added to the rest, the result will be an outcome whose benefits exceed the cost one incurs. This is true as well for agents who proceed on the basis of the PIR. But if an agent of this latter sort believes that there will be enough contributions without his participation, he will not contribute himself. The PCR, by contrast, directs contribution whenever enough others will contribute to ensure that the benefits produced exceed the cost of contribution. So if all in a group accept it, and each believes that at least the minimum necessary will contribute, all will contribute. The greater common benefit (or reduced cost to each) associated with general cooperation in a chicken game will thus be realized.

I have said that an agent who accepts the PCR compares the net gain, from her point of view, that the scheme will produce with what she would receive in the noncooperative outcome. This is the outcome in which everyone defects from the scheme in question – uses in some other way the resources the scheme directs him or her to contribute – and thus the scheme, understood as a combination of actions, does not exist (even in part). I assume that behavior in the noncooperative situation is guided by a principle of rationality. The simplest case is that in which everyone finds defection indicated by the PIR, and acts accordingly. The noncooperative outcome is the outcome of all these actions in accordance with the PIR, taken together – the outcome of this combination. But defection from a particular target scheme can also be justified by the PCR if there is some other scheme which an agent could join instead, and she judges the outcome that will result if she does so (the outcome of the combination that will result) to be more valuable than the outcome of the target scheme. Thus, when employing the PCR to determine whether to contribute to a particular scheme, one compares the outcome of this scheme with the best one could do from the standpoint of one's values, either as an individual or by joining some other cooperative scheme, if the target scheme did not exist.

Unlike the principle of fairness, the PCR does not require that the benefits (given an agent's principles of value) produced by a cooperative scheme be voluntarily accepted. According to it, *there is* sufficient reason for an agent to make her assigned contribution to a cooperative scheme if, from the point of view of her values, its outcome, after she joins it, would be preferable to the best she could do if that scheme did not exist. And an agent *has* sufficient reason under the PCR to contribute if she justifiably believes this to be the case. It must be emphasized, however, that it is not enough that the target scheme produce something to which the agent attaches a value that exceeds the direct cost of her contribution (the disutility of her labor, for example). It must produce an outcome that is better, from her point of view, than what she could accomplish by defecting. And as we have just seen, this includes joining an alternative scheme. So the fact that benefits need not be voluntarily accepted does not mean that an individual is required to contribute to any scheme that assigns her a contribution the direct cost of which is less than the benefit the scheme produces.

I have been describing the ideal case in which the PCR gives all the members of a group sufficient reason to make their assigned contributions to a chosen scheme. If this situation does not obtain, the PCR will justify some in defecting. This complicates the picture I have sketched, but not unduly so. Defection deletes some contributions from the chosen scheme, creating a new scheme. The PCR will give the remaining members of the group sufficient reason to make their originally assigned contributions if the gain, from the point of view of each, that the new scheme produces exceeds what each could realize in the noncooperative outcome.

It should be clear that although the PCR is a principle to be employed by individual agents in determining what to do when a cooperative scheme assigns them a contribution, it is not individualistic in a sense that would deny the existence of social factors in shaping many features of individuals, including the values they hold. All that is necessary is that the operative social factors work in such a way that different people accept different principles of value. When this happens, the members of a group may find themselves in situations where promoting their values as the PIR directs will lead to an outcome that each regards as less desirable than the outcome of cooperation.

Of course, if it is to succeed in its task of enabling agents to avoid the collectively disadvantageous consequences of action on the PIR, the PCR must take precedence over the PIR when they conflict. To be more precise, it must take precedence in any situation in which general conformity with the PIR threatens to produce a suboptimal outcome.[25] In presenting the PCR as a formulation of the practical requirement accepted by cooperatively disposed people, I am assuming that this relation of priority is appropriate.

Now let us return to the problem discussed earlier. We saw that when agents have moral reasons for defecting from a cooperative scheme, many may judge the reason of fairness for contributing – that not doing so would be unfair – to be outweighed. Yet if they all act accordingly, the result could be an outcome that each finds worse, from the standpoint of his moral values, than the cooperative outcome (which results when all make their assigned contributions).

When contribution is guided by the PCR, this problem does not arise. The PCR does not introduce a new principle of value that must compete with the values justifying defection. It simply views agents as assigning the same value to defection that they assign to the non-cooperative outcome. In particular, an agent's decision whether to contribute to a cooperative scheme is made by comparing the degree to which her principles of value will be satisfied if she adds her contribution to the others that will in fact be made with the degree to which they would be satisfied if nobody were contributing and she did the best that she could in that situation. She has sufficient reason to contribute if the former degree of satisfaction exceeds the latter, and sufficient reason to defect in the converse case. This means that the PCR will direct an agent to defect from a cooperative scheme only when she would be willing to pay for her defection with the loss of the benefits produced by that scheme. And no matter how many find defection from a cooperative scheme justified in this way, the result cannot be suboptimal. For no defector will judge any of the alternatives in which she rejoins the scheme, along with some or all of the other defectors, to be preferable from the standpoint of her values.

We should be clear about what is being claimed here. As we have seen, there are reasons to question the applicability of the notion of fairness to the issue of cooperation when the parties have moral concerns. But my argument does not depend on this. We can remain open to the possibility that defection from a cooperative scheme for moral reasons would be unfair. The important point is that the moral reason agents have to avoid unfairness will not always be sufficient to justify cooperation, given that it must sometimes compete with moral reasons for defecting. Thus, if we wish to describe the reason that guides cooperatively disposed people, we would do better to invoke the PCR.

It might be replied, in defense of the principle of fairness, that while it may sometimes allow suboptimal outcomes in cooperative contexts, the PCR has drawbacks as well. The principle of fairness makes the fairness of a particular cooperative scheme a condition of the existence of a reason to contribute to it. The PCR does not do this. Substantive moral considerations enter only through the principles of value that rational cooperators may hold, the principles that determine the value for each agent of the relevant outcomes (the cooperative and noncooperative outcomes). Thus, the PCR can apparently require an agent to contribute to a scheme that is unfair to him, provided only that the noncooperative outcome would be worse. This problem arises in its clearest form when agents are cooperating to realize a self-regarding gain.

In fact, however, the PCR can accommodate the main intuitions that support the idea that the fairness of a cooperative scheme is a condition of rational cooperation. As we have seen, people who care about morality will often be able to make the world a better place, from the standpoint of their respective moral values, by cooperating. To say this is not to presuppose any objective standard of moral improvement. Each may find the world morally better for different reasons. But, of course, these reasons can include reasons of fairness. Thus, to the extent that a given cooperator cares about fairness, he may judge that he is justified, under the PCR, in contributing to a certain cooperative scheme because it makes the world a fairer place (as he understands this).

Similar reasoning establishes that someone who cares about fairness may lack sufficient reason to contribute to a cooperative scheme that he regards as unfair. According to the PCR, one has reason to defect from a cooperative scheme if the noncooperative outcome would be preferable, in light of one's values, to the outcome produced by the scheme. But even if a scheme constitutes an improvement over the noncooperative outcome from the standpoint of one's *self-regarding* values, one may judge the noncooperative outcome to be preferable from the standpoint of one's *moral* values, including the value of fairness. Suppose, for example, that a cooperative scheme that involves slavery or serfdom is preferable from the self-regarding standpoint of everyone involved, including the slaves or the serfs, to the situation that would obtain in the absence of the scheme. Nevertheless, both those assigned the role of subordinates and those assigned the role of superiors may judge that the noncooperative outcome would be *fairer* than cooperation to implement such a scheme and, thus, that they have no reason under the PCR to contribute to it. The problem of unfair initial conditions can be handled the same way. A scheme that mitigates this unfairness will effect an improvement, from the standpoint of fairness, over the noncooperative outcome. But the PCR will give an agent who cares strongly about fairness no reason to contribute to a scheme that does nothing to mitigate initial unfairness.[26]

These points can be framed within the method of reflective equilibrium. I have said that this method seeks a way to accommodate the justificatory force of two different kinds of elements: considered judgments and general theoretical considerations. A natural initial assumption is that the considered judgments that underwrite contribution to mutually beneficial cooperative schemes are judgments of fairness. It is thought that acting as a free rider would be unfair. This idea is reflected in the principle of fairness. But as we have seen, when agents have moral reasons for defecting, understanding the requirement to contribute in this way runs afoul of the relevant *theoretical* consideration that general acceptance of the requirement should not threaten the achievement of Pareto optimal outcomes. The PCR solves this problem, but initially seems to give no role to the considerations of fairness that many people think germane to mutually beneficial cooperation. The solution is the one that I have just described. The reason to contribute is provided by the PCR, but for those who care strongly about fairness, whether the PCR justifies contribution will depend on whether they can regard the scheme at issue as fairer than the noncooperative outcome.

VI. RATIONALITY OR MORALITY?

Succeeding chapters will discuss other aspects of the PCR in more detail. But one issue should be addressed now. This concerns the sense in which the PCR is a principle of rationality. My project employs the method of wide reflective equilibrium to determine the best way of understanding the requirement that guides the choices of cooperatively disposed people. I have noted that, at least in its wide form, this method is not simply an exercise in descriptive psychology. Because it brings general theoretical considerations to bear, it has normative force. It establishes what cooperatively disposed people *ought* to do (to realize this disposition). I have argued that the relevant considered judgments and theoretical considerations together establish that the PCR is preferable to the principle of fairness as a characterization of the requirement to contribute to mutually beneficial cooperative schemes acknowledged by cooperatively disposed people.

But why speak of the Principle of Collective *Rationality*. Earlier I suggested that this label is appropriate because the PCR does not itself invoke any substantive values. Rather, it is a formal principle. It provides a method for correlating actions with states of affairs that takes the appropriateness of a particular action to be determined by the substantive value – as established by the agent's principles of value – of the associated state of affairs. In this respect, the PCR works the same way as the PIR. But does this suffice to show that it is a principle of rationality?

Two objections might be made to this claim. The first is that the PCR would be better regarded as a *moral* principle of a formal, rather than a substantive, kind. The thought here can be brought out by considering a common form of universalization. This is the form that directs one first to describe what one proposes to do as the performance of a certain action in certain circumstances, and then to consider whether one could endorse (given one's values) the performance of that action by everyone in those circumstances.[27] The account of rational cooperation that I have developed makes use of this form of universalization. I have suggested that we interpret cooperatively disposed people as assigning to defection the same payoff they assign to the noncooperative outcome. But this is, in effect, to assign it the payoff it would receive if everyone else defected as well. And the PCR explicitly directs an agent considering whether to defect to ask the question, "What would happen if everyone did that?" So if universalization is a sign of moral thinking, it seems to follow that the PCR should be regarded as a moral principle.

If this is right, our earlier discussion has been entirely intramoral. The argument has shown that while the reason that cooperative people accept for contributing to mutually beneficial cooperative schemes is indeed a moral reason, it is not best understood as one that derives from a particular substantive moral value that must compete with other moral values. In particular, it does not derive from the value of fairness. Rather, it involves a form of universalization.

I do not deny that the previous discussion can be viewed in this way, and I think that even so described, the result obtained is important. But I nevertheless believe that the PCR is best understood as a nonmoral principle. The first thing to notice is that the PCR does not make as much use of the device of universalization as it might. We have seen that it directs agents to assign a value to defecting by asking the question, "What would happen if everyone did that?" A principle governing participation in cooperative schemes could also direct agents to assign a value to contribution in this way – by assuming counterfactually that everyone will contribute. The PCR does not do this. It directs an agent to consider how the realization of her values will actually be affected by the scheme she is considering contributing to, and it enjoins contribution only if these values will be better realized than they would be in the noncooperative outcome. But this focus on the actual realization of an agent's values is characteristic of what we ordinarily regard as rational action.[28]

Similar points can be made in connection with another feature of the PCR that has apparent moral force, the element of reciprocity involved in acting as it directs. Each of the other contributors has done, or will do, something that benefits one slightly. In making one's contribution, one pays them back by doing something that benefits each slightly. It is possible to pay all back with a single act because what is typically at issue is contribution to the production of a public good valued by all in the group.

The notion of reciprocity should not, however, be seen as underwriting the normative force of the PCR. In the first place, the value of reciprocity is a form of the value of fairness. Thus, interpreting the PCR in terms of a requirement of reciprocity runs afoul of our argument against invoking substantive moral values to justify contribution to cooperative schemes. These can be outweighed when the parties have moral reasons for defecting.[29] And second, the notion of reciprocity does not provide a complete description of action in accordance with the PCR. The PCR dictates contribution only when the value (from one's own point of view) of the outcome produced by a scheme *exceeds* the cost of contribution. The notion of reciprocity does not capture this fact. The participants in a system of gift exchange in which each gave gifts to the other members of a group and received a gift of equal value in return would display reciprocity. But leaving aside the spiritual benefits, no one would be better off than she was at the start. So to capture the full force of the requirement articulated by the PCR, we must add to reciprocity an element that is characteristic of rational (in contrast to moral) action.

I believe that these considerations show that the PCR is not best understood as a moral principle. We can, then, view it as a principle of rationality in the following sense. It states a practical requirement that is not a moral requirement. But one might also make a different objection to the claim that the PCR is a principle of rationality. One might argue that nothing that I have said forces us to abandon the standard conception of rational choice presented by utility theory. Acceptance of the PCR can be accommodated within the standard conception. We can suppose that people who acknowledge a requirement of moral universalization are standardly rational agents who have a decisive second-order preference to assign utilities to actions on the basis of the procedure of universalization. And similarly, we can suppose that agents guided by the PCR are standardly rational agents who have a decisive second-order preference to assign utilities to actions in the way characteristic of that principle.[30]

These observations are correct. But I nevertheless think that insofar as we are attempting to characterize the practical requirement accepted by cooperatively disposed people, it is preferable to distinguish two principles, the PIR and the PCR, with the PCR taking precedence when general adherence to the PIR would threaten suboptimality. This yields the same result as the possibility just described, and models the dispositions of cooperatively disposed people in a more straightforward way.

VII. GENERALIZING THE ACCOUNT

In concluding this chapter, I shall defend the generality of the account I have offered. Two issues are germane here: explaining how the account accommodates incommensurable values and explaining how it can be extended to noncausal forms of production.

The model I have presented is compatible with a wide range of approaches to evaluative reasoning. I have been assuming that each agent acknowledges a number of different basic values (holds a number of different principles of value), but I have said nothing about how a judgment of the comparative value of two outcomes is derived from these principles. It could be a matter of simple intuitive balancing, in which some principles of value applicable to a given case are viewed as outweighing others. But more sophisticated methods, for example, Henry Richardson's specification of norms, are also possible.[31] On this view, instead of regarding one of two conflicting norms (that is, principles of value) as possessing greater weight than the other, we seek to explain its precedence by qualifying it or the other norm in a way that makes clear how, in the case at hand, their conflicting claims are to be resolved. As qualified, one of the norms applies to the situation while the other does not. The process is saved from being as ad hoc as intuitive balancing by the further requirement that the specified norms must fit within an evolving practical theory that is ultimately justified on coherentist grounds. But the end result is still a judgment that certain outcomes are more worthy of promotion than others, and this suffices for the application of both the PIR and the PCR.

Views that deny that states of affairs – or outcomes of action, which may include the action performed – are the ultimate objects of evaluation can also be accommodated. Elizabeth Anderson has proposed one such theory.[32] On her view, while we often choose between alternative states of affairs on the basis of their relative value, evaluative reasoning is not fundamentally a matter of establishing a ranking of states of affairs. In the first instance, we value objects, such as people, rather than states of affairs, and states of affairs come to have the value they do, good or bad, because promoting them expresses these prior valuings of objects. Lying behind this thinking are considerations relating to the sort of person one wants to be, which introduces a further kind of evaluative element, ideals of the good life. Our ultimate practical goal is not to maximize value but to lead a meaningful life – one which expresses a coherent and worthwhile ideal.

On this view, there is no place for maximization based on a context-independent ranking of all possible states of affairs. Maximizing reasoning plays a role only after evaluative reasoning of these other sorts has established a ranking of the states of affairs available as outcomes in a particular context. Nevertheless, we can still distinguish between the way the PIR derives a conclusion about what to do from the ranking of outcomes in a particular context and the way the PCR does this. And the argument that the disposition to cooperate is better modeled by the PCR than by the principle of fairness still goes through. General employment of the PCR prevents the realization of lower ranked states of affairs.

Now let us turn to the issue if incommensurability. Utility theory presupposes that outcomes can be weakly ordered. This means that in pairwise comparisons, one outcome is preferred to the other, or the agent is indifferent between them. If we suppose, as I have been doing here, that the value of outcomes is determined by an agent's principles of value, a weak ordering of outcomes is possible if and only if these values are commensurable. Indeed, commensurable values can be defined as values that engender a weak ordering of outcomes. A weak ordering of the possible outcomes of action is necessary if we are to interpret rationality as the maximization of value. Incommensurable values, by contrast, create situations in which we can say neither that one outcome is more desirable than another nor that they are equivalent in desirability. A number of recent theorists, including Richardson and Anderson, have defended the existence of evaluative incommensurabilities.

There are many interesting issues here, but for present purposes we do not need to go into the details. Writers who allow incommensurability do not typically conclude that there is, thus, no such thing as practical rationality. They take it for granted that the notion of practical rationality has legitimate application. They simply seek a way of understanding it that does not require maximization. Anderson's theory illustrates this. She makes two main points. The first is that when incommensurability seems to incapacitate a consequentialist approach to practical rationality (as the production of the most preferred outcome or state of affairs), the valuing of objects that we express by our actions may still give us reasons to prefer one action to another. The second is that the expressive approach provides a way that we can be reconciled to such incommensurability as remains. We can regard it as an expected part of a meaningful life, rather than a sign that something is amiss from the standpoint of practical rationality.

There is nothing here that threatens the employment of the PCR. When an agent is trying to decide whether to make his assigned contribution to a cooperative scheme, the PCR directs him to compare the value (from his point of view) of the outcome of that scheme with the value of the best outcome he could realize if the scheme did not exist. If the relevant values make these outcomes incommensurable, the situation can be handled as Anderson has suggested. In the first place, expressive considerations may make cooperation preferable to defection, or vice versa. I do not mean here that what one expresses by simply adhering to the PCR (namely, rational cooperativeness) provides a reason for doing so. Rather, what one expresses by choosing one way or the other within the framework of the PCR – by aligning oneself with one of the combinations to which the principle directs our attention rather than the other – may make that alternative more worthy of choice than the other. That is, the contrast between focusing on combinations and on focusing on actions understood as individual events remains when we introduce expressive considerations. Indeed, the fact that the PCR directs one to compare just two alternatives may make the expressive dimension of choice clearer. And second, if within the context of the *PIR* we can adopt the line that dilemmas in which no alternative can be taken to be right are an expected part of a meaningful life, we can do the same within the context of the PCR.[33]

Now let us briefly consider the production of outcomes. In the typical case this involves causation. On the standard account of causation, there are a number of causally necessary conditions of the caused outcome, and we identify as *the* cause of this outcome the condition that is salient, given our explanatory concerns. If we interpret production causally, then, a scheme for the production of some cooperative benefit B is to be understood as a combination which would be salient as the cause of B, were it realized. An example would be the general installation of pollution-control equipment, which causes the air to become cleaner. Conversely, a combination of actions counts as noncooperative, relative to a cooperatively producible benefit B, if it is salient as the cause of the nonrealization of B (salient as the reason why B does not obtain). Establishing that combinations have causal properties of these sorts often plays a large role in securing a collectively rational response to the opportunities or problems that a group faces.

We need not, however, restrict ourselves to cases where rational cooperation involves harnessing the collective causal power of combinations of actions. There can also be what might be called "constitutive promotion." One can promote an outcome by performing an action that constitutes the realization of that outcome. Thus, someone authorized to perform marriages can bring it about that two people are married by saying "I now pronounce you husband and wife" – together with the rest of the conventionally prescribed procedure. And there are also cases in which groups can cooperate to promote certain outcomes by creating combinations that constitute those outcomes.

Such cases need not involve conventions. Perhaps the most important constitutive relation is the part–whole relation, and the members of a group may contribute to the collective promotion of an outcome by performing actions that are parts of an identifiable whole. An example would be the "wave" effect sometimes created by fans at football games when all the fans located in a particular section raise their hands over their heads and then quickly bring them down, with this action then being repeated by those next to them on one side, until a circuit has been made around the stadium. But conventions can also play a role in the constitutive promotion of an outcome by a group. Thus, if a large group of people are marooned on an island after a shipwreck, they might form themselves into a pattern that spells "SOS" whenever an airplane is spotted overhead. If there are free-rider problems in cases of these sorts, the PCR can justify participation when the PIR supports defection.

Chapter 2

Cooperative Structures

Now that we have explored the reason that individuals have to contribute to cooperative schemes, we can consider some specific cooperative structures. First, I examine the formation of collective agents and the general issue of how the members of a group can regard the choice of a cooperative scheme as guided by reason. Then I take up the phenomenon of independent contribution. Next, I briefly discuss the topics of collective wrongdoing and collective intention. Finally, I provide an account of authority and promising. States and governments, viewed as cooperative structures, are treated separately in Chapters 3 and 4.

I. COLLECTIVE AGENTS

In the discussion of the PCR in Chapter 1, I simplified by supposing, in effect, that there was just one cooperative scheme available – one combination that would produce the benefits of cooperation. The case we considered concerned the choice whether to adhere to an established convention. Often, however, there will be several different cooperative schemes that could be realized by a group of cooperatively disposed people, and they must choose which to implement. This presents us with an additional aspect of rational cooperation. How can we understand the choice of a cooperative scheme as guided by reason?

For cooperatively disposed people, as I have characterized them, a situation displaying the features of the prisoner's dilemma is transformed into a coordination problem. The matrices in Figure 2.1 provide an illustration of a two-person case in which there is more than one cooperative combination.

		B					**B**	
	C₁	C₂	D			C₁	C₂	D
C₁	7,7	0,0	−5,9		C₁	7,7	0,0	−5,0
A C₂	0,0	3,3	−5,9	A	C₂	0,0	3,3	−5,0
D	9,−5	9,−5	0,0		D	0,−5	0,−5	0,0

Figure 2.1a (left) and Figure 2.1b (right).

Figure 2.1b depicts the situation as it looks to cooperatively disposed people. They will not be able to achieve cooperation until one of the cooperative combinations has somehow been designated as the focus of their efforts.

In Figure 2.1b, the cooperative combinations are Nash equilibria. So the problem faced by cooperatively disposed people could also be described as that of selecting among Nash equilibria. The theory of bargaining games provides solutions to this problem, but these solutions make various assumptions that may not always be satisfied.[1] As in Chapter 1, my strategy will be to see what can be said without getting into the technicalities of game theory. Our goal is to determine how those engaged in cooperation can regard it as guided by reason. Chapter 1 examined how the reason to contribute that is accepted by cooperatively disposed people should be understood. The present problem concerns how the members of a group of cooperatively disposed people can regard the choice of a cooperative scheme as guided by reason.

Before exploring the details, however, it will be useful to describe a simple multiperson case. Suppose that there is a particular cooperatively producible benefit B and various cooperative schemes by which it might be produced, each securing different amounts of B on the basis of a different pattern (or vector) of contributions. For each group member, some subset of these alternatives will be feasible under the PCR, in the sense that if the others make the hypothesized contributions, he will have sufficient reason to make the contribution stipulated for him. As we have seen, whether the PCR yields such a reason is determined by comparing the value for the agent of the outcome of the scheme in question with the value for him of the noncooperative outcome. All the cooperative schemes for producing B that pass this test constitute the agent's feasible schemes.

Normally there will be several schemes that are feasible – that pass the "yes or no" test imposed by the PCR – for all the members of the group. These are the *jointly feasible* schemes.[2] A group all of whose members accept the PCR must find a way publicly to designate as the scheme to be implemented one of the jointly feasible schemes. It must also find a way to provide assurances that the members of the group

35

(or sufficient number of them) will make their assigned contributions to the chosen scheme. Satisfaction of this last condition is crucial, since the PCR gives an agent sufficient reason to contribute to a cooperative scheme only if enough others will contribute so that when his contribution is added to theirs, the result is an outcome to which he assigns greater value than noncooperation. The provision of assurances is, perhaps, most easily accomplished if the mechanism that designates a scheme for the group is commonly known within it to possess de facto authority. A source of directives possess de facto authority in a group when the members are prepared (within limits) to allow its directives to preempt their own judgments concerning what is required in the situation. Authority will be considered more fully in Section V.

The members of a group of cooperatively disposed people can regard the choice of a cooperative scheme as guided by reason if they can regard it as justified by the principles or values that they accept as appropriately governing such choices. Pareto optimality and fairness are commonly invoked in this connection. That is, the members of a group often want the chosen scheme to be optimal and fair. Let us consider in more detail how these values might support the choice of a scheme.

In some situations, securing optimality and fairness in the choice of a scheme is unproblematic. For cooperatively disposed people, as I have characterized them, a prisoner's dilemma situation is converted into something resembling a coordination problem, in that the cooperative combinations are Nash equilibria. The simplest case that presents the problem of choosing a scheme is that in which there are two cooperative equilibria, and each party (consulting his principles of value) ranks the same one highest. When this happens, the group will still need a mechanism that selects one of the corresponding schemes and provides assurances that each will do his part. This could be agreement (if each accepts the trustworthiness of the others). If the mechanism chooses, and provides assurances with respect to, the inferior of the two schemes, all will have sufficient reason to contribute to this scheme. But the mechanism's choice can be criticized as failing to achieve optimality, where optimality is understood by reference to the principles of value held by the members of the group (which they employ to rank schemes).

In the case just described, the parties rank the same scheme highest. Thus, there will be no disputes over which scheme should be chosen, and the choice will not raise issues of fairness. But we can imagine cases where fairness would play a role. An example is a case in which the nonmoral values held by the members of the group lead to conflicting preferences concerning which cooperative scheme to implement, but a shared conception of *substantive* fairness grounds a consensus that one of the candidate schemes is fair – or fairer than the other candidate schemes.

Situations in which a group must choose a cooperative scheme can have a different structure, however. The nonmoral preferences of the members regarding the feasible schemes may conflict, and there may be no shared conception of substantive fairness that supports the choice of one over the other, or the schemes may be deemed equally fair. The parties are thus confronted with an impure coordination (or "battle-of-the-sexes") problem. The following matrix illustrates this case. As before, we can imagine it embedded in a prisoner's dilemma to illustrate the effect of cooperative dispositions.

		B					B		
		C_1	C_2	D			C_1	C_2	D
	C_1	7,3	0,0	−5,9		C_1	7,3	0,0	−5,0
A	C_2	0,0	3,7	−5,9	A	C_2	0,0	3,7	−5,0
	D	9,−5	9,−5	0,0		D	0,−5	0,−5	0,0

Figure 2.2a (left) and Figure 2.2b (right).

In a case of this sort, the parties must find some way to settle on one cooperative scheme, despite the fact that their preferences concerning schemes differ and no scheme is salient from the standpoint of substantive fairness. But here, too, there is a way that shared values can provide a basis for the choice of a scheme. Convergence on one scheme can be achieved if the members share a conception of *procedural* fairness that supports the adoption of a particular procedure for choosing one of the competing schemes.[3] As David Copp puts it, "there may be a consensus on *how* to decide, even if there is not a consensus on *what* to decide."[4] Procedures that could be employed include a lottery or voting. Each might, for example, regard a particular procedure as providing morally required equal consideration of all the members of the group, and accept its results for this reason. General acceptance of a procedure can also be achieved without a shared conception of procedural fairness if the different conceptions held by the members of the group point toward the same ranking of procedures (or the same first choice) – that is, if they yield a kind of overlapping consensus.[5] The democratic choice of cooperative schemes will be considered further in Chapter 4.

We have been examining the way the PCR operates in conjunction with a mechanism that chooses cooperative schemes – that assigns contributions. But on the approach I have been developing, the rationality of contributing to a scheme does not depend on whether it has been rationally chosen, in the sense of being chosen in accordance with whatever principles or values govern the choice of cooperative schemes. This constitutes an important difference between my theory and that developed by David Gauthier in *Morals by Agreement*. He employs the notion of "constrained maximization" to do the work that the PCR does on my approach. Basically, the requirement of constrained maximization is a requirement to contribute as provided to a scheme (or in Gauthier's terminology, a joint strategy) to which it would be rational to agree. Gauthier's theory thus presupposes an account of rational agreement, which he supplies with his principle of minimax relative concession. Schemes that satisfy this principle are nearly (Pareto) optimal and fair.[6]

On the view that I am presenting, by contrast, we first delimit a set of jointly feasible schemes, to any one of which the members of a group would have sufficient reason, under the PCR, to contribute (if the others did so as well). Such schemes need be neither optimal nor fair. For example, in the matrix depicted in Figure 2.1b, combination (C2,C2) is a jointly feasible scheme that is suboptimal. And the differences between the payoffs associated with different jointly feasible schemes could be much more radical than those depicted. The payoffs to the combination (C1,C1) might, for example, be 100 units of benefit to each party. In this case, (C2,C2) would be seriously suboptimal, yet if it were designated for the group by a mechanism that solved the assurance problem, each would have sufficient reason under the PCR to do her part in realizing it. As for fairness, we saw in Chapter 1 that whether the PCR gives agents sufficient reason to contribute to an unfair scheme depends on whether they value fairness, and on how cooperation on the basis of that scheme compares with the noncooperative outcome from the standpoint of fairness (as each understands it).

Unlike Gauthier's theory, then, the PCR does not make the (near) optimality and fairness of a scheme a condition of the existence of a reason to do one's assigned part in it. The securing of optimality and fairness is not the task of the principle governing the decision whether to contribute to a scheme (the PCR). Rather, this objective is addressed separately, in the choice among the jointly feasible cooperative schemes – on the assumption that the parties value optimality and fairness.

Support for detaching the reason agents have to contribute to cooperative schemes from considerations of optimality and fairness can be obtained by examining ordinary coordination problems. As was noted in the Chapter 1, in a coordination problem, the PIR gives the parties sufficient reason to converge on one of the equilibria if the assurance problem is solved. But a combination that produces an outcome that is neither fair nor optimal can be an equilibrium in a coordination problem. So in the case of ordinary coordination problems, there is no requirement that rational cooperation be restricted to the production of outcomes that are nearly fair and optimal. Understanding rational contribution in prisoner's dilemma situations in terms of the PCR simply extends this point to these cases.

I have been presenting the problem of choosing a scheme in a way that satisfies the values of fairness and Pareto optimality (or some other notion of efficiency that may be thought important by the members of the group) in a highly simplified form. In any actual case of multiperson cooperation to produce a public good, a number of issues germane to fairness and efficiency will have to be addressed by the mechanism that chooses a scheme. One is that some may benefit more from the good than others, in which case fairness might require that they contribute more, and so might efficiency (if the alternative is uniform contribution at a lower level that even those who attach little value to the good could accept). Another point is that the good at issue may sometimes be better realized if only some of the members of the cooperating group make a contribution. One reason for this is that the cost of producing an additional increment of the good may rise as the number of contributors increases. In these latter cases, efficiency requires restricting contribution to a proper subset of the members, but fairness will have something to say about how this is done. The solution might be to employ a lottery.[7]

I have identified two aspects of rational cooperation, two places where reason is relevant to cooperation. First, individuals must have a reason to contribute to a cooperative scheme even when they could benefit as free riders. I have argued that we should understand this reason as provided by the PCR. But a group that is thus given the potential to act cooperatively will not do so unless a single cooperative scheme, from among those that are jointly feasible in light of the PCR, is somehow established as the one the group is to implement (and each member is provided with sufficient assurance that enough others will do their parts to make contributing as directed rational under the PCR). The members of the group will be able to regard this choice, too, as guided by reason if it is in accord with various values – substantive or procedural – that they hold.

It should be emphasized that what is at issue here is how the individual members of the relevant group view the choice of a scheme. They may share values in light of which the choice of a particular scheme is appropriate. But it may also be that while some hold values that enable them to take this view of the situation, others holding different values (or different conceptions of a shared value such as fairness) cannot endorse the choice that has been made. I explore these issues further in the next section.

Let us say that when the cooperative potential created by general acceptance of the PCR within a group is actualized by the designation of a scheme, the group constitutes a *collective agent*. A collective agent could come into existence to perform a single cooperative task and then immediately go out of existence. An example would be a group of bystanders who cooperate to save someone who has fallen through the ice on a pond. Here one person's taking the initiative and presenting a plan to the group may suffice to crystallize the cooperative potential inherent in the group.

But a collective agent can also be brought into existence when the members of a group anticipate that they could benefit by acting cooperatively in a variety of different contexts, and thus create an *established choice mechanism* that generates schemes to be implemented whenever an opportunity to cooperate arises. The establishment of a choice mechanism can be viewed as a form of second-order cooperation that itself involves the acceptance by the group of a scheme that has somehow been proposed. We can call the cooperative scheme underlying the creation of the established choice mechanism associated with an abiding collective agent that agent's *constitution*. The constitution might envisage a dictator as the choice mechanism, and specify how someone can acquire this role. Alternatively, the mechanism could be a procedure, such as voting or a lottery. The second-order cooperation involved in creating an established choice mechanism will be rational under the PCR for a member of a group if the benefit derived from the existence of the resulting collective agent exceeds the best result she could obtain if that collective agent did not exist. Relevant here will be the cost of maintaining the choice mechanism and the benefits associated with implementing the various schemes it adopts for the collective agent. There might also be "spiritual" benefits derived from membership in an established community.[8]

II. THE CHOICE OF SCHEMES AND MORAL DISAGREEMENT

In the previous section, I suggested that when the members of a group disagree for self-regarding reasons about which of the jointly feasible schemes to implement, a shared substantive or procedural value, such as fairness, can provide a basis for resolving the disagreement. The case becomes more complicated, however, if fairness is invoked to resolve disagreements that are grounded in divergent moral values. In Chapter 1, we saw that when fairness conflicts with other moral values, we must either admit that fairness will sometimes be outweighed, or else accept the demotion of moral concerns to mere interests. The role of fairness is to resolve conflicts of interest. So when it is applied to moral disagreements, the associated moral concerns are demoted to interests. Moral values become considerations the satisfaction of which is important primarily because it satisfies those holding them. An individual may judge that the moral values underlying her particular concerns outweigh fairness, in which case the demotion of these concerns to interests that fairness effects will be irrelevant. But if she regards fairness as possessing, in the cooperative context at issue, greater moral weight than the values underlying her particular concerns, the status as interests that fairness gives these concerns will be the final status they have in that context.

I shall not be too precise about what makes a value a moral value. Mainly, I have in mind the role an agent gives it in her practical thinking. First, she treats it as making claims on her that could require her to sacrifice her personal good. And second, she regards it as potentially conflicting with other values that could require such sacrifices. The state or condition promoted by action in accordance with a moral value could be a feature of individual lives (the meeting of a need, for example), of groups (the development of a culture), or of the world at large (saving the rain forests). If the agent in question has a realist bent, we could add that she regards the state or condition as one the realization of which would make the world a better place even if no one had a corresponding desire; but we should not exclude the possibility that people who reject evaluative realism can have moral values.

When the concerns grounded in moral values, so understood, are demoted to interests, it may still be possible to view them as formally distinct from self-regarding reasons. Self-regarding reasons are agent-relative, while moral reasons are often agent-neutral. But when considerations of fairness govern the satisfaction of moral concerns, they are accorded the same normative status as self-regarding reasons. They may not become formally agent-relative, but their normative significance consists in the fact that satisfying them will satisfy the person whose concerns they are.

In Chapter 1, I argued that when what is at issue is the decision whether to contribute to a cooperative scheme that has somehow been chosen for a group, the PCR enables us to avoid this undesirable result. It does not provide a substantive reason to contribute that competes with other moral values. Rather, it provides a way of correlating actions with (genuinely) valued outcomes. It thus competes with – and in cooperatively disposed people, prevails over – the alternative way of correlating actions with genuinely valued outcomes provided by the PIR. But as we can now see, the threat of demotion looms again at the level of the choice of a cooperative scheme. If the moral values held by the members of the cooperating group lead to divergent preferences among the jointly feasible schemes, some members will regard any choice that is made as presumptively objectionable on moral grounds. Since fairness is the characteristic moral virtue of cooperative schemes, it is natural to reply by invoking it to justify the choice. The adoption of a particular scheme might be justified on the ground that it fairly resolves the competing claims, or that it has been chosen by a fair procedure. But this will only work – will only reconcile an objector to the scheme in question – if he can regard fairness as prevailing over the moral values that support the adoption of a different scheme. And this means accepting the demotion of the concerns grounded in these values to interests. By contrast, if he cannot do this – if he regards the other moral values he holds as prevailing over fairness – he will not be able to view the choice that has been made as justified.

We should be clear about what is at stake here. We are not talking about a global demotion of all one's moral concerns, in any employment, to interests, but only about the demotion of particular moral concerns for the purpose of solving a specific problem that may confront a group of potential cooperators (the choice of a cooperative scheme). And as we have seen, the reason the PCR provides for contributing to a cooperative venture does not force the demotion of moral concerns to interests. So given that the scheme chosen is feasible, under the PCR, for all the members of the group – given that each regards it as preferable to the noncooperative outcome – even those members who cannot view its choice as guided by reason will still be able to regard themselves as genuinely making the world a morally better place, in light of their values, by contributing as directed to that scheme. The problem is simply that it will be impossible to attain the ideal condition in which all in the group view not only their participation, but also the choice of the scheme, as justified, unless some are prepared to demote their moral concerns (as they bear on this choice) to interests. In Chapter 1, I said that we should avoid the demotion of moral concerns to interests if we can. But from what we have seen so far, it appears that some demotion may be unavoidable if people with divergent moral concerns are to cooperate in a way that they can regard as *fully* guided by reason. I take up this issue again in Chapter 4.

One further point should be mentioned here. I have said that an agent can have sufficient reason (under the PCR) to *contribute* to a particular cooperative scheme even if he cannot view the choice of that scheme as guided by reason. He may deem cooperation on the basis of that scheme preferable to the noncooperative outcome. But whether the members of a group can take the *choice* of a scheme effected by a decision procedure to be guided by reason is not similarly independent of whether they have sufficient reason to make the contributions it assigns to them. Decision procedures presuppose cooperatively disposed people. A decision procedure is a way of choosing among cooperative schemes that are jointly feasible within a group of cooperatively disposed people. So if the members of a group do not have the requisite cooperative dispositions, going through the procedure – voting or conducting a lottery, say – is an empty exercise. It cannot realize the procedural values, such as fairness, normally associated with it. I shall have more to say about this in Chapter 3.

III. INDEPENDENT CONTRIBUTION

So far, we have been focusing on cases in which a choice mechanism of some sort, which may be agreement within the group, decides among jointly feasible cooperative schemes, and thus assigns a contribution to each member. Given that the schemes are jointly feasible, each member of the group will have sufficient reason under the PCR to make whatever contribution the chosen scheme fixes for her. But there are cases of mutually beneficial cooperation that do not have this structure. The contributors to a listener-sponsored radio station, for example, must decide independently how much to contribute. The result of all their decisions will be a cooperative scheme – a pattern or vector of contributions – but no choice mechanism will have selected this scheme. Rather, it will be the resultant of a number of independent decisions. How are these cases to be accommodated within the model that I have proposed?

The key to that model is that cooperatively disposed people treat situations that have the structure of the prisoner's dilemma as if they were actually coordination problems. The PCR describes rational behavior on the part of such people. A cooperatively disposed person should make a particular contribution to a cooperative venture if the value to her of the cooperative outcome exceeds the best she could do with the resources at issue if the scheme did not exist. But the PCR does not tell each how much to contribute. It sets an upper bound; the amount contributed must not be so great that the noncooperative outcome would be preferable to cooperation on that basis. And we can perhaps suppose that the PCR requires those who accord some value to the cooperative outcome (who prefer the station's existence to its nonexistence) to contribute something. But precisely how much each is to contribute must be determined in some other way.

On the model I have been developing, the decision how much each is to contribute is made in choosing a cooperative scheme for the group. This suggests that we should approach independent contribution as involving the independent choice of cooperative schemes – as involving the choice, by each individual, of the cooperative scheme on the basis of which she will contribute. This may seem to be only notionally different from choosing a particular action, but it is not. Each chooses a scheme in the sense that she decides how much to contribute in light of her expectation regarding how much the others will contribute. And as in the case of the selection of a scheme by a common choice mechanism, values germane to the choice of a scheme will have to be brought to bear. The most obvious candidate is fairness. Each decides how much to contribute on the basis of some understanding of what would be fair, given how valuable she finds the radio station, how much she expects others to contribute, and perhaps how much she can afford.[9] The resultant of all these independent choices then constitutes the particular pattern of contributions that actually supports the station.

This much is relatively straightforward, but there is a further problem that must be confronted. It can be brought out by posing the following question. If a group has selected a scheme using some common choice mechanism, why should the members make the contributions assigned to them, rather than deciding independently what they will contribute? Or to put it another way, why should cooperatively disposed people employ a common choice mechanism to select a cooperative scheme, as opposed to letting each individual decide independently the scheme on the basis of which she will contribute (and thus the contribution she will make)?

The answer is that each may find cooperation on the basis of an explicitly chosen scheme preferable to the outcome produced by independent contribution. One important reason for this is that cooperation is likely to be inefficient when each decides her contribution independently. For individuals who are guided by fairness, contribution will be determined in large part by how much others are contributing. But initially, it will be appropriate for each to doubt that others will contribute much. And if each makes a correspondingly small contribution, it will be difficult for the group to move to a higher level, for each will have evidence that no one is prepared to contribute much. In this case, the problem the group faces is essentially an assurance problem. Each would be willing to contribute more, but only if she could be sure that others will do this as well. Where contributions are assigned by a common choice mechanism, however, it can direct the larger contributions that would be desirable from everyone's point of view. And if it is an established choice mechanism that has authority in the group – or if the mechanism is that of explicit agreement backed by a promise – the assurance problem will be solved. Thus, the group will be able to produce the more desirable outcome. I discuss the use of authority and promising to solve the assurance problem more fully in later sections of this chapter.[10]

We should be clear about how the choice between these two alternatives, independent contribution and the employment of a common choice mechanism, is to be framed. We might envisage it as being made by a higher-order choice mechanism. For example, a government might enact laws constituting a common choice mechanism for a group. But the transition from independent contribution to the employment of a common choice mechanism can also be made without resorting to a higher-order mechanism. The PCR directs an individual to contribute as provided to a cooperative venture so long as the value to him of the outcome that results, when his contribution is added to the rest, exceeds the best he could do if the venture did not exist. But the alternatives available in the noncooperative outcome may include joining other cooperative enterprises. This means that a given cooperative enterprise is always in competition with other actually operating cooperative enterprises, and must calibrate the contributions it assigns to reflect this fact. But it also means that if individuals participating in a given enterprise can organize an alternative enterprise that they would find preferable – which would mean solving the assurance problem – they will have sufficient reason, under the PCR, to abandon the first enterprise for the second.

So if, as I have suggested, independent contribution is often inefficient, the members of a group employing this mode of cooperation will have sufficient reason to abandon it for cooperation on the basis of the explicit choice of a scheme, if they have reason to believe that enough others are prepared to cooperate on that basis as well. The requisite assurances might be provided by promises. It should be borne in mind, however, that the costs involved in setting up a common choice mechanism – for example, the cost of identifying and communicating with all others listening to a particular radio station – may be greater than the benefit that could be expected.[11]

IV. COLLECTIVE WRONGDOING AND COLLECTIVE INTENTION

Two further topics related to the phenomenon of collective agency deserve mention. First, the discussion in this and the preceding chapter has assumed that the relevant values are those of the particular cooperating agents, the values established by each agent's principles of value. There is no assumption that we, looking at the situation from the outside, know what the correct values are and can use them to appraise the performance of a group. But, of course, it is possible to adopt such a posture. If we do, we may regard the members of a group as engaging in collective wrongdoing, as realizing combinations that are undesirable from the standpoint of the putatively correct set of values.

I shall examine only the case where the wrongdoing at issue takes the form of the realization of what might be called an "incremental bad" – an outcome that is deemed bad from the standpoint of the values held to be correct by the observer and to the badness of which each member of the group in question makes an incremental contribution. In such cases, what the correct values require is the realization of a "countercombination," an alternative combination of actions that lacks the bad-making feature of the original.

An incremental bad may be produced by a combination of actions of a particular type. An example would be the case in which the combined effect of many acts of littering is the creation of an eyesore. In this case, the desirable countercombination is that in which all refrain from littering. Alternatively, an incremental bad may be created by collective inaction, in which case the pernicious combination is a set of failures on the part of the members of the relevant group to perform an action of a particular type. An example would be the case in which the failure by the members of a group to construct a barrier out of sandbags is responsible for serious flood damage in a city. Here, the desirable countercombination is general participation in the requisite sandbagging project.

In some cases of these kinds, each member of the group may have sufficient reason to withdraw from the pernicious combination – to refrain from performing an action of the pernicious type or from displaying inaction of the pernicious type (which means performing an action of the desired type) – whether others do so or not. For although the action or inaction of each agent accounts for only a small part of the associated badness, she will be responsible for none if she behaves in the opposite way.

In other cases, however, individual withdrawal from the pernicious combination may have no discernable effect on the realization of the presupposed values. Each will have sufficient reason to withdraw only if his withdrawal can be coordinated with that of others. Cases in which the pernicious combination involves inaction are especially likely to display this feature. One person's sandbagging efforts will almost certainly accomplish nothing. In situations of this sort, the avoidance of collective wrongdoing requires the formation of a collective agent to realize the countercombination. This fact has implications for the extent to which individuals can be said to have acted wrongly through participating in a pernicious combination. If the formation of a collective agent is required for the creation of a countercombination, then the assurance problem must be solved. But this means that no member of the group can be said to have a reason to act differently unless there is something that can support the belief that enough others will do so as well. Still, if they could take steps to produce the

requisite assurances and do not, their failure to create a suitable countercombination will be open to criticism.

What is the role of the PCR in an account of collective wrongdoing?
The PCR is designed for the case in which people have different values
– or to be more precise, value the available outcomes differently. But
in considering collective wrongdoing, we are invoking a certain set of
values that is taken to be correct. That is, the relevant values are not
those actually held by the members of the group, but those held by
the person asserting collective wrongdoing. He is presupposing that
the members of the group ought to be guided by these values. If all
the members of a group are appropriately guided by the same values,
however, the problem they face in collectively acting as they should is
a straightforward coordination problem. And as we saw in Chapter 1,
the PIR suffices to enable agents to solve coordination problems –
assuming that something provides the requisite assurances.

Still, there may be a role for the PCR in explaining the wrongness
of collective wrongdoing in cases where each component of a pernicious combination has, considered alone, no discernable effect on realization of the presupposed values. This fact means that there is
something like a free-rider problem. Since the realization of the presupposed values will not be reduced if a single agent fails to participate in the desirable countercombination, the PIR will dictate withdrawal if there is the prospect of producing a tangible gain from the
standpoint of these values. Yet if all act in this way, the countercombination will not be created, which may constitute a loss greater than
the aggregate gain produced by all the defections. The PCR enables us
to avoid this result. If the assurance problem is solved, it directs the
members of the group to contribute to the countercombination. That
is, it has the consequence that, given the presupposed values, they
have sufficient reason to contribute to the countercombination.

The PCR does not provide the only solution to the problem we have
just considered. In his book *Reasons and Persons*, Derek Parfit presents
a theory of rational beneficence.[12] He notes that a serious negative
effect on human welfare may be produced by a combination of actions,
each of which, considered alone, has no discernable welfare consequences. He thus incorporates into his theory a principle calling on
beneficent agents to consider what they do *together* – that is, to consider the consequences for human welfare of combinations of actions.[13]
Parfit's principle must not be confused with the PCR, however. The
PCR works as well as Parfit's approach in cases where certain values
are presupposed. But unlike Parfit's principle, it can also be employed
in the case where the members of a group hold different values. Indeed, as I have said, this is its primary role. The PCR seeks to characterize the dispositions of people who are prepared to cooperate with

others holding different values. Since value pluralism is the situation that we almost always confront in large-group contexts, the PCR is indispensable.

The second topic that deserves mention in connection with the phenomenon of collective agency is collective intention. For individuals, the coordination of action over time is often facilitated by the existence of intentions. Recently, several writers have discussed the phenomenon of collective intention.[14] The main issues in this literature concern (1), whether a group can be said to have an intention that is not reducible to the intentions of its individual members, and (2) whether, if we suppose that individual intentions must be involved, an individual can intend that a group do something, or is instead restricted to intentions concerning his own actions (so that a group intention must be understood as a structure built up out of intentions that individuals have concerning their own actions). I do not propose to enter into these controversies here. Generally speaking, shared or collective intention exists when the members of a group can be said to intend to do something together.[15] It thus presupposes that the members have sufficient reason to participate in some sort of cooperative endeavor. The point I want to make is that the PCR, by extending the range of cases in which individuals have sufficient reason to participate in a cooperative endeavor, can extend the range of cases in which collective intention might be found. To keep the discussion brief, I will make the case for this within the framework of Michael Bratman's theory of intention.[16]

As characterized by Bratman, intentions are partial plans. We make plans to achieve certain outcomes, but rarely do we map out in advance exactly how we will achieve them. We leave until later those decisions concerning the particular means to be employed, or the specification of some more general goal. This strategy is an appropriate response to our limited rationality. Often we will not have available until later the information that is required to fill in the plan. But neither will we be able at that later time to do all the reasoning necessary to determine how to proceed. Thus, we divide the labor of deliberation among different temporal points. If intention is to do its job, the agent must remain committed to the associated plan in the face of new reasons for action that might arise between the time it is formed and the time action on it is completed. This element of commitment is one of the features that distinguishes intention from desire.

Shared or collective intention involves the adoption and progressive specification of a partial plan by the members of a group. This could be accomplished by a formal choice mechanism, and I believe that in such a case, it would be appropriate to speak of shared or collective intention. That is, I believe that we can ascribe a collective intention to a group when it is prepared to act on a particular scheme chosen by a formal choice mechanism, and an intention, in Bratman's sense, can be ascribed to that mechanism. But the most interesting cases – and those that have been the focus of attention in the literature – are those in which the members of a group accomplish these tasks, the adoption and specification of a plan, without employing a formal choice mechanism. They simply fall into a cooperative activity through a process of mutual adjustment of their respective intentions, thus "spontaneously" establishing a collective agent.[17]

The PCR can play a role in this phenomenon. Where shared activity crystallizes because a number of individuals fall in together, the maintenance of the activity over time requires that each observe the behavior of others as the project unfolds and adjust her actions accordingly. A simple example is the case where two people go for a walk. They may repeatedly choose a route at forks they encounter, without any explicit proposal from either of them, through a process of attention and adjustment to each other's behavior.

Shared cooperative activity can, as in the example of going for a walk, take the form of temporally extended coordination underwritten by the PIR. Forks in the path present junctures where coordination could continue to be achieved (if both go down the same path) or be lost (if they go down different paths). Since each wants to go where (wherever) the other goes, mutual observation secures mutual responsiveness. And rationality as characterized by the PIR suffices to underwrite this. The parties will be worse off, from the standpoint of each one's values, if coordination fails.

But there will be situations where temporally extended coordination is threatened by free-rider problems. An example might be a case in which some individuals spontaneously form a group to fight a wildfire facing their neighborhood. Here, the general acceptance of the PCR within the group enables the requisite intentions to be formed and maintained. As was described in the first section of this chapter, cooperatively disposed people, people prepared to act on the PCR, are prepared to contribute to any of the jointly feasible schemes chosen for a group of which they are members, even though they could do better as free riders. The choice among the feasible schemes can be made by a formal choice mechanism, but it need not be. If all the individuals in a group accept the PCR, they will sometimes be able to form a mutually beneficial cooperative enterprise in a prisoner's dilemma situation by simply falling in together. The observance by each of the behavior of the others provides the requisite assurances. And if junctures arise where the members of a group cooperating on the basis of the PCR must, if they are to continue in accordance with a particular plan, further specify that plan, they could do this by monitoring

49

each other's behavior and making corresponding adjustments, just as in cases of simple coordination.

We can, then, understand cooperatively disposed people – people whose behavior in cooperative contexts is guided by the PCR – as sharing intentions, as cooperating in a way that involves the progressive specification of a common plan. And this expands the range of possible situations in which the members of a group could share an intention. Sharing an intention will be possible not only in cases where the members must solve simple coordination problems, but also in cases having the structure of the prisoner's dilemma, in which the PIR would justify defection.[18]

V. AUTHORITY AND COOPERATION

Cooperative enterprises often display an authority structure. Some mechanism issues directives to the cooperating group, and the members regard themselves as having sufficient reason to do what they are directed to do, simply because it is directed. How does this phenomenon fit into the picture of rational cooperation that we have been developing?

The first step in answering this question is to distinguish de facto authority from de jure, or legitimate, authority. As a social phenomenon, authority exists whenever most of the members of some group are prepared (within limits) to defer to the directives emanating from some source, even when they seem to be mistaken. That is, a source of directives has de facto authority within a group if most of its members are prepared within limits to implement its directives even when they judge that, all things considered, some other course of action would be better in the circumstances. Let us call this form of authority "subordinating authority." Subordinating authority is legitimate, for a particular member of a group on a particular occasion, if she is actually justified in deferring to the authority's directive on that occasion.[19]

So described, subordinating authority presents a puzzle. To say that an individual is disposed to act against an all-things-considered judgment regarding what to do in a situation seems to be to attribute to her a certain kind of irrationality. Weakness of will or irresistible impulse are common examples. Yet the concept of legitimate authority implies that accepting authority can be in accordance with reason. How, then, can one have sufficient reason to act contrary to an all-things-considered judgment regarding what one has sufficient reason to do?

Clearly, some distinctions are required. The judgment that a subordinate acts against is not exactly *all*-things-considered, because she judges that she has sufficient reason to act against it. But we fail to capture the "bite" that authority can have if we suppose that the legitimacy of authority is to be understood in terms of the existence of a reason for complying with a directive that outweighs the reasons that support noncompliance. Being disinclined to implement a directive, and then judging that one should do so after all because it emanates from a legitimate authority, is not just a species of the more general phenomenon of thinking that one has sufficient reason to refrain from doing something and then, on further reflection, discovering a reason that tips the balance in favor of it. It is part of the phenomenology of authority that authoritative directives are capable of being experienced as constraints. But discovering a reason that changes one's mind about what to do need not be experienced as constraint.

We can make some progress here by complicating our picture of the way that reasons are related to one another. We do not have to view them has having a certain weight that is balanced against the weight of other reasons. As Joseph Raz has noted, some reasons operate by excluding others.[20] They are reasons for not taking certain reasons into account when making a decision. Such exclusionary reasons withdraw certain reasons from consideration, letting the result be determined by the reasons that remain.

This provides some assistance in the attempt to understand legitimate authority. The reasons that establish the legitimacy of authority can be regarded as excluding the reasons that support noncompliance. But this is not quite the whole picture. The reason to comply with the directive of a legitimate authority also has a positive component, which directly supports this action. The point is just that in providing this support, it also removes other reasons from consideration. Raz calls such reasons "preemptive."[21]

Armed with this idea, we can make sense of the structure of subordinating authority, of its appearing to involve the existence of a reason to comply with directives that defeat an all-things-considered judgment about what there is the best reason to do. We can suppose that the all-things-considered judgment is preempted by a reason that supports deferring to the authority's directive, making the directive itself a preemptive reason for action. De facto subordinating authority exists when most of the members of a group accept the existence of such a preemptive reason for complying with the relevant directives.[22] And authority is legitimate for an individual on an occasion when there actually is a sound basis for the preemption, by the authority's directive, of that individual's judgment concerning what to do on that occasion.

The PCR provides one way of understanding legitimate preemption. As we have seen, achieving the benefits of cooperation requires

that the PCR be given precedence over the PIR when general acceptance of the PIR would lead to suboptimal results. We can now say
that this precedence is not to be understood in terms of outweighing.
Outweighing is a relation that can obtain between particular substantive reasons, viewed from the standpoint of either the PIR or the PCR,
but it is not the relation that obtains between these two principles
when they derive conflicting conclusions from a given set of substantive reasons. The PCR preempts the PIR. It excludes and replaces the
practical judgment authorized by the PIR.

Given this, there can be legitimate subordinating authority if compliance with a de facto authority's directives is justified by the PCR.
And if, in addition, the situation is one in which the PIR justifies
disobedience, we have all of the elements of the paradigm of authority.
The agent makes an all-things-considered judgment, grounded in the
PIR, that he has sufficient reason not to comply with the authority's
directive. It is all-things-considered because it takes into account all of
the substantive values the agent acknowledges. Nevertheless, he has a
reason to act contrary to this all-things-considered judgment and comply with the authoritative directive. This reason is provided by the
PCR, operating with these same substantive values. And since the PCR
preempts the PIR when they conflict, the authority's directive preempts the all-things-considered judgment grounded in the PIR. To
repeat, however, this can happen only when doing what the authority
directs is justified by the PCR. So this way of understanding legitimate
authority establishes a condition the satisfaction of which enables a de
facto subordinating authority to claim legitimacy. Authority will be
legitimate if what is directed can be regarded as a contribution to a
cooperative scheme that is justified by the PCR.

The PCR gives us a way of accounting for the authority structures
that are often found as a part of cooperative enterprises. But a puzzle
remains. We have explained how authority can be legitimate, but we
have not explained why we need it in the first place. Authority, understood as a social phenomenon – de facto authority – is a matter of the
existence, within a group, of dispositions to comply with the directives
emanating from some source. But what does a group gain by having
these dispositions? What use is a habit to obey that can be underwritten by the PCR if one already has the ability to make sound judgments
regarding when, according to the PCR, one has sufficient reason to
contribute to a cooperative scheme?

The solution is to be found in the fact the PCR gives the members
of a group sufficient reason to contribute to a cooperative scheme only
when enough others will contribute to produce an outcome that each
can view as preferable to the noncooperative outcome. That is, the
PCR provides a reason for action only when the assurance problem is

solved. This can be accomplished in a variety of ways. If realizing a particular cooperative scheme is a continuous, ongoing process, each member of a community might be given in childhood a habit of contribution to it. Here we could say that a social norm or convention supporting contribution exists in the community.[23] Common knowledge of the existence of this convention would provide each with the required assurances, so that she had sufficient reason, under the PCR, to contribute as provided by the convention. This is the case we considered in Chapter 1.

But when a source of directives has de facto authority within a group, we can say that there exists within the group a norm or convention of deference, understood as a habit of obeying the directives emanating from that source. Common knowledge of the existence of such a habit provides another way that the assurance problem can be solved. The members need not wait for a concrete social norm underwriting a particular cooperative scheme to crystallize as a result of the usual social processes that generate norms. Rather, any directive issued by a de facto authority will fall into a social situation in which there is already a disposition on the part of the members of the group to obey it. So if the existence of this disposition is common knowledge within the group, the assurance problem that must be solved if the PCR is to provide each with a reason to contribute to a cooperative scheme will be solved – by the mere fact that the contributions associated with the scheme are directed by (what is commonly known to be) a de facto authority.[24]

The existence of such a convention of deference will be especially useful when a group must respond to new situations in which its members could benefit from cooperation, or when it must modify cooperative schemes already in force to ensure that they remain mutually beneficial. The fact that each is disposed to do whatever the source of directives says, and that this is common knowledge in the group, means that each can be confident that the others will do their part in any novel cooperative scheme satisfying the PCR that the source promulgates.

De facto authority, then, enhances the flexibility of mutually beneficial cooperation. It is not the only mechanism that can do this. If a source of directives can make effective coercive threats, this provides another way that the assurance problem can be solved, at least if the ability to coerce most members is common knowledge within the group. These threats give each a sufficient self-interested reason to comply, but for agents who accept the PCR, this is not the reason on which each acts. Rather, each acts on that principle, and the coercive threats merely serve to provide assurances that others will do their parts. De facto authority and coercive force are both forms of what can be called *directive power*, the ability to get people to do things by telling them to do these things. It is plausible to understand the notion of legitimate subordination more broadly, so that what is at issue is the underwriting of directive power of any sort, including coercive power. The PCR can be used to explain the legitimacy of all forms of subordination, including those effected by coercion. The ability to coerce is legitimately exercised only if it supports actions that are underwritten by the PCR.[25] Maintaining the ability to coerce is expensive, however. So de facto authority is a preferable device for solving the assurance problem.

To sum up, the directive of a de facto subordinating authority is taken by those subject to it as providing a reason for acting in a certain way, a reason that they did not previously have. When authority is legitimate, the rational situation is what the subordinates take it to be; there really is a reason for complying with the authority's directives. On the account I have provided, the PCR can ground the legitimacy of de facto authority. When a source of directives commonly known to possess de facto authority directs each to do something he or she would be justified in doing under the PCR if the assurance problem were solved, the fact that it is directed by that source gives each a reason to do it. It does this precisely by solving the assurance problem.

VI. PROMISING AND COOPERATION

On the account I have just presented of subordinating authority, it is a mechanism by which the cooperative potential of a group of people who are already cooperatively disposed can be more fully realized. I believe that promising, too, is best viewed in this way. It is not a source of reasons designed to justify cooperation on the part of people not otherwise cooperatively disposed, but a device for facilitating cooperation among people who are already cooperatively disposed.

As Bratman understands intention, it has some of the features of promising. It is a commitment that is, to some extent, resistant to emerging reasons to abandon the associated plan. Nevertheless, it is customary to distinguish a declaration of intention from a promise. While morality requires that one speak truthfully when declaring an intention, intentions can be lost – either as a result of psychological processes operating extrarationally, or through the rational process of reconsideration. When this happens, the agent loses the reason for doing what she said she would do in expressing her intention. Promising can be understood as a mechanism that enables an agent to give herself a reason for action capable of replacing an intention if it is lost, or perhaps of preventing its loss through reconsideration.

In traditional accounts of mutually beneficial cooperation, promising is assigned a large role. Promising to behave cooperatively in situations having the structure of the prisoner's dilemma is presented as a way of creating a reason that is capable of defeating the reasons one would ordinarily have for being a free rider. This mechanism operates within the framework of individual rationality. The promise transforms the payoffs, so that contributing is the rational course.

But so understood, promising confronts the same problems that beset the principle of fairness. If agents have moral reasons for defecting from a cooperative scheme, promissory obligations to contribute to it could be outweighed, with collectively disadvantageous consequences. In Chapter 1, I argued on these grounds that the PCR is preferable to the principle of fairness as an account of the reason we have to contribute to cooperative schemes, and for similar reasons it is preferable to promising. But while we must regard rational cooperation as underwritten by the PCR, there is still a way that the practice of promising can play a role. Promising does not create cooperative dispositions but, rather, enables cooperatively disposed people to overcome certain obstacles to cooperation.[26]

The first step in understanding promising is to notice how rarely we actually use the words "I promise." The standard situation in which an agreement is struck involves, rather, the making and acceptance of what I shall call a *coordination proposal*. Paradigmatically, a coordination proposal is made with the locution "let us" ("let's") – for example, "Let's go to the movies." If the proposal is found agreeable, it will be accepted with an expression such as "okay" or "all right."

As the term implies, in the standard situation, the agreement made by the offer and acceptance of a coordination proposal solves a coordination problem. The preferences or values of the parties are such that there are a variety of action-combinations that would constitute the realization of a coordination equilibrium – a variety of combinations such that both would be worse off if either departed from them unilaterally. Thus, the two parties in our example may want to engage in some recreational activity together, and have a variety of options. In an ordinary coordination problem, given that the exchange of utterances is common knowledge among the parties, the offer and acceptance of a coordination proposal makes one of the available equilibria salient and provides each with assurances that the other will do his part in realizing it. The PIR then justifies the corresponding contributions.

Many situations in which cooperation is desirable, however, are not ordinary coordination problems. They, rather, have the structure of the prisoner's dilemma. But as we have seen, for cooperatively disposed people, as I have characterized them – people whose behavior in cooperative contexts is determined by the PCR – a prisoner's di-

55

lemma situation acquires the features of a coordination problem. So where there is common knowledge that the parties are cooperatively disposed, it may once again be possible for them to achieve cooperation through the offer and acceptance of coordination proposals. One especially common case of this sort is that in which there is a first performer and a second performer. Such cases have the same payoff structure as the prisoner's dilemma.[27] The offer and acceptance of coordination proposals can, then, occur even in cases of temporally discontinuous cooperation, if it is common knowledge among the parties that both accept the PCR. "If you scratch my back, I'll scratch yours," could be a coordination proposal.

It should be noted that the offer and acceptance of coordination proposals is not restricted to cases where the parties have self-regarding ends. Coordination may be required if an agent is to act on altruistic ends. Thus, if I want, for purely altruistic reasons, to water the plants of a neighbor while she is away on vacation, I will still need her consent. So we would get the exchange: "Would you like me to water your plants while you are away?" "Yes, thanks."

Normally, informal agreements (those not secured with a legal contract) take place between people who know each other well enough that each can be confident that the other will act in accordance with the agreement – that the intentions expressed in the offer and acceptance of a coordination proposal will not be lost. But for various reasons, the situation may not conform to this pattern. An example is the case in which, while both parties truly intend to do their parts, one has doubts about the reliability of the other. One suspects that although the intention expressed by the other party is sincere, something will undermine it. Alternatively, one party may suspect that the other's expression of intention is insincere. And in prisoner's dilemma situations, which are not coordination problems from the standpoint of individual rationality but have that structure for cooperatively disposed agents, fear of nonperformance may arise from the suspicion that the PCR will not, in the end, prevail in the contest with the PIR.

When there is a lack of confidence in the sincerity of an expression of intention, or the stability of the intention expressed, the offer and acceptance of coordination proposals will just involve the uttering of words, not the provision of the assurances required for cooperation. It would thus be useful if there were available some mechanism by which a party to a proposed interaction could create the missing assurance by increasing, in a way that was evident to the other, her motivation to perform.

Basically, this is the function of (explicit) promising. Promising is a conventional device that enables an agent to increase her motivation for performing a certain action, thus providing the assurances that are required if a coordination proposal is to be accepted. A simple exchange might be: "Let's go to the movies." "Do you promise that you will show up on time?" "Yes." "Okay." There could also be cases where assurances are required from the person to whom the proposal is made: "We could go to the movies, but I want you to promise that you will show up on time." "I promise." "Okay." And altruistic ends can be served the same way: "Would you like me to water your plants while you are away on vacation?" "Do you promise to follow the schedule I will give you?" "Yes." "Okay, thanks."

In light of these points, we can sum up the operation of promising as follows. It is a mechanism that enables agents whose beliefs do not permit cooperation to proceed on the basis of the offer and acceptance of a coordination proposal to create the motives that will allow such a proposal to be made and accepted. Once this is done, the prior reasons each had to participate in the arrangement, which might find expression through the PCR, are activated, and the promise is usually redundant. Basically, it just solves the assurance problem by providing each with a reason to believe that the other will do her part.

But how does explicit promising create the additional motivation to perform that enables it to provide the required assurance? Hume suggests that to promise is simply to invite the punishment of not being trusted in the future if one fails to perform.[28] But since this would be a feature of the ordinary case where coordination proposals are exchanged as well, it is not distinctive of explicit promising. The usual suggestion is that the reason created by a promise is a moral reason, but it is puzzling how promising can create a moral reason for action.

Here it is important to make a distinction. The mere offer and acceptance of a coordination proposal, unbuttressed by a promise, can give rise to moral obligations on the part of either party if one of them incurs costs in the expectation of the other's performance. In this case, we can say that one of the parties has induced the other to rely on his performance, and that the intentional induction of reliance gives rise to moral obligations not to disappoint the reliance induced. The moral mechanism at work here can be viewed as a specification of the general requirement of fair treatment. To disappoint reliance that one has intentionally induced is to treat the other party unfairly.[29]

Agreements can, then, give rise to moral obligations even in the absence of promising. If promising is a source of moral obligations, it is an additional source. The idea would be that promising creates a moral obligation to perform as one has promised, and the existence of this obligation provides the assurance that leads the other party to do his part – and thus to make himself vulnerable to one's nonperformance, thereby generating a further moral obligation not to disappoint reliance. But this still leaves us with the puzzle of how one can create the initial obligation simply by using a form of words.

The most common answer points to the status of promising as a mutually beneficial practice. It is a kind of public good that each can consume by speaking the words "I promise." Writers who take this approach have invoked the principle of fairness to explain why promises create obligations. Keeping promises that one has made is how one pays one's fair share of the cost of maintaining the public good constituted by the practice of promising. Not to do so would involve a kind of free riding. Of course, from the standpoint of the present study, we would want to appeal to the PCR, rather than the principle of fairness, to underwrite contribution to this public good.

But a closer look reveals problems with this account. The value of the public good constituted by the practice of promising lies in the ability of a promise to provide the promisee with the requisite assurance. If promises are typically kept, then by making a promise, one creates an expectation that one will do what one has promised to do. Here one benefits from the many acts of promise keeping performed by past participants in the practice. The reason to keep the promise is that otherwise one will be guilty of riding free on their contributions. This view has some unwelcome consequences, however. First, one's ability to give oneself a reason for action by promising depends on the general health of the practice. If most people do not keep their promises, then promising cannot create an expectation of performance. Second, insofar as keeping a promise involves contributing to a mutually beneficial cooperative scheme, the other participants are those who maintain the practice of promising by making and keeping promises. But there is no reason why the promisee need be in this group. He may never have made a promise, or he may always have broken all the promises he has made. Yet it seems odd to regard the reason we have to keep a promise as an obligation (of fairness) owed to a group of people that need not include the promisee.

I believe that we can provide a more adequate account of how promising gives rise to reasons for action by modeling promising on authority. In the account of authority in the previous section, I introduced a distinction between de facto and de jure – or legitimate – authority. De facto authority exists when the members of a population are disposed to comply with the directives emanating from some source. In such a case, we can also speak of the obtaining of a convention, or practice, of deference, grounded in the existence of motivational dispositions of a certain sort in the members of a group. Authority is legitimate (for a person on an occasion) when these dispositions are underwritten by a valid reason that justifies doing what they dispose one to do. On the account of authority provided earlier, this reason was supplied by the PCR.

We can look at promising the same way. Talk of a practice of promising is a way of summarizing the motivational dispositions of the members of a group. Each is motivated to do whatever she promises to do. We can imagine this motivation to be inculcated as a part of the upbringing of children, much as respect for authority might be inculcated. Individuals who are known to have this disposition can create expectations concerning their behavior by making promises. It is important to note that the ability of a promisor to create such expectations depends on the beliefs that the promisee has about *the promisor's* motivational dispositions. Even if most people fail to keep their promises, knowledge that a given individual has the dispositions characteristic of promising – is true to her word – will be enough to enable her to create assurances in this way. Of course, if many in the population have the requisite dispositions, then it may also be possible to create (on inductive grounds) an expectation that one will act as one has promised, even when those with whom one is dealing have no previous knowledge of one's character.

Having taken this view of the disposition to keep promises as a kind of (de facto) trustworthiness, we face a question parallel to the question regarding the legitimacy of authority. Someone who finds himself, as a matter of brute psychological fact, motivated to do something that he has promised to do, might want to know why he should act as he is motivated to act. This question will arise with special force if he could benefit by breaking his promise. We can answer this question the same way we answered the corresponding question about authority. It was argued that de facto authority can be seen as a device that enables the members of a group to have the assurance, regarding the behavior of the other members, that is required for mutually beneficial cooperation under the PCR. And when the actions directed indeed constitute mutually beneficial cooperation – when the condition stated by the PCR is satisfied – authority is legitimate.

Similarly, promising can be seen as a motivational device that facilitates cooperation by solving the assurance problem. And when the motivational dispositions involved support action that is justified, in light of the PCR or the PIR, by the other reasons that are operative in the situation, we can speak of a "legitimate promise." It is especially in situations where the PCR is the relevant principle that assurance will be required. As was noted earlier, one typical case is that in which promising makes possible a mutually beneficial exchange between a first performer and a second performer. When the second performer's disposition to act as he has promised is indeed underwritten by the PCR, in the sense that contribution to the particular cooperative

59

scheme at issue is justified by the PCR, his promise will be legitimate. There will genuinely be sufficient reason for him to act as he has promised (as his promise motivates him to act).[30]

Two contrasting objections might be made to this account. The first is that if one promises to perform an action that is part of an exchange to which the PCR does not justify contribution, one will have a strong motive to do something that there is no good reason to do. I concede that my account could have this consequence. An agent might experience something like weakness of will, finding himself effectively motivated to keep a promise that there is no good reason for him to keep. This problem can also arise in connection with subordinating authority. An agent may find himself strongly motivated to comply with directives when there is no good reason, under the PCR, for doing this.

This possibility can explain why some people might feel compelled to keep even coerced promises. But there is no need to accept it. The dispositions underlying explicit promising can be made conditional on the presence of good reason, under the PCR, to perform the actions in question. That is, in the process of socialization, parents could reinforce a disposition to keep promises that is sensitive to whether there is sufficient reason, under the PCR, to do so.[31] All that is necessary is that promising create a motive to contribute to (genuinely) beneficial schemes when one could do better by acting as a free rider on the contributions of others. This will suffice to create the requisite assurances (when the scheme in question will benefit the promisor). The same approach could be taken to the habits of deference associated with legitimate authority. They could be made conditional on the authority's directing actions that are underwritten by the PCR.

The other objection proceeds from this reply. If the reason, in contrast to the motive, that we have to keep promises is provided by the PCR, and thus tied to the possibility of mutually beneficial cooperation, the disposition to keep a promise will be legitimate only when the promisor can regard the outcome of the combination facilitated by the promise as preferable to the noncooperative outcome (in which no component of the combination exists). So if the situation changes and this condition ceases to be satisfied, the promisor will have no reason to keep her promise. Yet it seems that a promise rightly maintains its force in such cases.

In considering this objection, it must be borne in mind that a promisor could have an altruistic end. But even when her objective is purely self-regarding, it does not follow that she may ignore her promise if she comes to regret having entered into the arrangement that it makes possible. If a promise induces reliance, the promisor will often have a sufficient moral reason to act as she has promised, even when it would have been better, from her point of view, had the agreement never been made. And if a promise has not induced reliance – if it merely provides an assurance of future participation in a plan in which the parties have invested nothing – it is unclear why either party should perform if the situation changes so that she would prefer the noncooperative outcome. It would, however, probably be advisable for the promisor to take steps to verify that there has been no detrimental reliance, and to notify the promisee that the promise will not be kept, so that there will be no detrimental reliance in the future.[32]

Of course, there will be people who have not been effectively socialized to the practice of promising – have not acquired the dispositions normally associated with promising – yet who can pretend to have this attribute by using the linguistic formulas, and thus take advantage of others. But we can still say that there is good reason deriving from the PCR, and perhaps from the induction of reliance as well, for such a promise to be kept. So the account I have provided does not prevent us from criticizing the misuse of the practice of promising.

From the standpoint of the general theory of rational cooperation that I have presented, social norms or conventions, authority, and promising are all of a piece. They are all ways of giving cooperatively disposed people – that is, people who are already cooperatively disposed – the assurances required for mutually beneficial cooperation. When what constitutes mutually beneficial cooperation is relatively stable over time, a social norm or convention, understood as common knowledge within a group of a general disposition to perform a certain specific action in certain specific circumstances, can provide the assurance that makes participating in the associated cooperative scheme rational under the PCR. And when a group of cooperatively disposed people finds that what constitutes mutually beneficial cooperation changes often – because changing circumstances require new patterns of cooperation to meet the group's goals, or because the goals change – common knowledge of the possession by each member of a further disposition to comply with the directives promulgated by an established choice mechanism can provide assurance that each will contribute to any novel cooperative schemes instituted by that mechanism in response to these changes. That is, where there is a convention of deference to authority, a group of cooperatively disposed people can achieve cooperation without waiting for the emergence of specific norms or conventions geared to particular cooperative schemes.

Promising also facilitates the formation of new cooperative ventures by cooperatively disposed people. But instead of enabling a given group of such people to adjust its cooperative behavior to changing circumstances, it enables cooperatively disposed people to form themselves into new groups for cooperative purposes. It facilitates the grouping together of people for cooperative purposes in new ways. The making and accepting of simple coordination proposals gives individuals a way of constituting a new group and choosing a scheme for it, and if the members could benefit by defecting, the PCR supplies a reason for them to do their assigned parts. But the assurance problem must be solved. Promising – that is, the disposition to act as one has said one will when one uses the words "I promise" – is a conventional mechanism for solving the assurance problem connected with the offer and acceptance of coordination proposals.[33]

Chapter 3

States and Governments

In this chapter and the next, I consider a further kind of cooperative structure, the state. Of course, it will not be possible to provide a complete political theory. Instead, I describe how certain political phenomena look to cooperatively disposed people, as I have characterized them.

I have distinguished two aspects of rational cooperation. One concerns the reason individuals have to contribute to cooperative schemes. I have argued that the PCR provides the best account of this. In a group whose members accept the PCR, there will be a set of jointly feasible schemes, schemes to which each would be willing to contribute if he expected the others to do so as well. The second aspect of rational cooperation concerns the choice among the jointly feasible schemes. I have suggested that substantive or procedural values held by the members of the cooperating group establish a basis on which they may be able to regard the choice of a scheme as guided by reason.

In applying these ideas to the political case, we can view the state as the cooperative enterprise and the government as the mechanism the selects cooperative schemes by enacting laws underwriting them. This means that the state is a collective agent. This fits well with the idea, common since the seventeenth century, that states are artificial persons.[1] In this brief chapter, I focus on contributing to the maintenance of a state by obeying the law. The democratic choice of cooperative schemes is treated in Chapter 4.

I. POLITICAL OBLIGATION

The idea that the state can be understood as a form of mutually beneficial cooperation is associated with the contractarian tradition in political thought. Theories of this type compare life within a state with life in a condition in which there is no political cooperation, the "state of nature." It is argued that the relative desirability of life within a state gives each of the members of the territory in question sufficient reason to enter into an agreement to form a state. Such theories are best understood not as attempts to provide an historically accurate account of the emergence of states, but rather as offering a way to vindicate compliance with the laws of existing states by showing that their members would have sufficient reason to create the corresponding cooperative enterprise if it did not exist.[2]

A similar story can be told within the framework of the PCR. Roughly, if a given member of a state, viewing it as a cooperative enterprise, finds life within it preferable to the best she would be able to do (with the resources she is called upon to contribute) if it did not exist, she has sufficient reason to make her assigned contribution. The resources contributed are both monetary and "practical" – the capacity to act in certain ways. Since the assignment of contributions is accomplished by the issuing of directives having the status of laws, contribution takes the form of obeying the law. This general approach is compatible with the value-pluralism that is usually taken to be a feature of modern states. The members of states need not share a commitment to particular substantive values. They need only accept the PCR and the suitability, in light of their values, of the state's procedures for enacting laws (that is, the suitability of the state's constitution). The view of rational cooperation developed in the earlier chapters provides, then, the basis for an account of states and governments that is broadly contractarian in spirit.

The picture just sketched of the PCR's role in justifying political society might be challenged on the ground that the normative powers claimed by actual states go well beyond what can be vindicated by reference to the PCR. The state claims obedience to all its laws from everyone living within its territory, yet the PCR will not give all who live within the territory of any actual state sufficient reason to obey all its laws. Thus, the PCR cannot provide the normative foundation for a modern state.

It will be useful to begin the discussion of this issue by examining the problem of political obligation. This can be understood as follows. A state claims a right to the obedience of all the people residing in its territory, in the sense that all are expected to obey all laws that apply to them. The problem of political obligation is that of vindicating this claim by finding a moral principle that gives all the members of a state a corresponding duty or obligation to obey all its laws. John Simmons, whose work on this problem is the focus of most recent discussion of it, has added a further desideratum. The moral principle must tie an individual to the particular state of which she is a member, giving her a reason to support it, by obeying its laws and in other ways, that she does not have to support other states.[3]

Simmons has argued that none of the moral principles that might be regarded as underwriting political obligation can satisfy these conditions. He thus embraces what he calls "philosophical anarchism."[4] The individuals in a given territory may have a moral reason to obey some of the laws that apply to them, but this will depend on the content of the laws – on whether they (1) direct something that these individuals independently have sufficient moral reason to do, or (2) provide independently desirable coordination. What philosophical anarchism denies is that most members of states have a sufficient moral reason to obey the law as such, simply because it is the law.

The PCR puts these issues in a somewhat different light. We can accept Simmons's arguments against the principles he considers – the principle of consent, the principle of fairness, the natural duty of justice, and the principle of gratitude. Indeed, we can add a new argument to his. Simmons's basic contention is that these principles will not give most individuals even a presumptive reason to obey the law. But in Chapter 1 we saw that even if all the members of a group *do* have sound moral reasons of this sort for contributing to a cooperative endeavor, this may not be enough to secure the optimal level of cooperation. Moral principles cannot reliably block morally motivated defection. This means that they cannot reliably block morally motivated disobedience to the law. The argument was made in connection with the principle of fairness, but it is applicable to any principle that purports to supply a substantive moral reason for contributing to a cooperative scheme.

I have suggested that the PCR provides a solution to the problem of morally motivated defection. Does this suffice to refute philosophical anarchism? The verdict is mixed. Philosophical anarchism says that one need obey only those laws that direct the performance of actions that one independently has sufficient moral reason to perform. If this means that one should obey only when the Principle of Individual Rationality (PIR), working in combination with one's moral values, would dictate doing what the law requires, the PCR requires a greater level of compliance. In this sense, it can be regarded as justifying compliance with the law just because it is the law.

Further support for this conclusion can be derived from the phenomenon of political authority. In Chapter 2, I characterized de facto subordinating authority as a form of directive power, common knowledge of which can solve the assurance problem associated with the PCR. It has a special role to play when a particular group could benefit from sustained cooperation but must often adopt new cooperative schemes or modify old ones. In the normal case, it will be an established choice mechanism that possesses such authority. The essence of subordinating authority is preemption, an individual's deferral to a directive even when what it directs is something that he would not otherwise regard himself as having sufficient reason to do. I argued that the PCR can underwrite preemption because (1) it gives agents a reason to comply with a directive that they would not have reason to comply with if they considered the matter solely from the standpoint of the PIR, and (2) the PCR itself preempts the PIR. But to vindicate the preemption associated with the exercise of de facto political authority is – in one sense at least – to justify obeying the law as such, just because it is the law.[5]

Directive power is the ability to get people to do things by telling them to do these things. De facto authority is a form of directive power, but a source of directives can also possess such power by virtue of its ability to coerce compliance with its directives. Common knowledge that a source of directives has the ability to coerce compliance provides another way of solving the assurance problem that arises in connection with action on the PCR. This possibility is, of course, especially important in political contexts. It should be noted, however, that it is difficult for a government to coerce everyone in a society, especially if it eschews terror. Thus, a government's ability to coerce normally presupposes that it has de facto authority with respect to a large segment of the population. As I mentioned in Chapter 2, when subordination is at issue, it is not very important to distinguish de facto authority from the ability to coerce. So I shall use the term "legitimate authority" to designate any mechanism for choosing and promulgating cooperative schemes that is commonly known within a group to possess directive power of either sort, and which uses this power to support (by solving the assurance problem) cooperation that is in fact justified by the PCR.

The PCR, then, has some potential to underwrite obedience to the law and political authority. But as in the case of the PIR, what an individual has sufficient reason to do ultimately depends on his or her principles of value. Thus, if the conclusion of philosophical anarchism is that one should obey the law if and only if doing so is justified in light of one's values, there is a sense in which my account supports philosophical anarchism. The PCR expands our understanding of rational action in light of one's values, thus expanding the instances in which compliance with the law is justified, but the values of some of the individuals residing within the territory of a state could be such that compliance with the law remains unjustified.

It should be noted that the PCR does not tie individuals to a particular state. It gives them a reason to obey the laws of whatever state they happen to be residing in – if the benefits of political cooperation there, judged by reference to their principles of value, exceed what could be achieved in the noncooperative outcome. Still, the PCR can be regarded as providing some support for the idea that only one state can claim an individual's allegiance. Because political cooperation is localized to particular territories, an individual will typically be receiving the benefits of only one political cooperative scheme at a time, that which is in force in the territory in which she resides. It should be borne in mind, however, that there is no reason in principle why a state could not pass laws governing the behavior of its citizens while they reside in other states (to be enforced by the threat of punishment upon a citizen's return).

In light of our discussion of promising in Chapter 2, there is a further aspect of these issues that should be discussed. The traditional contract theories ground political obligation in a promise to obey, or in consent that has promissory force. If this is understood as a way of generating a particular substantive moral reason for action, it falls to the argument I gave in Chapter 1. The reason will be less effective in underwriting cooperation when individuals have moral reasons for disobeying the law. But in Chapter 2, I presented a different account of promising, according to which it is basically a device by which those who accept the PCR can solve the assurance problems that arise in connection with the formation of new cooperating groups. On this theory of promising, the normative work – the reason, in contrast to the motive, to behave cooperatively – is provided by the PCR. So on the account of promising that I have presented, it appears that promising could, after all, underwrite obedience to the law.

It will, however, usually be possible to dispense with promising for this purpose. De facto authority is another social mechanism that can solve the assurance problem associated with the PCR. It is useful when a cooperating group has already been established but must often change the schemes guiding its actions. This means that in established states, where the dispositions underlying de facto authority have been reliably inculcated (and coercive mechanisms are in place to deal with those who lack these dispositions), there will be no need to invoke promising to activate the PCR as a reason for complying with the law. Common knowledge of the directive power of the government will suffice.

If there is a role for promising in political contexts, then, it arises only in connection with the largely hypothetical case in which a state is created ab initio. This can be understood as follows. A group of people occupying a given territory, all of whom are cooperative disposed, recognize that in certain respects their lives would be better if they could institute an established choice mechanism that would dictate various forms of cooperation throughout the territory (so that everyone in the territory would be involved). Their immediate task is to adopt a constitution for such a choice mechanism. We can suppose that an exchange of proposals and counterproposals brings the members of the group to the point where each would find compliance with the laws promulgated by a particular choice mechanism justified, under the PCR, provided that enough others would also comply. Each would regard general compliance with laws enacted in accordance with that procedure as preferable to the noncooperative outcome. But since each has no reason to suppose the others will comply, the corresponding cooperative enterprise (a state) cannot be formed.

If, however, the inhabitants have been socialized to the practice of promising, acquiring a disposition to keep promises they have made, the required assurances could be provided by a set of promises, made by each to all, to comply with any laws enacted in accordance with the designated procedure. Of course, this story presupposes a totally unrealistic ability on the part of each resident of a large territory to communicate with all the rest. But for present purposes, the important point is that if this scenario could be realized, the real normative work – the work of *justifying* obedience to the laws promulgated by the new government – would be done by the PCR. On the account of promising I presented in Chapter 2, this is always the case when promises are made. The socially inculcated disposition to keep a promise merely solves the assurance problem. And if the founders create in their children the habits of deference that enable us to speak of de facto authority, this will soon replace promising as the means by which the assurance problem is solved.[6]

II. OBEYING UNJUST LAWS

We should note the implications of this account of justified compliance with the law for the question whether there is sufficient reason to obey unjust laws. To simplify matters, I shall assume that reasons of justice are the only relevant moral reasons.

This issue can be approached in the same way we approached, in Chapter 1, the question whether an agent who accepts the PCR has sufficient reason to contribute to an unfair cooperative scheme. The answer to that question depended on how the cooperative scheme in question compared with the noncooperative outcome from the standpoint of the agent's understanding of fairness. Similarly, whether an individual who accepts the PCR has a sufficient reason to obey an unjust law depends on how cooperation on the basis of the relevant scheme compares with the noncooperative outcome from the standpoint of that individual's conception of justice.

There are, however, two different ways of understanding the relevant scheme in political contexts. One possibility is that by complying with a law, an individual contributes to the legal order as a whole, so that in applying the PCR, she must determine whether the legal order as a whole is preferable, from the standpoint of her conception of justice, to the situation in which there is no legal order – the state of nature. When the legal order contains many laws that an individual deems unjust, or a few that she deems egregiously unjust, she may judge the state of nature preferable. While it would doubtless be marked by injustice of various kinds, she may find the legal order worse. In this case, she will have no reason to obey the law as such, although she may still have sufficient reason to obey particular laws directing actions that she takes to be morally appropriate in themselves. But if the legal order contains many laws that she regards as just and only a few that appear unjust, it is plausible that she will find it preferable, from the standpoint of justice, to the state of nature.[7] This means that she will have sufficient reason, under the PCR, to obey even unjust laws. Of course, the fact that one has sufficient reason to comply with a law that one regards as unjust does not mean that one must accept it in the sense of refraining from efforts to change it.[8]

The alternative is a piecemeal approach that involves comparing, from the standpoint of one's conception of justice, the particular aspect of social cooperation underwritten by a given law with the situation in which there is no law responding to that opportunity for cooperation. When the relevant question is posed this way, the PCR is more likely to dictate disobeying a law that seems unjust. But for people who care about justice, this will probably not be the right way to look at the matter. Basically, we are talking about two forms of political cooperation: piecemeal compliance with the law, in which each obeys only laws that she regards as just, and holistic compliance, in which each obeys all laws. As we have seen, some may judge the state of nature preferable to holistic compliance, especially when they find legal order egregiously unjust. But any cooperatively disposed person who finds holistic compliance preferable, from the standpoint of justice, to the state of nature will probably find it preferable to piecemeal compliance as well. Piecemeal compliance would make it impossible for the group to adopt any fixed policy on issues the justice of which was controversial, and thus would have some of the objectionable features of the state of nature. So in considering whether there is sufficient reason to obey an unjust law, cooperatively disposed people who care about justice should normally apply the test associated with the PCR to holistic compliance, asking whether the legal order as a whole is preferable to the state of nature.[9]

There is a further point that supports holistic compliance. We must consider procedural as well as substantive justice. In particular, we must take into account the possibility that justice supports democratic decision making – that democracy, including voting, is a just procedure for enacting laws (and thus for choosing cooperative schemes). Democracy will be discussed in more detail in Chapter 4, but the procedural values that support it strengthen the case, from the standpoint of justice, for holistic compliance over piecemeal compliance. We should remind ourselves of some points made in Section II of Chapter 2. Decision procedures presuppose cooperatively disposed people. If the members of a group are not prepared to act on the schemes chosen by a given procedure, employing it is an empty exercise. This means that democratic procedures can realize the procedural values associated with them only if people are disposed to comply with the laws enacted, even those they have voted against. But if the members of a state decide whether to comply with democratically enacted laws by employing the PCR in a piecemeal fashion, those in the minority on a given issue will often be able to judge that they have no reason to comply in that case. So the values of procedural justice that support democracy will be less fully realized when the members of a state adopt the posture of piecemeal compliance. This gives us a further way that the world can be better from the standpoint of justice if the members of a state adopt the posture of holistic compliance. Our earlier observations about holistic compliance remain, however. If democratic procedures are used to enact egregiously unjust laws, many may conclude that the state of nature would be preferable, all aspects of justice considered.

The conclusion that there can be sufficient reason to obey unjust laws runs contrary to the trend of much recent philosophical discussion, which holds that one need not obey morally pernicious laws.[10] But we must bear in mind that these are claims about what morality, properly understood, requires. What is being claimed is that if a law is in fact unjust, one is morally permitted – or perhaps required – to disobey it. Thus, the problems posed by moral disagreement are swept aside. With respect to any issue about which morality has something to say, there will be morally correct and morally incorrect policies. If a morally correct policy is enacted, one must obey; but if a morally incorrect policy is enacted, disobedience is at least permissible.

Actual political cooperation, however, cannot proceed on the basis that one of the parties to a dispute is right while the others are wrong. This point is familiar from discussions of liberal political theory, where it is said that one cannot expect political cooperation to be premised on the fact that one's conception of the good is correct. What often goes unnoticed is that many of the most contentious issues in contemporary political life do not involve competing conceptions of the good but, rather, competing understandings of what justice or fairness requires (or of what can be reasonably rejected). Both sides in the affirmative action debate, for example, think that fairness requires what they advocate. This means that one cannot expect political cooperation to be premised on the fact that one's conception of justice or fairness is correct, either. Political cooperation must be understood as cooperation among people who have different views about what is just or fair. The upshot is that the maintenance of a state will usually require everyone to comply with at least some laws that seem unjust. I have tried to show how people who accept the PCR and also care about justice might conclude that they have sufficient reason to behave in this way, but as I have also indicated, there is no guarantee that such a result will always be achieved.

III. THE MANDATORINESS OF THE LAW

In some respects, the problem of justifying voluntary compliance with the law is less interesting than another problem, the problem of justifying what I shall call the *mandatoriness* of the law. The mandatoriness of the law consists in the fact that coercion is employed to secure the compliance of all to whom the law is addressed. As we have seen, it will probably not be possible for all the cooperatively disposed members of the territory comprising a state – all those who accept the PCR – to regard the government of that state as exercising legitimate authority every time it promulgates a law. Even when what is at issue is whether holistic compliance is preferable from the standpoint of justice to the state of nature, some will not find obeying the law appropriate. What, then, can justify the use of coercion to enforce general compliance with all laws?

The fact that a state might be justified in coercing compliance with its laws, even if it cannot claim legitimate authority over everyone within its territory, has not gone unnoticed. As Leslie Green puts it, "the state can legitimately coerce those over whom it has no authority in order to protect those over whom it does."[11] And Christopher Morris, who regards the claim to sovereignty (authority over all in a territory) that states make as dubious, thinks that nevertheless a state can claim a right to rule, which includes a right to issue directives backed by coercive threats, if it is reasonably just and minimally efficient.[12] But on the whole, there has been little discussion of precisely how the coercing of people over whom a state does not have legitimate authority might be justified. And if Morris's view can be taken as representative, the question has been approached as one about what morality (properly understood) requires or permits. This creates the same problems that confront attempts to invoke putative moral truths

71

to answer the question whether there is sufficient reason to obey the law. Political cooperation is cooperation in the face of moral disagreement. Thus, we need an account of justifiable coercion that is anchored not in what morality truly requires, but in what the members of a state can regard as morally justified (from their respective standpoints).

The model of rational cooperation with which we have been working makes possible such an account. The key is to refine our understanding of the cooperation engaged in by those who view the PCR as giving them sufficient reason to obey the law (on a holistic interpretation). We now understand this cooperation as taking the form not only of their obeying the law themselves, but also of their participation in a collective effort to coerce compliance with the law from those who do not have sufficient reason under the PCR to comply. We can take this latter form of cooperation to be among those supported by the law. As was noted earlier, it is not usually possible to coerce the compliance of all those resident in a state's territory. Some residents – and in states without extensive and intrusive policing, most of them – must obey the law voluntarily. The assumption we are now making is that the cooperation these people engage in is, in part, cooperation to coerce the rest. Typically, this will take the form not of active participation in coercive activities but of providing resources that support the state's coercive efforts, and of noninterference with these efforts. Vindicating the mandatoriness of the law is a matter of explaining what could justify this form of cooperation.

The main hurdle confronting this project is provided by the fact that there is a strong moral presumption against coercion; other things being equal, it constitutes impermissible treatment of people. What we need if we are to vindicate the mandatoriness of the law, then, is some way that the voluntary cooperators can regard coercion as justified, despite the fact that there is a moral presumption against it.

We should be clear about the relation of justified mandatoriness to legitimate authority. When we consider the legitimacy of authority, we are looking at compliance with directives from the standpoint of those to whom they are addressed. There must be sufficient reason, from the point of view of these people, to accept the preemption of their own judgment about what is required in the situation. I have argued that the PCR gives us a way of interpreting this. We may speak of legitimate political authority, then, when the state's directive power – its de facto authority and its coercive power – is used to support laws compliance with which can be justified by the PCR. But as I have said, it is doubtful that modern states can claim legitimate authority in this sense over all the people within their territory.

When we consider mandatoriness, by contrast, we look at the situation from the standpoint of those who control the coercive apparatus of the state. *They* must be able to regard the state's efforts as justified. In a democracy, it is ultimately the voluntary cooperators – those who accept the state's authority – who control the coercive apparatus of the state.[13] The people who actually apply the state's coercive power will be their agents. To mark the contrast with authority, we can introduce the notion of legitimate *government*. Government is legitimate when the use of coercion to enforce the law against all in a state's territory is morally justified, despite the presumption against it. The relevant question for the voluntary cooperators in a democratic state, then, is whether they can regard government as legitimate, in this sense. But they need not agree on why it is legitimate. It need only be the case that each, consulting his own moral values, can conclude that the coercion to which he is contributing has the requisite moral justification.[14]

How might the mandatoriness of the law be justified? Basically, there are two possibilities. First, with respect to some laws – those securing social peace, for example – people who are unwilling to participate in the cooperative scheme underwritten by the law can be seen by those who are willing to do this as dangerous. Thus, the people in the latter group will have a sound reason of self-defense to use coercion to support such laws, and they can plausibly take this consideration as having a moral force sufficient to outweigh the moral presumption against coercion. By enforcing the laws ensuring social peace throughout the territory encompassed by their cooperation, the cooperators extend the protection of the law to those who do not take themselves to have sufficient reason to participate. But these people will be getting something that they think is not worth the cost of their (coerced) contributions. So the only reason for them to obey will be the reason provided by the coercive threats.

In contemporary societies, however, the law does more than secure social peace. It also directs the members of states to contribute, in various ways, to a wide range of public goods – or, if we regard social peace as a public good, to a wide range of other public goods. Where a public good takes the form of the avoidance of the negative externalities associated with certain actions, such as the dumping of pollutants into air or water, it may be possible to justify coercing contribution in the same way this is justified in the case of social peace. The dumping of pollutants, in aggregate, harms or damages the legitimate interests of other people. So those who control the coercive apparatus of the state can take the presumption against coercion to be outweighed by considerations of self-defense and the defense of others. But this argument cannot be employed to justify coercing participation in the state's efforts to produce public goods that merely constitute a positive benefit (for those holding certain values).

This brings us to the second way that those in control of the coercive apparatus of the state may be able to regard coercion as justified despite the moral presumption against it. They may be able to suppose that, regardless of what those coerced might think, there is sufficient reason for them to do what they are coerced into doing. Coercion would then be justified as, in effect, correcting a defect of rationality on the part of those coerced. As I said, in a democracy, it is ultimately the voluntary cooperators, acting through democratic procedures, who control the coercive apparatus of the state. The idea we are now considering, then, is that these people may be able to regard coercion as justified by the fact that it forces those coerced to do what there is actually sufficient reason for them to do. Of course, this means that the voluntary cooperators or their agents, the members of the government, must take themselves to be well positioned to determine what others have sufficient reason to do – indeed, as better positioned than these others.

For people of certain political persuasions, this would present no problem. But it can be awkward for liberals, who accept the fundamental liberal idea that coercive impositions must be justifiable to those coerced. On the narrowest reading of this requirement, those coerced would have to accept, at the very time coercion was applied, that it was justified. For the most part, this would restrict justifiable coercion to the case where it was employed to solve the assurance problem within a group of people who accepted the PCR. Legitimate government would be reduced to legitimate authority. But more expansive readings of the requirement of justifiability are possible. Somewhat less restrictive is the requirement that those coerced could be brought, at some point after the imposition of coercion, to accept that it was justified. And less restrictive still, we might understand the requirement of justifiability to those coerced as satisfied if the values they accept support, in conjunction with the PCR or the PIR, their doing what they are being coerced to do, even if they could never be brought to see this. The final possibility is that there are certain values that all competent reasoners must accept, and thus that coercing behavior supported by these values satisfies the requirement of justifiability to those coerced, whatever their actual evaluative commitments.

The liberal requirement that coercive impositions must be justifiable to those coerced can, then, be interpreted in ways that would allow liberals to coerce compliance with the law from people who do not regard themselves as having sufficient reason to comply. But no matter how it is interpreted, the liberal position reflects a concern to bring legitimate government, as much as possible, into line with legitimate authority. Although the people coerced do not accept the authority of the state, those in control of the state's coercive apparatus take themselves to be constrained by how things look from the standpoint of the coerced, as this is *properly* understood. They aim to govern in a way that those coerced would regard as involving the exercise of legitimate authority, were it not for various cognitive shortcomings.[15]

Perhaps the simplest possibility of this sort is coercing compliance with the PCR. The idea here would be that people who have sufficient reason under the PCR to contribute to a cooperative scheme (given their values) can justifiably be compelled to make this contribution. The unwillingness to contribute that coercion could overcome could arise from a temporary inability to appreciate the force of the PCR or from a general lack of a cooperative disposition – from an inclination to ride free. How far would this take us?

Basically, we are talking about using coercion to prevent people from making mistakes about what they have sufficient reason to do, given the PCR. It is predictable that individuals will err on the side of supposing that the public goods provided by the state are not worth enough to justify the designated contributions, when in fact the PCR would support contribution, given their values. Still, it is not plausible that this consideration could justify the state in coercing contribution to all of the public goods it provides. For each resident, there will be some goods that are clearly worthless.

Here I am supposing that in deciding whether those coerced have sufficient reason, under the PCR, to comply with laws supporting the production of public goods, we can consider each good separately. It might be suggested that by drawing on the earlier argument for holistic compliance, we could obtain a stronger result. But it is unclear whether this is so. The principal argument supporting holistic compliance was that piecemeal compliance would make it impossible to put in place fixed policies on issues the justice of which was controversial. But the promotion of most public goods produced by the state is underwritten by values other than justice, and with respect to these values, the argument against piecemeal compliance – against contributing only when the benefit associated with the particular good at issue exceeds the cost one incurs – is less compelling.

Still, these points may not be decisive. When compliance with the PCR can be achieved by voluntary efforts, there seems to be no justification for a holistic approach to the production of positive public goods. There is no reason that a population cooperating successfully on a piecemeal basis to produce positive public goods should shift to a holistic form of cooperation, in which each regards the total social effort as a single cooperative scheme and applies the PCR to it. But we are now considering the use of coercion to secure participation that would be justified by the PCR but is not occurring. Basically, this is a matter of enforcing the payment of taxes. And it may be that those in control of the coercive apparatus of the state can regard a holistic posture – coercing the payment of taxes supporting a single package of public goods for the whole society – as more appropriate than a piecemeal posture.

Enforcing compliance with the PCR on a piecemeal basis would mean establishing a separate tax for each public good and then determining, for each person, whether that good had sufficient value to outweigh the cost of the tax. This would be beyond the reach of any conceivable administrative apparatus, and since voluntary compliance would err on the side of noncontribution, it could be predicted that many contributions that were in fact justified by the PCR would not be made. Coercing holistic compliance, by contrast, is administratively much simpler. Thus, undercontribution can be largely eliminated. True, this will mean requiring some people to contribute to goods they regard as having little or no value. But those in control of the coercive apparatus of the state may be able to regard this as justifiable because enforcing the PCR on a holistic basis will secure an outcome closer to what this principle actually requires – each person's making, with respect to each public good, all and only those tax payments that are indicated given his values – than trying to enforce it on a piecemeal basis (or not enforcing it at all). It should be noted, however, that this involves assuming that everyone in the population can regard the whole package of governmentally produced public goods as worth the cost of his or her total contribution.

There may, then, be a way of viewing the enforcement of laws imposing taxation to produce positive public goods as justifiable by reference to the PCR when it is employed in conjunction with the values the people coerced actually hold. But if there remain cases that this strategy cannot handle, to vindicate the mandatoriness of the law in all its aspects – to justify coercing compliance with all laws by everyone residing in a state's territory – we must expand the rational defects that those in control of the coercive apparatus of the state can regard themselves as justified in correcting by coercion. In particular, we must suppose that there are certain values, procedural or substantive, that all normally functioning rational agents will acknowledge. Coercion can then be understood as correcting the rational defect involved in failing to be responsive to these values.

John Rawls's political liberalism provides an example of this approach. He formulates the following liberal principle of legitimacy: "Our exercise of political power is fully proper only when it is exercised in accordance with a constitution the essentials of which all citizens as free and equal may reasonably be expected to endorse in the light of principles and ideals acceptable to their common human reason."[16] The idea of what can be *reasonably expected* in light of principles *acceptable* to common human reason obviously introduces a standard that those coerced need not actually accept. And Rawls's talk of political power indicates that we are in the domain of what I have called mandatoriness (legitimate government, rather than legitimate authority). Political liberalism acknowledges the fact of reasonable pluralism, the fact that under conditions of freedom, the free play of reason will result in the emergence of a variety of reasonable comprehensive moral doctrines.[17] But a liberal society will require some common normative ideas on the basis of which it can make important political decisions – for Rawls, decisions concerning constitutional essentials and questions of basic justice. Rawls terms this common basis for decision making in a pluralistic society *public reason*. Its content is provided by a political conception of justice. The political conception must be such that each reasonable member of the society could expect all other reasonable members to accept it as the foundation for their common life. The underlying idea appears to be fairness. The political conception provides a fair basis for organizing the common life of a pluralistic society where people hold different comprehensive moral doctrines.

I shall have more to say about public reason in Chapter 4. For present purposes, it is enough to point out that if the political conception of justice provides a basis for cooperation that all reasonable members of a pluralistic society would accept, people who do not accept it can be seen as displaying a rational defect – unreasonableness.[18] Thus, coercing compliance with laws giving expression to the political conception can be justified as forcing people to do what there is sufficient reason for them to do, whether they acknowledge this or not.[19]

This approach can solve a problem that is probably beyond approaches based solely on enforcing the PCR: justifying the coercion of people who hold conceptions of justice in light of which the state of nature is preferable to the legal order. In this sort of case, what is at issue is not compelling payment for public goods, but forcing people to contribute to what they regard as injustice. And the problem may be exacerbated if the legal order embodies a commitment to – and thus directs contribution to – a variety of efforts to promote social outcomes deemed by those in control to be required by justice. People holding opposing conceptions of justice may regard making such contributions as worse than wasting money on public goods they think valueless. But if the political conception of justice that all reasonable people will accept is relatively determinate, other conceptions can be dismissed as deviant.

It may also be possible to invoke the political conception to justify enforcing laws that require contribution to the full social package of positive public goods. Rawls makes use of the political conception of justice primarily to justify the adoption and maintenance of a constitution for a pluralistic society, not to justify particular laws (except where they concern questions of basic justice). But he appears to suppose that cooperation to maintain the constitution involves compliance with any laws enacted in the requisite way (and within the constraints of basic justice). If this is right, there will be sufficient reason for each person to obey laws supporting the production of positive public goods. Thus, those in control of the coercive apparatus of the state will be able to regard the use of coercion to secure compliance with even these laws as correcting a rational defect.

The reasoning here should be spelled out more fully. Rawls formulates his liberal principle of legitimacy as a necessary condition only. But I take it that this is because he wants to be able to say that the enactment and enforcement of laws that violate basic justice is not legitimate (does not constitute legitimate government) even when it proceeds in accordance with an acceptable constitution. If so, it would seem that where basic justice plays no role, the liberal principle of legitimacy can be understood as stating a sufficient condition, in which case it would establish the legitimacy of enforcing laws underwriting the production of positive public goods. It is worth noting, however, that in *A Theory of Justice,* Rawls discusses the possibility of providing public goods not required by justice through a branch of government that he calls the "exchange branch," which appears to be intended to work in such a way that only those who value a particular public good would contribute to its production, and only in amounts calibrated to ensure a net gain (from their points of view).[20] But he mentions that the idea may be impractical.

The Rawlsian approach to legitimate government in terms of public reason may seem to enable us to dispense with the PCR, but this is not so. The argument should be familiar by now. Each individual is presumed to accept the values derived from the political conception of justice, and also some moral values that potentially dictate defection. Rawls clearly supposes that the values derived from the political conception of justice have greater weight than any moral values with which they might conflict.[21] But if we use the PIR to determine what all the applicable values give agents sufficient reason to do, we will not get a satisfactory result. In employing the PIR in a particular case, we must consider not only the relative weights of the applicable reasons or values, understood abstractly, but also the degree to which their realization will be affected by the various alternatives that are open. And it seems unlikely that a single individual's failure to comply with any law, or even all laws, would have an appreciable effect on the degree to which a particular state realizes fundamental political values. In particular, the injustice brought into the world by one individual's noncompliance with the law would not be very great, as injustice goes.[22] By contrast, an individual might be able to accomplish a lot from the standpoint of the other moral values she holds by defecting – by breaking the law. Thus, the great weight of political values must be brought to bear through the PCR. It must be argued that each has sufficient reason to obey the law since she must regard general cooperation to promote public values – the political conception of justice – as preferable to what she could accomplish in the noncooperative outcome.[23]

If we invoke public reason to vindicate the full mandatoriness of the law in a liberal society, then, we are supposing that those in control of the coercive apparatus of the state can regard coercion as correcting a composite rational defect: failure to be responsive to the PCR when it operates in conjunction with a political conception of justice that all reasonable people will accept.

IV. SECESSION AND ANNEXATION

A further aspect of political cooperation that deserves discussion concerns changes in the composition of the groups engaging in such cooperation. Although traditional contract theories tell a story about the formation of states out of groups of individuals not previously members of any state, in the actual world, most people are born into states. The PCR provides an account of when they can regard the authority established in their area as legitimate and when the voluntary cooperators are justified in imposing political control on those who do not regard authority as legitimate (the issue of mandatoriness).

But while the formation of states out of individuals not previously living in any state is basically a fiction, we do confront the formation of new states out of old ones. Sometimes political revolution in a given territory can be understood this way, at least if it results in a change of constitution. There are also, however, cases in which a previously existing political unit breaks up into smaller units, or a previously existing unit expands to encompass other previously existing units. These are the cases of secession and annexation. We can approach these phenomena either from the standpoint of legitimate authority or from the standpoint of mandatoriness.

Secession becomes an issue when the individuals in a territorial subpart of a larger political entity find that an alternative scheme of political cooperation involving only them would be preferable, in light of their values, to continued participation in the larger scheme. Under such conditions, the PCR may justify their withdrawing and establishing the new scheme. It will do this if they can judge that continued participation in the larger scheme would give them less of what they value than establishing the new scheme.

It is important to note, however, that even if secession is indicated by the PCR when the issue is posed from the standpoint of the self-regarding concerns of the members of the relevant group, it may not be indicated when the issue is posed from the standpoint of their moral values. One important moral issue is whether they are justified in removing from the larger unit the land on which they reside. And this issue may be further complicated by questions of distributive justice. If the territory in question contains most of the economic basis of the larger entity, those residing in it may judge that there are reasons of justice for remaining a part of the larger entity. Still, they could also accept moral considerations that support secession. They may believe that those who would be left behind have no right to what they lose (perhaps because it was acquired by conquest), or that secession is required to preserve a distinct culture.[24]

Here we are examining secession from the standpoint of legitimate authority. It appears in a somewhat different light if we look at mandatoriness. One aspect of this concerns what can justify supporters of secession in using coercion to enforce the cooperation of those in their territory who do not wish to secede. But we must also allow for the possibility that moral values held by the residents of the remaining territory may justify their forcibly opposing secession. The position of the North in the American Civil War might be interpreted in this way. From our contemporary standpoint, the goal of abolishing slavery has the most promise here. Forcing the South to remain in the union so as to effect the legal abolition of slavery could be justified, if not by the value of self-defense then by the value of defending others. This is probably not a historically accurate characterization of the situation, however, despite the role played by the abolitionists. At the start of the Civil War, at any rate, the North was fighting only to preserve the union. It is an interesting question whether this goal can be put in a moral light sufficient to justify the use of coercion to prevent secession.[25] As the case of the American Civil War shows, when secession is at issue, the question of what can justify coercing compliance with the law merges into the question of what can justify war.

Similar points apply to the phenomenon of annexation. The PCR can underwrite this. Suppose that two states, A and B, border each other. State A might issue directives to the residents of state B who occupy the border area, directives that, if complied with, would involve those individuals in a scheme of political cooperation proposed by state A for the larger territory encompassing it, plus the bordering parts of state B. If these individuals found participation in the larger scheme – that is, joining the proposed new state – preferable in light of the PCR to remaining in state B, they would have sufficient reason to start obeying these directives and cease obeying the directives of state B. It would be a simple case where the PCR justifies defection from one cooperative enterprise because another one yields greater benefits. The residents of the border area would thus be peacefully incorporated into a new, larger state A. Of course, this presupposes that they could regard themselves as justified in bringing with them into the new scheme the territory, formerly in state B, in which they reside.

Once again, however, when we look at the matter from the standpoint of mandatoriness, we get a somewhat different picture. We will need to consider what could justify coercing the cooperation of those residents of the border area who do not wish to join the new political unit. And consideration will also have to be given to what could justify state B in using force to maintain compliance with its laws in the area at issue, as well as to what could justify state A in meeting this force to effect annexation.

One final point should be made about these cases. The PCR directs an individual to compare how her values would be realized by a given cooperative scheme with how they would be realized in the noncooperative outcome. The noncooperative outcome is the outcome that would obtain if the cooperative scheme at issue did not exist. But as we have seen, the options that would be available if a particular scheme did not exist could involve participation in a different cooperative scheme. Thus, if an individual judges that her values would be more fully realized by scheme A than scheme B, the PCR will endorse leaving scheme B and joining scheme A. When the question of secession or annexation is being posed, it is appropriately presented in this way, as involving a choice, made by the members of a certain population, concerning which of two cooperative schemes to participate in. But if secession or annexation is effective as a matter of fact – if a new state, understood as a collective agent with a functioning choice mechanism, is created – the question the PCR poses to the individuals residing in the territory at issue will no longer involve the comparison of two cooperative schemes. They will have no realistic option of joining another scheme. They must, rather, compare cooperation on the new basis with the noncooperative outcome, understood simply as the state of nature. This means that successful annexation or secession may be able to constitute a political entity as a legitimate authority for certain individuals who could not have regarded it this way when they still had a choice.

Chapter 4

Democracy

In Chapter 2, we saw how cooperative dispositions, as I have characterized them, create a framework within which a choice mechanism can operate, a mechanism that selects one of the cooperative schemes jointly feasible for all the members of the relevant group. At bottom, the method for the selection of schemes is (de facto) agreement – that is, coincidence of preference. In some cases, there may be agreement among the members of the group on the ranking of the feasible schemes, or at least on which scheme is ranked first. In others, the choice of a scheme is possible despite disagreement regarding which of the candidates would be best because the members can agree on a procedure for selecting a scheme. In the first kind of case, substantive values ground the agreement; in the second, procedural values. It should be emphasized that there need only be agreement on which scheme or procedure would be best. The members of a group need not hold the same values. That is, it will suffice if there is a kind of overlapping consensus.

In Chapter 3, we explored some implications of the PCR for political life on the assumption, associated with the contractarian tradition, that states are cooperative enterprises. An aspect of this interpretation of political life is that legislation can often be regarded as effecting a choice among candidate cooperative schemes, either by implementing a wholly new one or modifying an old one. To legislate a policy is to choose a cooperative scheme. In many modern states, it is widely supposed that the legislative process should be democratic. The choice among cooperative schemes effected by legislation should be made by a vote after discussion of the alternatives. In this chapter, I consider some different ways of understanding the desirability of democracy, giving special attention to the role that deliberation plays in it. The discussion will thus provide a transition to the topic of collective reasoning.

82

I. VOTING AND FAIRNESS

Democracy standardly involves the making of proposals, deliberation concerning their relative merits, and the selection of one by a vote. Let us focus first on voting by the method of majority rule. On the view I have presented, the employment of this procedure will be justified by moral values held by the members of a state. Since the paradigmatic virtue of mutually beneficial cooperation is fairness, we can begin by considering how this value might justify voting.

A procedure for accomplishing a certain task can be evaluated in two different ways. First, it can be regarded as having instrumental value. This means that its value as a procedure is derived from the value of the outcomes that it produces. If fairness is the operative value, the claim will be that voting has value as a decision procedure because it yields schemes that are fair – or fairer than they would be if chosen in some other way. It must be borne in mind that we are speaking only of the division of the benefits of political cooperation. The claim is that when cooperative schemes are chosen by a vote, the benefits of cooperation will be divided fairly, or more fairly than they would be if schemes were chosen by some other method. There is no suggestion that all sources of unfairness in life will be eliminated.

But procedures can also be assessed on the basis of their intrinsic value. In this case, we deem their mere employment to have moral value, irrespective of the value of the outcomes produced. Fairness can support voting in this way as well. This is, perhaps, easier to see if we gloss the requirement of fairness as a requirement to give equal consideration to each member of a group. We can regard voting as displaying intrinsic value because it gives each member equal consideration, in some way that is independent of the fairness of the outcomes produced. In particular, there is a sense in which it gives each member equal influence over the outcome, at least when each has one vote.

Unfortunately, these two ways of viewing the value of voting are somewhat at odds. It seems relatively unproblematic to say that making a choice among candidate cooperative schemes by the method of majority rule satisfies the value of fairness – or equal consideration – when we abstract from the outcomes produced. But it is less clear that voting secures outcomes that are fair. A paradigm of such an outcome would be a compromise that gives each a part of what he values and also satisfies a criterion of fair distribution. Voting by the method of majority rule, however, may give some members of a group exactly the cooperative scheme they want, while giving others a scheme that they judge to be decidedly inferior. If political cooperation is licensed by the PCR, each will regard the benefits associated with the legal order as exceeding the cost of his contribution. But on any given issue, those in the majority may find that the benefits of cooperation exceed the costs by a large amount, while those in the minority find that the benefits exceed the costs by only a little. Is there any way to derive an unambiguous verdict about voting from the standpoint of fairness?

The problem just described is mitigated if a group routinely chooses among cooperative schemes by voting and the people in the minority on one occasion are in the majority on others, so that over the long term, each finds herself in the majority about equally often. In this case – leaving aside the fact that more might be at stake in some votes than others – the outcome will have the features of a fair compromise. The share of the benefits of cooperation received by each will be approximately equal (over time). But we can expect this to happen only if the composition of majorities varies randomly from issue to issue, which may not be the case.[1]

When the composition of majorities does not vary randomly, there appears to be a telling objection to voting from the standpoint of overall fairness. A fair lottery to determine who gets to choose the scheme to be implemented by the group seems to have just as much intrinsic value, as a procedure by which to select a cooperative scheme, as the method of majority rule – to manifest equal consideration of each to the same degree. And it can be argued that a lottery is a more effective instrument for promoting overall fairness because the outcomes it produces will be fairer.[2] To be sure, in this case, too, we have the problem that some derive a greater benefit from cooperation than others. But if the lottery gives each an equal chance of winning, over time each should get what she wants about equally often – in the sense of winning the lottery equally often. As we have seen, we can expect voting to have this feature only if the composition of majorities varies randomly from issue to issue.

We should not be too hasty in declaring a lottery preferable to the method of majority rule from the standpoint of outcome-fairness, however. The case for the outcome-fairness of a lottery – for its giving each what he or she wants about equally often – seems of limited applicability in political contexts. It is plausible that in a small group that confronts many decisions, deciding among cooperative schemes by a lottery that gives the winner the right to choose a scheme for the group will, over time, make the preferences of each effective about equally often. But this is because the group faces many more choices than it has members. In a large society, the opposite will be true. Most will never win the lottery.

To be sure, in a large group, there is a feature of the situation that compensates for this. An individual does not need to win the lottery herself to find the choice of a cooperative scheme optimal from the standpoint of her preferences. This will also happen if someone who shares her preferences wins. But this does not ensure that outcomes will have the features of a fair compromise. The subgroups within which preferences are shared may not all be the same size. This means that the members of larger preference groups will have a better chance of finding their preferences put into effect (through having someone who shares these preferences win the lottery). Unless the composition of preference groups varies randomly over time, the upshot is that members of large preference groups will get what they want more often than members of small groups. So viewed as an instrument for promoting fair outcomes, a lottery of this sort has some of the shortcomings of voting. And as we have seen, if we suppose that the composition of preference groups changes randomly from issue to issue, the shortcomings of voting will be reduced.

It should be noted that there is one form of lottery that would be clearly superior to voting from the standpoint of outcome-fairness, a lottery over preference groups that gives each group an equal chance to win. On any given issue, this will give each individual an equal chance of getting what he wants, and could result in each actually receiving what he wants about equally often in the long run. But conducting a lottery on this basis in a large society – identifying all the different preference groups for each issue – would present insuperable practical problems.

It seems, then, that a reasonable case can be made for voting from the standpoint of fairness. It is not a matter of unambiguous triumph from both the intrinsic and the instrumental points of view. Voting has as much intrinsic value as a lottery. The procedure, abstracting from outcomes, is as fair as a lottery; it accords equal consideration to each. And, at least when we take practical exigencies into account, both procedures have shortcomings as instruments for producing fair outcomes.

Two additional points should be made here. First, it might be suggested that the problems that confront voting from the standpoint of outcome-fairness arise because we are viewing it as an instance of what Rawls calls imperfect procedural justice.[3] We have an independent criterion of fairness – exemplified by a fair compromise – in light of which we can see that voting sometimes fails to hit the mark, and is not superior to a fair lottery. But perhaps we can instead view voting as an instance of pure procedural justice. We can speak of pure procedural justice when we have a procedure the rules of which seem fair, as judged by some criterion that abstracts from outcomes, and we have no independent criterion by which to evaluate outcomes. Any outcome actually produced by the procedure counts as fair. A paradigm of pure procedural justice is a poker game, in which whatever distribution of winnings results from playing the game (in accordance with the rules) is fair. If we can view voting in this way, we can say that whatever scheme is chosen by democratic procedures is, ipso facto, fair.

To speak of pure procedural justice, however, it must be either impossible or inappropriate to apply an independent standard to the evaluation of outcomes. The latter is the case in a poker game. The players have voluntarily agreed to play the game, on the understanding that what each takes away from it will be determined by the game. This suspends the application of independent criteria of fairness. But this condition is not satisfied in the case of political decision making. Few have a real choice about playing the political game, and it is entirely appropriate to employ independent criteria to evaluate outcomes. Suppose that a government announced that henceforth it would distribute welfare benefits of a certain kind using poker games. Each person eligible for benefits would get a voucher good for a certain number of chips in a poker game, and the actual benefit each received would be determined by the outcome of the game. Clearly, the government could not legitimately reply to objections by saying that a poker game is an instance of pure procedural justice, and thus independent criteria of fairness have no application.

The remaining possibility is to defend the interpreting of voting as an instance of pure procedural justice by arguing that it is impossible – at least in the political case – to make an independent determination of the fairness of outcomes. The issues here are tricky. Certainly, many members of a society that chooses cooperative schemes by voting will have no difficulty judging, by reference to their own conceptions of fairness, that the society in which they live is unfair in some respect. The most we can say is that since people have different conceptions of fairness, for practical purposes we have no alternative but to regard whatever result a vote produces as fair.

But this goes too far. It is true that people disagree markedly about the substantive fairness of various policies that might be embodied in political cooperative schemes – for example, a progressive income tax. But a different application of the concept of fairness is at issue when we argue that there is no independent standard by which to evaluate the choice of cooperative schemes effected by the legislative process. We are concerned with whether the mechanism for choosing among schemes distributes the benefits and burdens of *political cooperation* – cooperation to create a state – fairly. And here there is much less room for disagreement about what fairness requires. If some people always cooperate on terms that are maximally favorable from the standpoint of their concerns – if the policies adopted are always the policies they want – while others always cooperate on terms that are minimally favorable from the standpoint of their concerns, the system of cooperation produces unfair outcomes in a relatively uncontroversial sense that all who possess the concept of fairness should be able to acknowledge.

In considering the value of voting as an instrument for promoting fairness, then, we are unavoidably in the domain of imperfect procedural justice. And here what is required is a comparative judgment. Is there any method for choosing cooperative schemes that is a more effective instrument for securing a fair distribution of the benefits of political cooperation than voting? I have given reasons for thinking that voting is at least as good as its most plausible rival, a lottery.

The second point that needs to be made is that there is another moral value, beyond fairness, that can be employed to justify voting, the utilitarian value of maximizing overall welfare. This leads unambiguously to a preference for voting over a lottery from the instrumental perspective. While a lottery may produce as much overall satisfaction as a vote if there is a majority on a given issue and a member of it wins the lottery, over the long term voting will be better, since it ensures that on each occasion when a decision must be made, a majority will favor the chosen alternative. Or at least this is so if the method of majority rule is employed, so that when a majority does not exist, new alternatives must be generated until one is found that is sufficient to attract a majority.

It perhaps reflects the influence of Rawls's critique of utilitarianism that contemporary discussions of the moral value of democratic procedures seldom consider welfare maximization. Yet even those who regard fairness as synonymous with justice, and regard justice as the first virtue of a society, will usually be prepared to accord some value to welfare maximization as a way of deciding among equally fair alternatives. So if, as I have suggested, voting and a lottery are roughly equivalent, intrinsically and instrumentally, from the standpoint of fairness in a large political society, it seems unproblematic to use considerations of welfare maximization to break the tie.

II. DELIBERATION AND FAIRNESS

Recently, there has been much discussion of what has become known as deliberative democracy. One prominent proponent of this approach, Joshua Cohen, has offered the following definition: "By a deliberative democracy, I shall mean, roughly, an association whose affairs are governed by the public deliberation of its members."[4] But this idea is open to two very different interpretations. The key phrase might be taken to mean that the affairs of the association are governed *only* by the public deliberation of its members. This would be possible if, every time the association faced the need to decide how to proceed as an association, it was able to deliberate to a consensus. Such associations can certainly be imagined, but in any plausible case they will be small and of short duration – for example, a group of friends on a camping trip. Alternatively, the key phrase might be interpreted to mean that deliberation plays *some* role in the process by which an association decides how to proceed. But even traditional views of democracy provide for debate or deliberation prior to the taking of a vote.

How, then, are we to make sense of deliberative democracy as an alternative to the standard view in large political societies, where deliberation to a consensus among all citizens on every issue the society faces is clearly out of the question? One natural possibility is to distinguish between the procedures by which a group decides and the substantive policies chosen. A group that frequently faced disagreements that did not yield to deliberation might still be able to agree on a procedure for generating decisions – for example, the method of majority rule. If we suppose that the consensus on a particular procedure is the result of deliberation concerning the merits of various procedures, there would be a natural sense in which the affairs of the group could be said to be governed by the public deliberation of its members. But again, this possibility is too close to the traditional view of democracy to constitute a significant alternative.

These observations suggest that the deliberative ideal is meant to be more ambitious, applying not just to the choice of procedures but to the enactment of particular laws. Cohen states that "outcomes are democratically legitimate if and only if they could be the object of a free and reasoned agreement among equals."[5] To explicate this idea, he introduces the notion of an ideal deliberative procedure. But he does not understand the legitimacy of outcomes in the manner of a constructivist account of truth – so that an outcome yielded by our actual procedure now is legitimate if and only if it would have been produced by the ideal procedure. Rather, the ideal procedure is meant to serve as a model for actual institutions; actual institutions are to approximate the model as closely as possible. The claim, apparently, is that if actual institutions do closely approximate the ideal deliberative procedure, we can – in the spirit of pure procedural justice – take whatever outcomes they produce as acceptable.

Cohen acknowledges that deliberation may not produce a consensus, and that in such cases, matters must be decided by a vote. But he goes on to say,

> the fact that it may so conclude does not, however, eliminate the distinction between deliberative forms of collective choice and forms that aggregate nondeliberative preferences. The institutional consequences are likely to be different in the two cases, and the results of voting among

those who are committed to finding reasons that are persuasive to all are likely to differ from the results of an aggregation that proceeds in the absence of this commitment.[6]

What we must consider, then, if we are to comprehend how the deliberative approach can depart from a more traditional approach, is why the results of a vote when democracy conforms to the deliberative model are likely to be different.

One possibility involves democracy's claim to be a fair procedure for resolving disputes. In our earlier discussion of this, we focused on voting. We saw that voting can be regarded as a fair procedure in two respects. It is intrinsically fair as giving each equal consideration in the decision-making process. And it produces outcomes that have some claim to be regarded as fair – or at least as fair as the outcomes produced by the alternatives. But it is easy to see that viewed in either of these ways, the merits of voting from the standpoint of fairness will be affected by features of the context in which voting is carried out. In particular, it will be affected by factors relating to the ability of group members to influence each other's votes. It seems that if democracy is to claim to be a fair procedure for resolving disputes, the ability of each to influence the voting behavior of others in the group must itself be fairly distributed.

These considerations point to the desirability of structuring the deliberation that precedes voting in various ways. I shall not consider all of the details, since they are not immediately germane to the principal themes of this book. But it is clear that in addition to ensuring the formal right to make proposals in a legislative assembly, either directly or through representatives, and to speak for and against the proposals made, steps must be taken to ensure the fair value of these rights. This involves equal access to education, to information, and to the means of communication.

It is important to understand, however, that the goal of these measures is a form of equality of opportunity – equal opportunity to influence voting behavior.[7] Enhancing effective participation in the deliberation preceding a vote is not the same thing as guaranteeing that each will actually have an equal influence on the voting behavior of others. If that were the case, the voting behavior of each individual would be the resultant of the same influences, and the outcome would presumably be unanimous. More important, equality of actual influence seems to be incompatible with the view that the discussion that precedes voting is a process of *deliberation* – that it involves the presentation of reasons. If reason is capable of deciding a matter about which people disagree, the reasons presented by some parties to the dispute will be stronger than the reasons presented by others. So even if all are equally competent in argument, some will hold, so to speak, a better hand. And if all the participants are as competent at appreciating arguments as they are in making them, the reasons offered by those who hold a better hand will have a decisive influence. In the ideal case, perhaps, the result will again be unanimous; but it will not be possible to say that each member of the group was equally efficacious in producing it. Those who presented the best reasons will have had a disproportionate influence.

Structuring deliberation to secure equal opportunity for influence is thus analogous to voting. Giving each member of a group one vote does not ensure that each will influence the resulting decision equally. Those in the minority will have no influence at all. Indeed, the whole point of voting is to resolve disputes in favor of one or the other of the positions held. Each has an equal input to the decision-making process, but the output reflects the rejection of some of these inputs. They are displaced by the collective force of other inputs. Something similar can be said about deliberation, even when it is structured so as to provide each with an equal opportunity to influence the decisions of the others. These decisions will usually involve the rejection of some of the inputs offered by the members of the group.[8]

There are, then, limitations on what can be accomplished by supplementing voting on the basis of one person one vote with various measures designed to equalize the capacity of each to make his or her case in the public forum. We can expand the claim of democracy to satisfy the relevant intrinsic value – to be a procedure that gives each equal consideration. But we cannot suppose that each will have equal influence on the outcome. Thus, democratic decision making retains the basic features described in Section I.

III. PUBLIC REASON

We have been exploring Cohen's claim that the deliberative model of democracy differs from the aggregative model even if, in the end, we must resort to voting. We have just seen that by structuring deliberation in certain ways, we can make the opportunity for political influence more equal. This is an important point, but I have argued that it does not represent a fundamental departure from the traditional model.

Another way of interpreting the claim that the deliberative approach constitutes a distinct alternative to the aggregative approach involves the Rawlsian notion of public reason. For Rawls, public reason consists of a set of principles and values that are appropriate for guiding the common affairs of a pluralistic society, where comprehensive moral doctrines differ. The connection with deliberative democracy arises from the fact that public deliberation in a pluralistic society must be conducted in terms of public reasons or values. It is plausible that if citizens vote their judgments concerning what these reasons or values require, the results will be different than if they voted their preferences.

We are accustomed to thinking that when interests conflict, a resolution can be found by appealing to moral reasons, especially reasons of fairness, that rise above such conflicts. Public reason seems intended to play the same role in connection with conflicts grounded in the comprehensive moral doctrines held by the different members of a pluralistic society. It is supposed to provide a basis on which they can rise above the competing claims of their different doctrines and resolve the conflicts these doctrines engender.

In Chapter 3, we explored the implications of the Rawlsian notion of public reason for the legitimacy of government. Our concern there was with the role that public reason might play in vindicating the claim that coercing compliance with the law can be viewed as correcting a cognitive defect. In the present context, however, the focus is on the connection between the political conception of justice imported by public reason and the choice of schemes of political cooperation.

The key concept underlying the notion of public reason is *reasonableness*. According to Rawls, public reasons are reasons that one can reasonably expect other reasonable members of a pluralistic society to accept.[9] Of course, shared deliberation will play an important role in shaping each person's sense of what constitutes a reasonable response to the reasonable commitments of others.[10] We need not suppose that public reasoning will result in a consensus about which policies are reasonable. As has been noted, it can still play a role if policies are determined by voting, provided that each votes only for policies that he finds justified by public reasons (by the shared political conception).

Public reason can be interpreted as having a more or less extensive employment. In its less extensive employment, citizens are to vote their judgments concerning what public reasons require only in cases pertaining to constitutional essentials and questions of basic justice.[11] Otherwise, they may vote their comprehensive doctrines. In a representative democracy, where most voting by citizens is for representatives of various sorts, it is a bit unclear what would be involved. Voting behavior would apparently be determined by judgments concerning the force of public reasons only when the representatives selected were expected to address constitutional issues or questions of basic justice. One suspects that on this less extensive view, the role of public reason in the lives of ordinary citizens is mainly to provide reassurance regarding the legitimacy of the democratic institutions they live under.

Routine decision making on the basis of public reasons is reserved for governmental officials, such as the justices of the Supreme Court.[12] On the more extensive employment of public reason, by contrast, citizens consult public reasons in determining how to vote whenever the relevant issues pose the question of what would constitute a reasonable response to the reasonable commitments of others. It may, however, be possible to bring the two interpretations more closely together by saying that the second one involves a more expansive understanding of what constitutes an issue of basic justice.

When public reason is invoked to ground constitutional essentials, it is being employed as a source of procedural values. When it is invoked to ground the judgments expressed in voting, by contrast, it is being given a substantive employment. In Chapter 2, we saw that fairness in its procedural employment can conflict with the substantive moral values that underwrite the preferences that the members of a group have for particular schemes. When a member of the group experiences such a conflict, he will be able to regard the choice of a scheme as guided by reason only if he is prepared to accept the demotion of his substantive moral concerns to interests. If the conflict between procedural and substantive values is less of a problem when votes express judgments regarding what public values (in their substantive employment) require, this will provide one way of vindicating the claim that deliberative approaches are fundamentally different from aggregative approaches. In the remainder of this section, I explore this possibility. A further respect in which public reason is connected with deliberative democracy will be discussed in the next section.

When interests conflict, bargaining and compromise can play a large role. But when comprehensive moral doctrines conflict, the search for policies that require the least concession by everyone will have greater urgency. In their recent account of deliberative democracy, Amy Gutmann and Dennis Thompson say, "In justifying policies on moral grounds, citizens should seek the rationale that minimizes rejection of the position they oppose."[13] They speak of this as economizing on moral disagreement. Nevertheless, Gutmann and Thompson – and other proponents of deliberative democracy – concede that disagreement will often remain despite our best efforts to find policies that satisfy everyone. It is here that public reason comes into play. It provides (in its substantive employment) a standard for determining what would constitute an appropriate resolution of disagreements grounded in conflicting moral commitments.[14] As I mentioned earlier, the fundamental concept of public reason is that of the reasonable. But how exactly is this to be understood?

The notion of the reasonable is ambiguous. Basically, to be reasonable is to be appropriately responsive to the relevant reasons. This is the sense in which the term is employed when people speak, for example, of proof beyond a reasonable doubt, or of (prudentially) reasonable precautions. I shall call this the competence sense of reasonableness (reasonableness-as-competence). But there is also a more substantive notion of the reasonable, a particular way of being responsive to the applicable reasons, which refers explicitly to the division of the benefits of cooperation. When we say to someone, in a cooperative context, "Be reasonable," we mean "Recognize that everyone has to find participation worthwhile, and thus that you must make some concession from your most preferred cooperative scheme." Here, the essence of reasonableness is fairness. Gutmann and Thompson connect public reason with fairness when they say, "the foundation of reciprocity [that is, deliberation on the basis of public reasons] is the capacity to seek fair terms of social cooperation for their own sake."[15] And Rawls explicitly ties the notion of the reasonable to fairness: "Persons are reasonable in one basic aspect when, among equals say, they are ready to propose principles and standards as fair terms of cooperation and to abide by them willingly, given the assurance that others will likewise do so."[16] I shall call this sense of reasonableness "reasonableness-as-fairness."

This latter value admits of a procedural-substantive contrast. Democratic procedures provide a reasonable (as fair) way of resolving disputes about which policies a group should follow. And, in the cases we are now considering, people are assumed to vote for what they judge to be a substantively reasonable (as fair) way of responding to the commitments of others. On the face of it, however, this places us in the same situation we explored in Chapter 2. Those in the minority will find that procedural reasonableness conflicts with substantive reasonableness. If they judge substantive reasonableness-as-fairness to prevail, they will not be able to regard cooperation as fully guided by reason, because they cannot regard one of its aspects, the choice of a cooperative scheme, as guided by reason. And if they judge procedural reasonableness-as-fairness to prevail, the moral concerns embodied in their judgments regarding what would be substantively reasonable-as-fair will be demoted to interests.

It will be useful to look at this problem in a little more detail. An individual who cannot view the choice of a cooperative scheme effected by democratic procedures as guided by reason, because she cannot view the value of fairness that justifies such procedures as outweighing the moral reasons for choosing a different scheme, may be powerless to do anything about it. If so, the PCR could still give her a reason to make her assigned contribution. This was explained in Section II of Chapter 2. But it may also be the case that she can alter the choice if she – or more likely, a group of which she is a member – can bring some form of social power to bear.

The most likely scenario involves the use of bargaining power at the deliberative stage. Bargaining power might be employed, instead of or in addition to arguments concerning what the relevant values support, in order to influence the voting behavior of the members of the group. If it is thought that procedural fairness requires that voting behavior be determined only by the exchange of arguments – as an aspect of equal opportunity for political influence, perhaps – individuals who could use bargaining power to influence voting will have to consider whether their reasons for doing so outweigh the associated procedural unfairness. But when these reasons are provided by substantive moral values, it seems plausible that they could frequently prevail over procedural fairness. To be sure, the employment of bargaining power to subvert deliberation will involve greater unfairness than that associated with a single individual's defection from a cooperative scheme (the case we considered in Chapter 1). Thus, a strong moral reason would be necessary to justify it. But what one can accomplish, from the standpoint of one's substantive moral concerns, by using bargaining power in this way will usually be greater than what one can accomplish by unilateral defection. If one succeeds in getting one's preferred scheme chosen, the whole group will be acting to promote one's moral values.

Earlier it was suggested that the problems created when procedural and substantive values conflict might be reduced when citizens vote their judgments concerning what public values require – concerning what would constitute a reasonable-as-fair response to the commitments of others – instead of judgments grounded in substantive values of other kinds. The argument would be that what we are talking about, in particular, is people voting their judgments concerning what a shared political conception of justice requires. But in this case, disagreements will not be very sharp. Each can acknowledge that the opposing views are backed by cogent reasons. Indeed, at the appropriate level of abstraction, the reasons invoked by one's opponents are the same reasons that one invokes. Thus, the conclusions they draw cannot be too alien. But this means that the moral loss associated with the choice of the scheme favored by one's opponents will be slight, and the reason for subverting a reasonable-as-fair decision procedure to block this choice correspondingly weak – too weak to justify the sacrifice of public values (in their procedural employment) that would be created by such an action.

But it is doubtful that this line of argument can succeed. In the first place, the disagreements about justice and fairness that we actually find are often quite intense, providing citizens with reasons for dissatisfaction that appear, if anything, to be stronger than the reasons provided by comprehensive moral doctrines. And while it might be replied that this is because, as things now stand, people are not operating with a single political conception of justice grounded in public reason, it is not clear how relevant this is. Rawls himself notes that it is more realistic to assume that a liberal society will contain different political conceptions that nevertheless have enough in common to deserve the label "liberal."[17] Under these circumstances, it can be expected that substantive disagreements about what justice and fairness require will remain sharp and widespread, with the result that the members will have strong reasons to subvert fair procedures.

Second, if public values in their procedural employment do prevail against the reasons that these values in their substantive employment provide for subverting the deliberative process, we will still be faced with the other horn of the dilemma. We will have to accept the demotion of certain moral concerns, those grounded in judgments regarding what would be substantively reasonable-as-fair, to interests – to considerations the satisfaction of which is important primarily because it satisfies those making these judgments.

It might be suggested that there are some respects in which moral conflicts, including conflicts about what justice and fairness require, bring with them conflicts of interest.[18] But this does not mean that it is unproblematic to resolve them as one would conflicts of interest. For the person holding a moral concern – whether grounded in a comprehensive moral doctrine or a political conception of justice – its importance is not exhausted by the fact that satisfying it satisfies her. It is taken to identify a feature that the world morally ought to have. This is compatible with accepting situations in which one's moral concerns are not as fully realized as one would like them to be. One does not demote one's moral concerns to interests by doing the best one can in an unfavorable situation. But acquiescing in the less than maximal realization of one's moral values because *fairness* requires this does alter the character of one's moral concerns. If one has the power to bring about a morally preferable alternative, but refrains for reasons of fairness, one treats one's concerns as interests. And it appears that the demotion of moral concerns to interests is something to regret.[19]

IV. EPISTEMIC DEMOCRACY

Deliberative democracy is sometimes said to differ from the standard understanding by virtue of the fact that while the standard view takes preferences as given, merely aggregating them into a social decision, the deliberative approach envisages the transformation of preferences through deliberation.[20] Presumably, the expectation is that deliberation will transform preferences by correcting mistakes, of fact or of reasoning, underlying them. Our discussion so far seems to show that only if the transformation is so radical as to produce a consensus will deliberation give democratic decision making a fundamentally different structure. If disagreement remains after deliberation, we will have to tell essentially the same story about why democratic decision making is desirable as we would tell if deliberation played no role. It is a fair – and utility-maximizing – way of resolving disputes between concerns that, regardless of how they may start out, must be seen as having a status like that of interests if the parties are to view cooperation as fully guided by reason. There is, however, one final way that one might try to salvage the idea that deliberative democracy represents a fundamentally different alternative, even when deliberation does not produce agreement.

In Section II it was noted that while equal *opportunity* for political influence seems to be a feasible goal, actual equality of influence is not to be expected if deliberation tracks the true force of the relevant reasons. Some participants in any controversy will have the weight of reason on their side. So if deliberation tracks the force of the relevant reasons, these people will wind up influencing the outcome more than others. But it is possible to look at the situation in a way that makes this seem less objectionable. If all in the group want its decisions to be guided by the relevant reasons, those who prevail need not be regarded as defeating those who oppose them. Rather, they serve the whole group by identifying the right course of action. This raises the possibility that, because of its deliberative aspect, we can view democratic decision making as having epistemic virtues – as getting the right answer, or getting it more often than not. This possibility is especially worthy of investigation in connection with decisions that have a moral dimension. It might provide a way that those in the minority can be reconciled to a democratic decision without demoting the moral concerns they express in voting to interests. They can instead regard these concerns as appropriately abandoned in favor of the democratic result.

It is useful to discuss this possibility within the framework provided by the concept of authority. In Chapter 3, I distinguished legitimate political authority, which concerns the reasons that those subject to the law have to obey it voluntarily, from legitimate government, which concerns the reasons that those in control of the coercive apparatus of the state have to coerce compliance with the law. I noted that liberal political theory brings the two notions more closely together, but still leaves them distinct. The idea that democracy might have epistemic virtues, however, seems intended to provide citizens with a reason to accept its results. In assessing this epistemic claim, then, we can focus on its implications for the legitimacy of authority

As we have employed the notion of authority so far, the focus has been on what I have called subordinating authority. This involves deferring to directives without changing one's mind about what would be the best course of action. I suggested in Chapter 2 that the PCR provides a way of justifying subordinating authority. But there is also another form of authority, the authority of experts, which works differently from subordinating authority. When someone who is legitimately viewed as an expert in some area expresses his or her considered opinion about a matter of that kind, this gives others a reason to change their minds.[21]

Expertise seems to be a threat to democracy. If there are moral experts, the members of a group should defer to them, rather than making up their own minds about the issues facing the group. However, even if we suppose that there is such a thing as moral truth, and that some people can know it, there will be problems establishing that these people should be accepted as experts on what morality requires. In general, expertise is established – and deference to experts justified – by a history of success. Thus, to acknowledge someone's expertise, one must be able to determine that her previous answers were correct. But this means that where there is abiding disagreement about what morality requires, there will be disagreement about who the experts are. It is for this reason that truth – moral truth – is "safe for democracy," in David Estlund's phrase.[22]

It is worth pausing to consider a little more fully why the generally accepted moral expertise of an individual or subgroup would be a threat to democracy. Certainly it would not prevent the group from taking a vote. Rather, the problem is that the vote would simply echo the judgment of the acknowledged experts. In presenting democracy as an alternative to government by experts, then, we are supposing that democratic decision making involves the construction of a social decision out of the *independent* inputs of each member.

Still, it may be possible to reconcile this fact with a role for expertise in democratic decision making. We may be able to view the group as a whole, deciding democratically, as possessing expert authority on moral matters, to which the group's members should defer by changing their minds. In posing this possibility, we must be clear about how the improvement is to be understood. There are at least three alternatives. The first and strongest is that each can regard the group's decision as more likely to be correct than his or her individual judgment about the matter to be decided. The second alternative is weaker. It restricts the comparison to other political choice mechanisms, holding that democratic government is more likely to produce correct answers to moral questions than are other forms of government, for example, dictatorship. But we do not suppose that an individual whose views depart from those of the majority will have a basis for regarding the group's decision as more likely to be correct than her own. Their deference to democratically generated decisions is grounded in acknowledgement of the government's subordinating, rather than expert, authority. The third alternative will be introduced shortly.

In considering the first two alternatives, we must distinguish between deliberation and voting. There is a classic source for the idea that voting can confer expert authority on a group, the Condorcet jury theorem. This shows that if the individual members of a group are more likely to be right than not about the answer to a yes–no question, the group as a whole is virtually certain to be right (that is, the majority opinion is virtually certain to be right) if the group is large enough.[23]

But while the correctness of the mathematical argument is not in doubt, there seems to be a consensus that it is of limited applicability to actual controversies. The main problem is the same one that confronts establishing a particular person as a moral expert for all the members of a group. Even when the group faces a yes–no question that virtually ensures that one alternative will get a majority, those in the minority must be able to regard the individual members of the majority as more likely to be right than not. Since each member of the majority will be expressing an opinion that each member of the minority judges to be wrong, the members of the minority will have a reason to regard the individuals comprising the majority as more likely to be right than not, on that particular occasion, only if they have found them right more often than not in the past. But in the typical moral case, those who seem wrong now will have seemed wrong in the past as well. Thus (in the judgment of the minority), one of the conditions specified by the theorem – that the individual voters be more likely to be right than not – will not be satisfied. Even if the group's decision is almost certainly right, for the reason the theorem suggests, the members of the minority will not be able to acknowledge this. So they will have no basis for deferring to the group's decision, determined by a vote, as the deliverance of an expert. This, of course, comports with our experience of democracy. Those in the minority do not change their minds when the result of a vote is revealed.

These points suggest that we should be less ambitious. We should not ask the putative epistemic virtues of democratic decision making to do all the work of justifying political authority, understood as deference to the official directives of the state (that is, the law). Rather, we should suppose that some forms of government can possess legitimate *subordinating* authority – perhaps on the basis of the PCR – and use epistemic considerations to determine which form of government is best. The claim would then be that among the possible forms of government possessing legitimate subordinating authority, democracy is more likely than the others to get the right answer to the questions faced by the political unit in question. This is the second of the alternatives that were distinguished.

In fact, however, this claim can be resolved into an even more modest one, the third alternative. The problems encountered by the Condorcet jury theorem, which focuses on voting, suggest that we should seek any epistemic virtues democracy might possess in the deliberation that precedes voting. But, of course, to justify democracy we must justify voting as well. It is possible to combine general social deliberation with dictatorship. The dictator could witness, and perhaps participate in, deliberation, and then make a decision. Let us, then, make the further assumption that voting, too, is justified on a nonepistemic basis. As has already been suggested, this basis might be provided by the value of fairness. From the standpoint of fairness (in both an intrinsic and instrumental employment), voting is at least as satisfactory a method for deciding among cooperative schemes as any alternative. This approach has the virtue of respecting the fact that compliance with the directives arising from a vote can involve contributing to policies that one regards as, in the last analysis, mistaken. The putative epistemic virtues of democratic deliberation come on top of this. The claim is simply that decisions made, for reasons of fairness, by a vote are more likely to be correct when they are preceded by shared deliberation than when not.[24]

But what basis is there for supposing that when a moral controversy is decided by a vote, the decision is more likely to be correct if it is preceded by shared deliberation? To answer this question, we need a better understanding of why, in general, shared deliberation might have epistemic virtues. Of course, it is plausible that each will find her own grasp of what morality requires improved by witnessing and participating in a process of shared deliberation. This will enable her to refine her personal view of which policies are morally appropriate. But what more can we say?

If we suppose that some of the comprehensive moral doctrines held by the members of a pluralistic society are correct and others incorrect, shared deliberation might slowly convert the members of the population to the correct view. But there is a sense in which this supposition is antiliberal. The liberal stance seems to be that the various comprehensive doctrines found in the population are, in some sense, equally legitimate. If we wish to preserve the characteristic features of liberal societies, then, we must restrict any claim that deliberated democratic decisions are epistemically superior to undeliberated decisions to cases where the issue is what public reason requires. I have suggested that the Rawlsian version of public reason, and the versions influenced by it, take the fundamental notion of public reason to be reasonableness-as-fairness. So for these views, disagreements about what public reason requires are basically disagreements about what is fair in a pluralistic society, where people hold different comprehensive moral doctrines. But why should the results of a vote concerning what would be a reasonable-as-fair response to the commitments of others be more likely to be correct if preceded by shared deliberation?

We should be precise about what we are asking here. Earlier, I introduced a distinction between substantive and procedural fairness. If voting is a fair procedure for making social decisions, we can regard democracy as securing a certain degree of realization of the value of fairness (procedural fairness), simply by virtue of the fact that it involves voting. And if the argument in Section I is correct, it may also be possible to regard this procedure as yielding fair outcomes – or at least, outcomes as fair as any alternative. But this will simply be a matter of people finding what they vote for put into effect about equally often. In the present case, where people vote their understanding of what public reason requires, this means that over time, the *views* of each concerning what would be substantively reasonable-as-fair will find some embodiment in the policies adopted. The claim that democratic deliberation has epistemic virtues must, then, go beyond this. The claim must be that when voting is preceded by shared deliberation about what is substantively reasonable-as-fair, and the members of the group express their opinion about this in their votes, the policy decided upon is more likely *actually to be* substantively reasonable-as-fair than it would be in the absence of deliberation. We do not just fairly respect different views of substantive fairness; we move closer to the correct view – on average, if not on each occasion.

How, then, could it be established that deliberation improves the epistemic "batting average" of voting? As was noted, it is plausible that each group member will take her own view of what would be substantively fair to be improved by shared deliberation. This means that each member of the majority will regard the policy adopted as having stronger moral support than the policy that group (that majority) would have adopted in the absence of deliberation. But on what basis can the members of the *minority* judge that the result of the vote more fully reflects the moral truth (about what would be reasonable-as-fair) than it would have in the absence of deliberation?

The most straightforward possibility is that while those in the minority have not convinced the members of the majority, they have at least produced some changes in the majority view. The members of the majority have modified their position as a result of criticism from the minority, with the result that the minority can regard the policies ultimately enacted as better, from the standpoint of their understanding of what public values require, than they otherwise would have been. We can extend this point to the case where the composition of the majority changes as deliberation proceeds, or a majority coalesces out of a variety of smaller subgroups as deliberation proceeds. So long as those who ultimately constitute the majority have modified their view as a result of criticism from those who ultimately constitute the minority, the minority will be able to regard the resulting decision as embodying an improved understanding of what is required by the relevant moral values. But this would be a matter of the minority's coming to regard the majority's view of what public values require as more likely to be correct only in the sense of being less *wrong*, not in the sense of being more likely to be right than not.[25]

There is a further effect of democratic deliberation that should be mentioned. If one sees those with whom one disagrees (about what substantive public values require) participating effectively in shared deliberation, providing plausible if not convincing replies to one's criticisms, this can increase one's confidence in their intellectual competence. This will not mean deferring to their judgment. One can acknowledge that a position is competently reasoned while still taking it to be seriously mistaken. But shared deliberation, in which the members of the group respond to one another's objections, holds out the possibility of at least enabling those in the minority to be satisfied that those in the majority are not crazy. They may thus be able to treat the issue that divides them from the majority as one about which reasonable people can disagree. This would be an epistemic benefit of sorts, but again not one that would enable the minority to regard the majority view as more likely to be correct than not.[26]

We have been assuming that the members of the minority compare the majority view with their own to determine whether deliberation has effected an epistemic improvement. It might be suggested that there could also be general grounds for supposing that an improvement has taken place. When a moral question first arises in a group, all or most of the members will deviate from the correct view to some degree. But as deliberation proceeds, the degree to which each deviates from the correct view will be reduced. So far, this possibility does not alter the general result we have obtained. Since the members of the minority will still regard the majority view as wrong, they will still need a reason for complying with a decision that seems mistaken. But, it might be held, there is more to be said. To suppose that shared deliberation reduces everyone's deviation from the truth is to suppose that over the long term, it causes the moral views of citizens to converge on the truth. But then the emergence of a majority for a particular view can be taken by the minority as a sign of where the process is heading – a sign of what the truth is.

This suggestion, however, is dubious. In a case in which what is initially the view of a small minority eventually becomes the majority view, whether voting will have the suggested epistemic implication depends on where in time the vote is held. The view that initially attracts a majority will differ from the one that ultimately does. A related problem is that this approach works only for what might be called the final majority – the majority that ultimately expands into agreement by all. It is possible that prior to reaching a consensus, there will be a sequence of different majority views, each of which is rejected as deliberation proceeds. And it is unclear how we could be sure in a given case that the majority view we see is the final one.

We seem, then, to be left with a relatively modest understanding of the epistemic potential of democracy. The relevant position for assessing such claims is that of the members of the minority – those who are outvoted. There appears to be no basis for them to change their minds upon seeing the result of a vote. Thus, they must approach democratic authority as a form of subordinating authority. If they view it in this way, they can treat voting as an adequately fair way of distributing the burden of contributing to policies with which some will inevitably disagree. The most we can hope to say, in addition, is that the members of the minority may be able to regard the result of a vote concerning the force of the relevant reasons – presumably public reasons – that is taken after deliberation as more likely to be correct than it would have been in the absence of deliberation. But this can only be understood as a matter of their regarding it as less wrong (where this means closer to their own view), not as more likely to be correct than not.[27]

This is the result we should expect if we accept that democratic procedures are justified partly by procedural values, such as fairness. If we could say that when the members of a group vote the judgments they are prepared to make after shared deliberation, the majority view is more likely to be correct than not, we could make a purely epistemic case for democracy. In particular, we would not need an independent justification, grounded in procedural fairness, for voting. The basic epistemic claim would be that deliberation does not have to attain a consensus to be regarded by each participant as identifying propositions that are more likely to be correct than not. It is enough if it produces a majority – if a majority comes to believe a proposition. But in that case, voting by the method of majority rule could be justified simply as revealing which proposition had attained a majority. That is, the case for majority voting would merely be that it is a more efficient way of exercising what is essentially expert authority than deliberation to a consensus.

We can relate this conclusion about the modest contribution that deliberation makes to the legitimacy of democratic authority to those reached earlier. I argued that if cooperatively disposed citizens who have moral concerns are to view the choice of a cooperative scheme for their society as guided by reason – and thus view cooperation as a whole as fully guided by reason – they apparently must be prepared to accept the demotion of these concerns to interests. The possibility that democratic decision making might have epistemic virtues initially seems to offer a way of sidestepping this unwelcome conclusion. The members of the minority can regard the choice of a scheme as guided by reason because it has been made in a way that tracks the force of the relevant reasons. But, in fact, the initial conclusion remains. Although the members of the minority may be able to view the decision made as better justified than it would have been in the absence of deliberation, they will not be able to view it as more likely to be correct than not. Thus, if they are to be reconciled to it, they will have to give their moral concerns a form that allows them to be governed by procedural fairness – which is to say, they will have to demote these concerns to something like interests. As I have indicated several times, we should try to avoid this conclusion if we can. The question of how it might be avoided will be taken up again in Chapter 7.

Chapter 5

Collective Reasoning

In Chapter 4, we considered democracy as a procedure for choosing among cooperative schemes. We saw that if fairness (or reasonable-ness-as-fairness) justifies democracy, those in the minority on a given occasion may not be able to regard cooperation as fully guided by reason unless they are prepared to demote their moral commitments to interests, the satisfaction of which is important primarily because it satisfies them. This result presupposed that voting would be required in the end. If the parties could instead deliberate to a consensus on the scheme to be chosen, they would be able to regard the choice as guided by reason (and thus cooperation as a whole as fully guided by reason). Still, this seems unlikely outside of small groups.

The phenomenon of shared deliberation is, however, worthy of consideration not just as a component of democratic decision making but also in its own right. What exactly are people doing when they deliberate together? Let us call cooperation to achieve epistemic goals cognitive cooperation. One aspect of this is cooperation in the gathering of facts that potentially constitute evidence germane to some issue. I shall have something to say about this, but the main focus will be on what I shall call *collective reasoning* – the cooperative assessment of the rational force of the (putative) facts offered as reasons. I speak of collective reasoning rather than shared deliberation to mark the fact that the phenomenon is being viewed as an instance of mutually beneficial cooperation. It thus raises the same issues explored in Chapters 1 and 2: the nature of the reason to contribute and the basis of the choice among different cooperative schemes. But discussion of these issues will be postponed until the final chapter. Before we consider them, we need an account of what the cooperative product is – of what those engaged in collective reasoning produce – and how the participants benefit from partaking of it. These topics will occupy us in the next three chapters. In the present chapter, I provide a general overview of the process of collective reasoning and distinguish two forms that it can take. The following two chapters explore in more detail the structure of these two forms of collective reasoning, focusing on moral and political contexts.

I. THE STRUCTURE OF COLLECTIVE REASONING

Collective reasoning, as I understand it, has certain defining features. It is a cooperative effort, involving linguistic exchange, to answer a question or solve a problem confronting a group. It presupposes that each member of the group wants the question answered or the problem solved. Collective reasoning must be distinguished from conversation. Conversation, too, involves linguistic exchange, but this is just the exchange of observations on a topic of mutual interest. If engaging in conversation is associated with a goal, it is internal to the process: the establishment and maintenance of a certain kind of social contact. Those who engage in collective reasoning, by contrast, have a separate goal: answering a particular question or solving a particular problem. This is not to deny that people engaged in collective reasoning may receive various benefits simply by virtue of participating, and these may make participation worthwhile even when the goal is not attained. But if those participating in a process involving linguistic exchange do not seek to answer some question or solve some problem, it is not a process of collective reasoning, as I am using this term.

Since solving a problem can be understood as answering the question of how it is to be solved, the two cases just distinguished can be reduced to one. I shall, then, focus on collective reasoning undertaken to answer a question. To regard this as an instance of mutually beneficial cooperation is to suppose that each participant seeks to obtain something of value that she could not obtain – or obtain as well – alone. It is natural to assume that this is true belief. The group faces a certain question, and its members reason collectively in the expectation that each will acquire a true belief concerning the answer. Nevertheless, I shall understand the benefit that each seeks to receive to be instead a *justified judgment*, a judgment that is well supported by the reasons actually relevant to the question being considered. Reasoning in general seeks to identify, and determine the force of, the reasons relevant to some question, and we can view collective reasoning this way as well.[1]

By regarding justified judgment as the benefit each seeks to obtain by participating in a process of collective reasoning, we are enabled, I believe, to avoid taking a position on controversial issues relating to truth. People who favor replacing talk of truth with talk of warranted assertibility will have no difficulty accepting the idea that the cognitive benefit derived from collective reasoning is justified judgment. But partisans of truth should be able to accept it as well. Even if the ultimate goal is true belief, insofar as we seek to attain it by reasoning, the proximate goal will be justified judgment. That is, since we are concerned with the cognitive benefits obtainable by a form of reasoning, we can adopt an epistemology according to which justification is the route to truth.[2]

In collective reasoning aimed at answering a question, then, each participant expects to acquire a justified judgment – one supported by the relevant reasons – regarding the question being considered. Or to be more precise, each expects to acquire a judgment that is better justified than the best justified judgment she could have made by reasoning independently. The parties are initially in a certain situation with respect to their ability to make justified judgments concerning some matter. There is a certain degree of justification that each could attain by her own efforts. The expectation is that by reasoning collectively, each will be able to make a judgment that is better justified.

Disagreement is often a sign that a group could benefit from collective reasoning. The existence of opposing views suggests that one's own view may be susceptible of improvement. To be sure, disagreement is not essential. The initial situation could be one of agreement. All could hold the same opinion, but each might suspect that if they all engaged in collective reasoning they would discover that some alternative was better justified. Still, the typical situation in which a group is prompted to reason collectively will be one of disagreement.

It is useful, however, to distinguish two ways of interpreting disagreement, within a group, about the rational import of a certain body of facts of which all are aware. On the first, disagreement about the correct answer to the question being addressed implies that there is cognitive malfunction somewhere in the group.[3] At least some of the members must be mistaken about what the relevant reasons imply. In this case, we can understand collective reasoning as reducing or eliminating malfunction. Often the cognitive malfunctioning displayed by an individual will take the form of the misemployment of concepts already in his possession. But it could also take the form of a simple lack of the relevant concepts. Appropriate functioning depends not only on the execution of a conceptual "program" but also on having the right program. In the latter sort of case, eliminating malfunction will involve bringing about the acquisition of the requisite concepts.

When collective reasoning eliminates cognitive malfunction – when it gives all the same concepts and ensures that they all apply them the same way – the result will be agreement about what the relevant reasons are and what they support. But it would be a mistake to say that agreement is the goal of collective reasoning in this sort of case. The goal – the goal of each participant – is justified judgment. If all successfully grasp the full rational import of a given body of facts, their judgments will agree. But this agreement will simply be a by-product of the attainment of the goal by each, not the goal itself. And conversely, the existence of agreement does not entail that the parties have attained justified judgments. A consensus about what is justified could be mistaken. The most that we can infer from agreement is that the cognitive resources available to a group have been fully mined. Thus, if what the members agree on is in fact unjustified, they will not be able to recognize this without some sort of exogenous input – new observations, or contact with some other group with which they can engage in collective reasoning.

The other case is that in which disagreement about how the question being addressed is to be answered does not imply cognitive malfunction somewhere in the group. There can be disagreement about the rational import of a given body of facts without cognitive malfunction. This can happen in two main ways. In the first, there is one set of concepts that is appropriately employed in formulating the reasons relevant to the question the group is considering, but a certain amount of variability in the application of these concepts is to be expected. It is an aspect of normal human performance in connection with the concepts at issue, and so cannot be regarded as malfunctioning. This is the sort of situation that Rawls means to capture with his notion of the "burdens of judgment" as they apply to public reasoning.[4] The burdens are various features of the human situation that make it virtually inevitable that even reasoners who employ the same concepts to characterize the reasons provided by a given body of facts will disagree about what conclusion these facts support.

The second possibility is that the parties may, without malfunction, invoke different reasons in answering the question they face. That is, we cannot say that there is only one set of concepts that can be appropriately employed to formulate reasons germane to the question being considered. Individuals may employ different sets of concepts, and so acknowledge different reasons. It is possible that they will nevertheless agree on the answer to the question the group faces, each having his own reasons for regarding that answer as justified. But it is also possible that they will not, and when this happens, their disagreement cannot be attributed to malfunction. This second possibility obtains with respect to many moral questions in a pluralistic society, where conceptions of the good differ. To accept the "fact of reasonable pluralism," as Rawls calls it – the fact that different reasonable comprehensive doctrines will emerge as a result of the play of reason under conditions of freedom – is to accept that one need not be manifesting cognitive malfunction in failing to acknowledge the reasons acknowledged by others.[5]

This second way there can be disagreement without malfunction introduces an element of relativism into the cognitive functioning of a group. The correct answer to a question is relative to the reasons invoked to answer it. It must be stressed, however, that the conceptual divergence cannot be too great. There must be enough overlap that the parties can understand themselves to be facing a common question.[6] It should also be noted that the relativism we are envisaging need not be understood subjectively. That is, we need not suppose that the ground of the reasons acknowledged by an individual is his or her "subjective motivational set."[7] Relativism is also possible if what counts as a reason is somehow objectively grounded – for example, in mind-independent normative facts, or in practices accessible to all – but the human situation is such that only a proper subset of all valid reasons can serve as the reference point for living a single human life or organizing a single human society. This means that each life or society must be based on a commitment to a restricted set of reasons or values, from which other reasons or values are excluded. A view of this sort is associated with the pluralism of Isaiah Berlin.[8] But for present purposes, the important point is that on either relativist view, disagreement about the correct answer to a certain question need not entail cognitive malfunction somewhere in the group.

When disagreement does not involve malfunction, there is still a role for collective reasoning. In the first place, the exchange of arguments may enable each to refine his understanding of what the reasons he acknowledges require. As I have mentioned, this might sometimes result in agreement about the appropriate answer to a particular question. But there is also another possibility that deserves consideration. This arises when a group can achieve a further cooperative benefit if it is able to settle upon a cooperative scheme. One way a group can choose a scheme when its members disagree without malfunction is to employ a decision-making procedure such as a lottery or a vote. But it may be that collective reasoning can accomplish something here as well. It may be that under certain circumstances, starting from disagreement that does not reflect malfunction, the members of a group can reason their way to agreement concerning which cooperative scheme to adopt.

These remarks are admittedly abstract. What is involved in the two main cases – where the initial disagreement is attributable to malfunction and where it is not – will become clearer in Chapters 6 and 7, where they are considered in more detail. First, however, we need to address some prior issues. In collective reasoning, the participants receive the benefit of justified judgment regarding some question. But – especially when disagreement indicates cognitive malfunction – there are two different ways of understanding the cooperative product (from which each derives this benefit).

These two alternatives can be introduced by noting the connection between reasoning and judgment. In the case of reasoning by an individual, the normal outcome is a judgment by that individual concerning which answer to the question being considered is best supported by the relevant reasons. That is, individual reasoning is followed by individual judgment.[9] But in the case of collective reasoning, we have a choice. We can understand the cooperation involved as focusing only on the first aspect of the process, or on both aspects. That is, one possibility is to regard individuals engaged in collective reasoning as cooperating in the reasoning they do – in gathering facts and assessing their rational significance – but then making individual judgments based on the common stock of reasons thus created. This process is just like the paradigm involving a single individual except that each party benefits from cooperation in the reasoning phase. Alternatively, we can regard the parties as extending cooperation to the act of judgment. After cooperatively evaluating the relevant reasons, they make a collective judgment concerning what these reasons support. This means that each suspends judgment about what the accumulated reasons support until a conclusion that all can accept has been found.

On the first interpretation, the cooperation involved in collective reasoning is essentially a matter of the *pooling* of reasons. In one respect, pooling goes beyond collective reasoning. Partly, it involves each offering to the group as a whole any presumptive facts thought to be potentially relevant to a particular issue. This was mentioned earlier. But another part involves the provision of arguments concerning these presumptive facts: arguments regarding whether there is good reason to believe that they actually obtain, and arguments regarding the significance they have (or would have, if they obtained) for the question being considered. Cooperation of this second sort takes the form of collective reasoning. This is pooling, too, because it has the effect of creating a common cognitive resource: a common pool of *criticized arguments* germane to the issue the group is addressing. We can also speak more generally of a pool of reasons, some of which may not be organized into arguments. The creation of this pool benefits each in that each can draw on it to make up her own mind about the question being addressed. The result will presumably be a judgment by each that is better justified than the judgment she would have made before the creation of the common pool.

We should note the contrast between cooperation of this sort and cooperation to produce certain familiar public goods, such as clean air. A pool of reasons is a public good in the sense that (1) it cannot be provided to any in the relevant group without being provided to all, and (2) one person's drawing on it to make a (better) justified judgment does not diminish the opportunities of others to do this.[10] But unlike the case of clean air, the benefit each derives from the good is not an immediate consequence of its production. Each must perform a specific act of "appropriation"; each must cash in the reasons as a judgment.

This description is oversimplified in two respects that should be noted. First, I have been characterizing collective reasoning in terms of its ultimate product, a pool of reasons or criticized arguments. But I have said nothing about how, in detail, reasoning should proceed. The philosophical literature contains attempts to formulate rules governing an individual's reasoning, and rules can also be formulated to govern the process of collective reasoning.[11] Alvin Goldman, taking the goal of epistemic practices to be the increasing of true belief in a group, has formulated rules of argumentation governing such things as anticipating objections and retracting claims previously made.[12] I shall say more about the choice among ways of conducting collective reasoning in Chapter 8. For the most part, however, the issues on which I shall focus in what follows do not require a detailed specification of what constitutes good reasoning. We need only suppose that each will be able to make a better justified judgment on the basis of a common pool of reasons than she could have made by investigating the issue alone.

The second oversimplification is that the common pool of reasons does not consist solely of reasons explicitly offered to the group by its members. The fact that an apparently competent reasoner has drawn a certain conclusion from a pool of reasons – that she regards a certain judgment as justified on the basis of the pool – is itself a presumptive reason to believe that conclusion correct. Thus, once this fact becomes known, it constitutes an addition to the pool. But this does not threaten the point that the determination of what the relevant reasons require is a matter of individual judgment. Each benefits from the common pool of reasons by being able to make a judgment about a particular matter that is more responsive to all the relevant reasons, including the reasons provided by the fact that others have made certain judgments, than it would otherwise have been.

The alternative to this view, as I have said, is that the appropriate outcome of collective reasoning is a collective judgment. That is, the act of judgment through which the pooled reasons are "cashed in" is itself an explicitly collective act, cooperatively generated by the members of the group. In the next two sections, I argue that the cooperation involved in collective reasoning is best understood in the first way, as undertaken to create a common cognitive resource on the basis of which individuals can make up their own minds.

II. COLLECTIVE JUDGMENT

Let us focus on the case where disagreement is attributable to malfunction somewhere in the group. Why would a group reasoning collectively in this sort of situation want to generate a collective judgment?

There might be moral reasons that support this. Simply creating a common pool of reasons on which each can draw does not guarantee agreement. Even after the construction of the pool, there may still be disagreement about what it actually implies. And this could seem undesirable from the standpoint of moral values, such as solidarity. If so, the members of a group might undertake a moral commitment to refrain from making judgments capturing the force of the pooled reasons so long as there is disagreement about this.

But at present, we are concerned with the *cognitive* benefits of various forms of cooperation. We are concerned with how cooperation might enable each to form a better justified judgment regarding the answer to some question. On the view according to which cognitive cooperation is merely pooling, each benefits from cooperation because the common pool contains more and better reasons and arguments on which he can draw in making a judgment than he could have generated by himself. The present suggestion is that this represents an incomplete understanding of how collective reasoning could produce the cognitive benefit of better justified judgment. The benefits will be even greater if the goal of collective reasoning is taken to be a collective judgment – so that each suspends judgment concerning what the pool supports until some conclusion that all can regard as correct has been identified. Or to be more precise, the benefits will be greater if each withholds *final* judgment until a conclusion all can regard as correct has been identified. The production of a collective judgment will require the formation within the group of tentative judgments that constitute hypotheses about what the pool implies. A collective judgment is made when one of these is collectively accepted by all.

We should be clear about what is being proposed here. We are understanding the benefit produced by collective reasoning to be the attainment of (better) justified judgments by the members of the group. That is, each party is able, as a result of collective reasoning, to form a judgment that is better justified than it would otherwise have been. If cognitive cooperation is more successful when the cooperative product is a collective judgment, there must be some extra increment of justification that each gains when collective reasoning results in a collective judgment. It must be that the judgment of each is better justified when he participates in a collective judgment. Making up one's own mind on the basis of the assembled reasons is a second-best option.

Associated with the two ways of understanding the goal of cognitive cooperation that I have just distinguished is a distinction between two kinds of consensus that could be the outcome of such cooperation. The first is what I shall call a *piecemeal* consensus. A piecemeal consensus is a de facto concurrence of judgments that can legitimately be made independently, and thus could be made by the members of a group of investigators at different times. Cooperation to construct an evidential pool – to gather presumptively relevant facts, and arguments pertaining to their force – could lead to a consensus of this sort, a de facto agreement of independent judgments. This will happen if, in addition to creating a common pool of reasons, collective reasoning brings it about that no member of the group is malfunctioning in his assessment of the force of these reasons. As I indicated earlier, the resulting piecemeal consensus will then be a by-product of proper appreciation by each of the force of the full set of relevant reasons.

Contrasted with this is what I shall call an *integral* consensus. An integral consensus in judgment has the feature that each of the constituent judgments accepting a proposition or principle is conditional on all the rest. Acceptance by all is a condition of acceptance by anyone. Collective reasoning can also end in an integral consensus. In this case, consensus is not a mere by-product of the successful tracking by each of the force of a common pool of reasons. Rather, each proceeds on the assumption that he can benefit most from cooperation to create a common pool of reasons by suspending judgment concerning what it supports until a proposition or principle that all can accept as justified by the pool has been identified.

When we say that the product of collective reasoning should ideally be a collective judgment, then, we are envisaging an integral consensus. We must be clear, however, that we are still viewing cognitive cooperation as a form of mutually beneficial cooperation. We are supposing that each participant, considered as an individual, gains something he values by participating – namely, a (better) justified judgment about some question of interest to him. The claim is that each individual will most fully attain the goal of better justified judgment if he incorporates his judgment into a collective judgment, if he suspends (final) judgment until something that all can regard as justified by the relevant reasons has been found.[13]

What basis is there for thinking that it is only through collective judgment – that is, integral consensus – that the true force of all the relevant reasons can be grasped? The most natural suggestion is that no one can attain a fully justified judgment in the face of disagreement. There is a legitimate point to be made here, one that I have already touched on. The fact that a competent reasoner has reached a certain conclusion concerning what a given pool of reasons requires constitutes a presumptive reason to believe that conclusion correct. Thus, if there is disagreement, each will have some reason to suppose that his own judgment, however well considered, is mistaken. I discuss the significance of this fact in the next section.

Here I want to consider a further suggestion regarding why collective judgment is cognitively preferable, one that does not turn on the reason for doubt created by disagreement. This is that by participating in a collective judgment one can get a better "grip" on the force of a body of reasons than one can by making an individual judgment. I am not aware that anyone has proposed this. But I think that considering whether it is true will help to solidify the conclusion that nothing is gained, from the cognitive standpoint, by holding out for a collective judgment.

To address the claim that independent judgment is necessarily inferior to collective judgment as a way of capturing the force of the reasons relevant to some question, we must consider the nature of reasons. Reasons have a normative dimension. They *justify* judgments. Thus, an account of the nature of reasons must somehow provide for this normativity.[14] There appear to be two main possibilities. The first involves a form of normative realism. We posit an independent realm of reasons, understood as abstract normative entities, and take judgments seeking to capture the force of the reasons relevant to a question to be true or false, depending on whether they accurately reflect relations in this realm. But this view provides no basis for supposing that the ideal outcome of collective reasoning should be a collective judgment. If reasons are normative entities, rational conviction of the appropriateness of a certain conclusion will involve making epistemic contact with relations in an independent realm of reasons. A realist view must provide an epistemology that explains how this is to be understood. But however it is understood, the contact with the rational import of a given pool of reasons that an individual attains by participating in a collective judgment cannot be superior to the contact that he could attain independently. A collective judgment is simply a number of individual judgments packaged in a certain way. Thus, the contact with the pool that each makes by participating in a collective judgment is still contact that he makes as an individual. And this means that he could, in principle, have made it alone.

The idea that reasons are abstract normative entities – the idea that relations in an abstract normative realm underlie the status of certain facts as reasons – brings with it cumbersome metaphysical and epis-temological baggage. This has led to attempts to find a place for normativity in the natural world. One way of doing this is to invoke the psychological facts of desire and aversion. The behavioral marks of normativity are striving and avoidance, and desire and aversion give us a way of providing a naturalistic interpretation of these behav-iors. But this does not appear to provide what is needed. There always seems to be room for the further question of whether we are really justified in acting in accordance with our desires and aversions. And it may even be that the notion of desire presupposes taking something to be a reason.[15]

A second, alternative way of trying to fit normativity into the natu-ral world is to invoke practices. Wittgenstein is often thought to have provided an account in these terms of the normativity involved in the use of language – of there being a right and a wrong way to employ the concepts our words express – and if it works, it could also find application in connection with the justificatory force of facts taken to constitute reasons.[16] A fact is constituted as a reason by a rule that licenses the drawing of a certain conclusion from facts of that kind, and these reason-constituting rules are grounded in practices. Simi-larly, to make a judgment capturing the force of the relevant reasons is to participate appropriately in such a practice.

There is a good deal of controversy about how the Wittgensteinian invocation of practices is to be understood. On Kripke's interpretation of Wittgenstein, the notion of a social practice seems merely to provide a way of accounting for the illusion of normativity, in contrast to naturalizing genuine normativity. John McDowell, on the other hand, has suggested that we cannot get beyond normative "bedrock," but we can see enough of what is below it to know that a general lack of uniformity in our practices would make the normativity associated with the employment of concepts impossible.[17] My discussion of col-lective reasoning presupposes that reasons are genuinely normative. So I shall proceed on the assumption that a practice-based account of reasons can somehow accommodate genuine normativity. I consider these issues further in Section V.

Like a realist view of reasons, a practice-based view provides no support for the idea that the force of a body of reasons is better grasped by a collective judgment. Since judgments of any kind grasp the force of reasons, we cannot speak of judgments unless reasons are already on the scene. On a practice-based approach, this means that rule-following practices of the relevant sort must already exist, prior to the creation of a collective judgment.[18] But the prior existence of a rule-following practice that grounds reasons of a certain sort is simply a matter of the existence of a particular history of judging, of accepting certain conclusions on the basis of certain facts. And if the reasons at issue have been sustained by a history of judging that does not involve collective judgments, it is difficult to see what basis there could be for supposing that by participating in a collective judgment, one could better capture their force. They are grounded in the practice underlying them, so one could do no better, in capturing their force, than to extend that practice.

These points are compatible with the possibility that a group could reap some ancillary benefits by imposing on its collective reasoning the goal of collective judgment. A group with this goal might thereby force itself to be extremely conscientious in its pooling – in its efforts to identify all relevant facts and determine their true force as reasons. Since the members would know that the force of the assembled reasons could only be cashed in by a collective judgment, they would exert extra effort to remove obstacles to understanding. But there is no reason why a group that eschewed collective judgment could not be equally conscientious in its pooling, seeking to provide the best possible basis for the resulting individual judgments.[19]

III. THE JUDGMENTS OF OTHERS

In this section, I consider in more detail the rational significance of the judgments of others. I have said that the fact that a competent reasoner has reached a certain conclusion regarding what the relevant reasons support constitutes a further reason in support of that conclusion. That is, we can distinguish two kinds of reasons supporting a judgment. First, there are the substantive reasons that are appropriately consulted by an individual in making up her own mind about some question. But in addition, there are the reasons provided by the fact that other apparently competent judges agree or disagree. Here what is at issue is not the arguments they offer, but the mere fact that they have reached certain conclusions – together with the assumption that they are generally competent. The fact that a competent reasoner has made a judgment constitutes a presumptive reason to believe that it is correct. Let us call reasons of this sort *interpersonal reasons*.

When there is a consensus – piecemeal or integral – the judgment each makes on the basis of the relevant substantive reasons accords with that of everyone else, and thus receives further support from the interpersonal reasons. Each can have greater rational confidence in her judgment than when others disagree, even though her substantive reasons remain unchanged. The judgments of the members are in a kind of equilibrium. When there is disagreement, by contrast, substantive and interpersonal reasons conflict. And in the limiting case where everyone else regards a particular opposing judgment as justified by the relevant substantive reasons, they conflict radically. What should an agent in such a situation do?

It is tempting to say that in a case of this sort, reason is overwhelmingly on the side of changing one's mind and adopting the majority view. As Michael Smith puts it:

> Other things being equal, the individual must therefore have a proper sense of humility when she finds herself in disagreement with the group. She must admit that she can rationally take a stand against the group only when she can construct a plausible story about why her own opinion is more credible than the opinion of her fellows.[20]

I believe, however, that this misstates the matter. It suggests that when an individual disagrees with everyone else, she has the burden of proof; she must be able to demonstrate, to her own satisfaction at least, that her view is more credible than that of the others. Actually, the burden of proof is on the others. An individual facing even widespread disagreement from others should stick to her guns unless she is given good substantive reason to believe that she is wrong.

The fact that many agree on some matter counts as a strong reason to suppose that their view is right only if their judgments are based on an *independent* assessment of the relevant substantive reasons. If their unanimous agreement is simply a result of their imitating a single person, it has little weight as an interpersonal reason. But if the force of interpersonal reasons depends in this way on independent assessment of the relevant substantive reasons, we have a kind of paradox. Interpersonal reasons strongly support a particular conclusion only if the members of a group generally discount them in deciding what to believe. Or more cautiously, interpersonal reasons are stronger the less attention the members of a group pay to them in deciding what to believe. Thus, the rationally appropriate response when faced with universal rejection of one's position is not to presume that one must be wrong unless one can find some positive reason to suppose that one is right. It is carefully to reconsider the evidence germane to the question, abandoning one's judgment if and only if one finds persuasive substantive reasons for thinking it is wrong.

If this is correct, the characterization of interpersonal reasons that I provided earlier requires qualification. I suggested that the fact that an apparently competent reasoner has reached a certain conclusion concerning what a body of reasons requires constitutes a presumptive reason for believing that this conclusion is correct. But when this reason conflicts with one's own assessment of the force of the substantive reasons, it cannot simply be weighed against them. It serves, rather, as a reason for considering whether the available substantive reasons in fact support the view expressed by the other person. Only by treating interpersonal reasons in this way does one do one's part in maintaining the integrity of the system of interpersonal reasons. Only in this way does one ensure that one's own judgment counts as a valid interpersonal reason for others.

It is useful to make a further distinction between two sorts of substantive reasons. *Primary* reasons are reasons that bear directly on the question being considered. Part of reconsidering an issue is considering whether one has overlooked some primary reasons or misinterpreted their significance. One might do this unilaterally, but it will often be of value to get some input from those who disagree with one's view. One can present one's reasoning to them and ask them to point out any mistakes they think it contains – facts overlooked or misinterpreted. Still, what is decisive here is not their conclusions but their reasons. What is their evidence that the facts they say one has overlooked actually obtain? What arguments support their interpretation of the significance of the relevant facts? One then adds these considerations to those one started with and tries to determine whether they support a change of mind.

But there are also substantive reasons of another sort that are relevant to the question of whether a judgment is correct. These are *debunking* reasons, reasons provided by facts that have debunking force. They reveal that a judgment has been formed by a process that is not reliable, without actually presenting evidence against the particular claim embodied in that judgment. Reconsideration of a judgment can take place at this level. One might consider whether one's disagreement with others reflects the influence in one's own case of factors that corrupt judgment, such as bias. The presence of such factors suggests that one would have believed what one does, regardless of what the primary reasons require. Debunking reasons can support the abandonment of a view, but one must still have primary reasons for adopting an opposing view. It should be noted that one must also consider whether the view of those who disagree can be explained in this fashion. It is only when the judgments of others are not subject to debunking that they constitute what I have called interpersonal reasons for believing something.

The main point, however, is that a decision is to be made on the basis of one's *independent* assessment of the force of all the relevant substantive considerations. If, upon a full review of the relevant reasons, including debunking reasons, one has found no basis for changing one's mind, the appropriate response is to retain one's initial position, despite the fact that others, even all others, disagree. To use Smith's terms, one need not construct a story about why one's own opinion is more credible than theirs. It is enough that one does not find any substantive reason to regard their opinion as more credible than one's own. To change one's mind, coming to believe what everyone else believes simply because they believe it, is to betray in one's own case the very independence of judgment that gives interpersonal reasons their force in the first place.[21]

Now we can return to the question of whether collective reasoning should aim at a collective judgment. The most plausible basis for supposing this is provided by the fact that when a judgment is collective, the substantive reasons for making it are reinforced by interpersonal reasons. That is, the equilibrium I mentioned earlier obtains. This means that the reason for doubt created by the mere fact that competent investigators disagree has been eliminated – or more accurately, reduced, since people outside a group engaged in collective reasoning may still hold opposing views. But in the first place, such an equilibrium will also obtain when there is a piecemeal consensus of independently generated judgments. And second, producing a collective judgment requires that each member of the group suspend judgment so long as anyone disagrees. Yet as we can now see, there is no cognitive justification for this. The integrity of the system of interpersonal reasons requires that the reason for doubt created by the disagreement of others be understood merely as a reason to reconsider what the applicable substantive reasons support. If, having done this, one (still) finds appropriate a judgment with which others disagree, one should go ahead and make it, despite their disagreement.

IV. AGREEMENT AS A GOAL

I have argued that individuals who engage in collective reasoning should be understood as cooperating to produce a shared pool of reasons, rather than a collective judgment. Each will then be able to derive from this pool a better justified individual judgment concerning the question being addressed. An individual can receive this benefit even if the group does not reach agreement. It might be objected that cases of this pure type are relatively rare. The best example is probably the collective reasoning characteristic of collaborative research in an academic discipline, or even better, of the proceedings of an academic seminar or discussion group. In most cases, people engage in collective reasoning because they need to generate a common answer to some question – to reach agreement about it – if they are to achieve some *further* goal. An example would be a jury seeking to reach a verdict.

I think that all of these cases are usefully regarded as having a certain general form. The members of the group each acknowledge a reason sufficient to justify their participation in a particular cooperative endeavor. The PCR may play a role here. But in order to realize the cooperative benefit, they must agree on a cooperative scheme. Collective reasoning is then undertaken to identify an acceptable scheme. Thus, in the jury case, the jurors are committed to producing a collective product, a verdict, for which unanimity is required. In a simple criminal matter, there are two "schemes" – combinations of actions – on the basis of which a verdict might be produced: agreement that the defendant is innocent and agreement that the defendant is guilty. The jurors reason collectively in an attempt to determine which of these cooperative schemes to adopt.[22]

Often when the members of a group face the problem of choosing a cooperative scheme to serve as the basis of some further cooperative endeavor, disagreement cannot be attributed to malfunction. Each legitimately brings different values to bear. This sort of case is especially likely to be encountered in large groups. It is discussed in Chapter 7. In this section, then, I shall focus on cases where disagreement is attributable to malfunction. The members correctly take it that there is a right answer to the question they face, and thus that disagreement means that at least some of them are mistaken. Nevertheless, they must agree if some further cooperative goal is to be attained. How does this affect the reasoning process?

One way that the members of a group can respond to the necessity of reaching agreement is to impose upon themselves a requirement of collective judgment – of integral consensus. This means that each suspends final judgment until something all can accept as justified by the relevant reasons has been found. Earlier, I argued that from the standpoint of the personal cognitive goal of acquiring a better justified judgment, there is nothing to be gained by extending cooperation beyond the construction of a common pool of reasons. But if there is an independent reason that the group must reach agreement, it can address this need by undertaking to achieve an integral consensus on what the relevant reasons support.

Piecemeal consensus, however, can also play a role when a group must agree if it is to achieve some further cooperative benefit. The notion of integral consensus gives us a way of understanding the requirement to reach agreement as a rule of the reasoning process itself – a constraint internal to the process that commits the parties to agreement irrespective of whether this is required for the choice of a cooperative scheme. The nature of piecemeal consensus, by contrast, is such that its attainment cannot be understood as a rule of the reasoning process itself. Piecemeal consensus is simply a by-product of the successful "tracking" of the relevant reasons by each. But when the members of a group must agree if they are to accomplish some task, a piecemeal consensus will suffice, and there is something they can do to bring it about. Each may feel comfortable, given the state of the common pool, in making a judgment about what the assembled reasons support, even though others continue to disagree. But in light of the need to reach agreement, each may deem it necessary to try to convince the others that the conclusion she has reached is the correct one, while at the same time remaining open to counterarguments. And as the exchange of arguments continues, minds may be changed, with the ultimate result that there is agreement – a piecemeal consensus – on which cooperative scheme to adopt.

There are, then, two ways in which a group that takes disagreement to indicate malfunction can respond to the need to agree on a cooperative scheme if some further task is to be accomplished. In the first, the aim of each is finding *something* all can accept. There is no cognitive basis for such a commitment, but its acceptance can facilitate cooperation in cases where a group must settle on a scheme if it is to achieve a further goal. In the second way of responding to the need for agreement, the aim of each is getting others to accept a *particular* conclusion – the conclusion he or she has already accepted. The need to decide on a cooperative scheme by which some further cooperative benefit can be produced leads each to try to convince others of the position that he regards as justified by the evidential pool. And if each is sensitive to the reasons offered by others, the group may be able to "grope" its way to agreement.

Still, a group that has some independent reason for reaching agreement on a scheme may not be able to attain it in either of these ways, especially if the question being addressed is complex. There may be no possibility of finding an answer to the question they face that all can regard as correct. It is interesting to consider what a group should do when it encounters an impasse of this sort. One possibility is to maintain the cognitive integrity of the process. Since disagreement indicates malfunction, the only cognitively respectable way of securing agreement is for all to become convinced that a particular answer to the question the group is addressing is justified by the relevant reasons. If this cannot be done, the group must forgo the opportunity for further cooperation that was present. For example, a jury that cannot agree on what the evidence supports should accept that it will not be able to produce a verdict.

There is, however, another possibility. In previous chapters, we saw that when people with competing moral concerns must agree on a cooperative scheme, the value of fairness can demote these concerns to interests. But something similar may take place even when considerations of fairness play no role. The parties may take the situation to be one in which cooperation will be attained only by bargaining and compromise, and convert their convictions into interests simply to give them a form suitable to these processes, accepting that the scheme to be implemented will be determined by the distribution of bargaining power.

Cases of this sort are easiest to envisage when disagreement is not attributable to cognitive malfunction, as in a pluralistic society. But we can also imagine such behavior when disagreement on some question germane to the choice of a cooperative scheme is attributable to malfunction. Each could treat the judgment that she regards as best justified by the relevant reasons as merely a kind of interest of hers, which she is prepared to compromise as necessary to reach agreement. That is, she is prepared to acquiesce in a judgment that she does not regard as justified by the relevant reasons because otherwise the further opportunity for cooperation will be lost.

On the face of it, it appears that a group's proceeding in this way could only be deplored. As we will see in Chapter 6, when collective reasoning is undertaken to eliminate malfunction, one of its primary goals is the identification and correction of factors distorting judgment. But what we seem to be envisaging now is the embracing of one sort of distortion, that introduced by the threat of failure to accomplish some further cooperative task.

Still, we may be able to put a somewhat better face on this sort of situation. By hypothesis, disagreement indicates malfunction. So if one finds that the assembled evidence strongly supports a particular judgment, one must apparently judge that others are malfunctioning. But further reflection may lead to a more modest conclusion. In the previous section, I argued that one should not adopt a view simply because many people hold it. The interpersonal reason provided by the disagreement of others is merely a reason to reexamine the evidence. But it may sometimes be possible to look at the reason for doubt created by general disagreement not just as a reason for thinking that one *may be* mistaken, but as a reason for thinking that everybody *is* mistaken – that no one has the right answer. And this could lead each of the members of a group that is seeking a common basis for cooperation to suppose that there is, after all, a kind of epistemic justification for making a concession from what he takes to be the judgment that is best supported by the available substantive reasons. If, in addition, the conflict is one to which considerations of fairness seem applicable, they could play a role in determining the particular pattern of concessions that results.[23]

It should be emphasized, however, that there would be no reason to treat judgments as interests to be compromised if the group faced no further cooperative task that required agreement. The question would simply be left unresolved, as it might be in a discussion group. So while it may be possible to give concessions that are not supported by the evidence a kind of epistemic rationale, this procedure is not fully in order from the standpoint of the cognitive goal of justified judgment. The observations in this section seem to show, then, that a group is in a difficult position when accomplishing some further task requires that it resolve a disagreement that is taken to arise from cognitive malfunction somewhere in the group. The members may have to choose between their cognitive integrity and whatever considerations support performing the further task. We shall return to this issue, in contexts where disagreement is not attributable to malfunction, in Chapter 7.

V. "NEGOTIATION"

In the discussion up to this point, I have been assuming that when a group could benefit from agreement, the alternative to collective reasoning is bargaining. The contrast here is between an approach in which the force of reason determines what is agreed to and an approach in which a form of power determines this. It might seem that there is a third possibility we should consider. It is often said that when a group needs a common conceptual basis on which to proceed, this should be "negotiated." The following observation from Ian Hacking illustrates this use of the term: "For purposes of the present discussion, I leave the categorization of such conjectured pathologies to future medical science, which will have to negotiate the ways in which they are to be described."[24] I shall argue, however, that negotiation in this sense is best regarded not as an alternative to collective reasoning but, rather, as a particular form of it.

The first step is to examine in more detail the normativity of concepts and reasons. Negotiation involves the creation of a common conceptual basis for action, and concepts are intimately connected with reasons.[25] So to reach conclusions about how negotiation is to be understood, we need to say more about the normativity of concepts and reasons.

Earlier, I suggested two different ways of understanding reasons: a realist view, according to which reasons are abstract normative entities of a certain sort, and the alternative practice-based view, which grounds reasons in rules that are themselves grounded in social practices. But both approaches leave something to be desired. Normative realism brings with it difficult metaphysical and epistemological problems. Yet if we assume that reasons are genuinely normative, that they genuinely justify, the practice-based view is problematic as well. It is questionable whether mere facts about how people "go on" – individually or in groups – can ground genuine normativity.[26] I shall propose a hybrid account of concepts and reasons that combines elements of both views. It provides for genuine normativity without positing an

122

inherently normative entity corresponding to every reason or concept we employ.

This view can be introduced using the distinction I have made between two main kinds of collective reasoning. That distinction turns, it will be recalled, on two different ways of interpreting disagreement. We can attribute disagreement within a group to cognitive malfunction (ignorance or error) somewhere in the group, or we can admit the possibility of disagreement without cognitive malfunction. This corresponds to a distinction that plays an important role in the practice-based view of reasoning and judgment, the distinction between the case in which a difference in judgment marks a substantive disagreement among people employing the same concepts and the case in which a difference in judgment reflects the fact that people are employing different concepts. The challenge faced by practice-based views is to preserve this distinction. How do we avoid the conclusion that when judgments differ, people are simply working within different practices?

This problem has been discussed by S. L. Hurley.[27] Her solution involves conceding that when simple concepts are at issue, such as sensory concepts like "red," and standard conditions obtain, different judgments mean that different concepts are being employed. But she argues that we can allow for substantive disagreement among people holding the same concepts when these concepts are more complex, being responsible to structured sets of potentially conflicting criteria. The evaluative concepts typically used to formulate reasons for action – for example, concepts like cruelty or injustice – are of this sort. With such concepts, agreement *about* certain exemplary cases, and *in* practices of theorizing about relationships among conflicting criteria, enables us to regard the members of a group as sharing the same concept (proceeding within the same practice) even when, in many cases, they disagree.

We can make this clearer by distinguishing a further way there can be substantive disagreement between people employing the same concepts.[28] Earlier I suggested that cognitive cooperation has two parts: identifying facts thought to be potentially relevant to a question, and collective reasoning per se, which involves the pooling of arguments concerning the rational import of the assembled facts. Sometimes substantive disagreement among people holding the same concepts can be attributed solely to ignorance of relevant facts. Thus, if two bird-watchers disagree about whether a bird they have seen is a bittern, this may be because they have been attending to different features of the bird. They both possess the concept of a bittern as it is employed in bird-watching contexts – they know the distinctive visual characteristics of a bittern – but they are not aware of the same facts. Substantive disagreement is not, then, always attributable to defective reasoning somewhere in the group. It can arise from a difference in "input." When it does, it is resolvable by a process that makes the parties aware of the same facts.

But there can also be disagreement, among people employing the same concepts, about the rational import of a given body of facts – for example, disagreement about whether, in light of all the facts about a certain policy, it manifests injustice. Here Hurley's suggestion comes into play. The relevant concepts are associated with structured sets of potentially conflicting criteria. Outside exemplary cases, these can generate conflicting reasons germane to the question of whether the concept at issue has application – whether the policy manifests injustice. The correct employment of the concept must thus be reasoned out.[29] If we are to attribute such disagreements to cognitive malfunction somewhere in the group, however, we must suppose that there is a right answer to the question of what these conflicting reasons, taken together, support. Outside the exemplary cases, we must engage in reasoning to identify the appropriate way to "go on." But there is just one appropriate way. If the parties agree to disagree, the case is no longer one of substantive disagreement among people employing the same concept, but rather one in which different concepts are in play, and thus disagreement does not indicate malfunction.

As has been noted, however, there are reasons for doubting whether a pure practice-based view can provide us with genuine normativity. So we should see whether we can find a different way of making these points. One issue that is useful to consider is whether an individual who dissents from judgments accepted by everyone else can be making correct use of a concept they all share. Hurley has shown how people who disagree can all be employing the same concept. But can a lone dissenter be using the concept at issue *correctly*? The practice-based view may seem to create doubts about this. As we saw earlier, McDowell argues that although we cannot get beyond normative "bedrock," we can see enough of what is below it (namely, practices) to know that disorderliness there would make the normativity associated with language impossible.[30] Hurley's account reveals how there can be order in disagreement. But when there is widespread *agreement* in judgment, the posited association between orderliness and normativity might seem to have the consequence that a lone dissenter – for example, someone who judges unjust virtually all the arrangements deemed just by the other members of his society – must be either mistaken or employing a different concept. Yet it seems desirable to keep open the possibility that radical dissent could involve substantive disagreement, and that the dissenter could be right about how the concept at issue is to be employed.

There is, I think, a way of interpreting McDowell's point that makes it compatible with the idea that an individual can be correct while everyone else disagrees. We accept that we cannot speak of a practice unless there is some sort of uniformity in judgmental behavior. But we also introduce the notion of *appropriate* participation in a judgmental practice (as it has existed up to that point). This enables us to say that an individual who disagrees with everyone else about how a particular concept is to be employed may nevertheless be correct. He may be participating appropriately in the practice while the others are not.

This view of correct reasoning and judgment is a hybrid of two elements. The first is an acknowledgement that judgmental practices are social practices. The repertoire of concepts with which an individual operates is mostly learned from others. It is a product of socialization. But the fact that judgmental practices are social practices does not mean that general agreement within the group of participants determines what constitutes correctly employing the associated concepts. We can distinguish between appropriate and inappropriate participation in a certain social practice of judgment – between proper and improper understanding of the extrapolative potential inherent in the practice. The notion of appropriateness constitutes the second element of the view. It introduces a form of normativity that is independent of practices, and this is what enables us to accommodate the idea that one person can be right while everyone else is wrong.

To maintain a distinction between appropriate and inappropriate participation, we must presuppose inherent normativity in some form. One possibility is to regard socialization to a judgmental practice as a matter of acquiring the capacity to produce certain inherently normative responses (responses that involve the grasping of reasons). It is plausible, however, that these responses will often be corrupted by various factors that distort judgment. This leads us to the idea of corrected responses, those that would be produced if the corrupting influences were eliminated by critical reflection. These in turn provide a standard by reference to which present practice can be criticized. Appropriate participation then becomes participation that accords with this standard, and we have the possibility that one individual can be right while everyone else is wrong.[31]

Here, however, I shall employ a different approach. This makes use of the notion of *proper functioning*. To participate appropriately in judgmental practices is to function properly as an animal whose conceptual capacities are acquired by socialization to such practices. Proper functioning in this application is basically a biological notion, the same notion that we employ in speaking of organs, such as kidneys and lungs. But in the case of conceptual functioning, it has a social dimension. Our conceptual capacities are (in large part, at least) not instincts; they are culturally acquired. So functioning properly as animals of the sort we are will include appropriate participation in certain social practices.[32] To put it another way, we cannot give in purely asocial terms a full characterization of what it is for a particular human being to be functioning properly. We must specify the practices to which he or she has been socialized. Yet there is still a distinction between proper and improper functioning as a being so socialized, and this distinction is not socially determined.[33]

As I am employing the notion of proper functioning here, it does not provide a naturalistic reduction of normativity. It is a biological idea, but to the extent that it is taken to have normative significance, it transcends biological facts. This can be brought out by considering the use of the notion made by Alvin Plantinga. He provides an epistemological theory that employs the idea of proper functioning in an appropriate environment to characterize warrant, understood as whatever has to be added to true belief to get knowledge.[34] But Plantinga argues that we cannot make sense of proper functioning naturalistically – for example, by reference to evolution. The notion of proper functioning presupposes the notion of a design plan; something's functioning properly is its functioning as it has been designed to function in the environment for which it was designed. And design requires a designer, which for Plantinga is God.[35] I do not believe that we need to go this far, however. Once we accept "the conceptual autonomy of normative notions," as Mark Johnston puts it, we are committing ourselves to an intranormative account of normativity that takes normativity in some form as given.[36] So we need only suppose that our access to inherent normativity is such as to enable us to employ the notion of proper functioning in a way that is independent of statistical norms.[37]

The hybrid view that I have been describing allows for the possibility that radical dissent from the generally accepted judgmental practice regarding a certain concept could actually manifest appropriate participation in that practice. But this does not mean that there is no social check on judgmental practice. It is provided by the interpersonal reasons introduced earlier. That is, we can obtain a social check on judgmental practice by supposing that all properly functioning humans will acknowledge a rule that constitutes the fact that another apparently competent reasoner has reached a conflicting conclusion as a *reason* to reexamine one's own reasoning.

On the hybrid view, then, the normative dimension of judgment, as it confronts an individual, has the following structure. It is grounded in an interplay between (1) the individual's own judgmental inclinations, understood as possessing a presumptive claim to correctness

grounded in his presumptive status as a properly functioning participant in the social practices grounding the concepts employed, and (2)
the judgments that others make with these concepts, which can generate interpersonal reasons for reexamining one's own employment of
them. As we have seen, such interpersonal reasons are not decisive.
After reexamination, one can legitimately conclude that it is appropriate to retain a judgment with which everyone else disagrees. Still, if
this picture is right, the overall effect of sensitivity within a group to
the full set of operative reasons will be a certain rational pressure
toward coordination in the judgmental practices of individuals who
share the same concepts.

Now we can turn to the phenomenon of negotiation. A recent
discussion by Philip Pettit of the rule following that is associated with
judgment provides a good place to begin.[38] Pettit argues that rule
following must be fallible. It must be possible for individuals to make
mistakes when they employ the concepts they possess. This means
that correctness in the employment of concepts cannot be understood
simply in terms of the actual extrapolative inclinations (dispositions)
of individuals. Pettit claims that we can supply the required normative
element by distinguishing between favorable and unfavorable conditions of application. What individual reasoners are inclined to do in
favorable (normal or ideal) conditions is definitive of correct application, but what they are inclined to do in unfavorable conditions is
dismissed as deviant.[39]

This leaves us with the problem of identifying favorable and unfavorable conditions. For Pettit, these are negotiated between different
loci of judgment. He allows for the possibility that the requisite negotiation could be intrapersonal, between the person-stages of a given
individual on different occasions of use. But he claims that it is a fact
of human life that we can, in principle, understand the conceptual and
reasoning practices of any human being. Pettit calls this feature of
human rule following *commonability*.[40] And he argues it is possible
only if the negotiation of normal or ideal conditions is, in fact, interpersonal.

But how is this negotiation to be understood? Pettit never says what
is involved. Clearly, it is a process that results in agreement of some
kind, but how is this agreement brought about? There appear to be
two possibilities. The first is that negotiation involves bringing to bear
something like bargaining power, which might be understood in terms
of social sanctions, such as exclusion and contempt. People will differ
in their susceptibility to these threats, and in their ability to move
others by making them. The agreement produced by negotiation is
simply the resultant of these forces, an equilibrium in a causal sense.

But if we view negotiation in this way, then correctness in judgment

– exercising judgmental dispositions under favorable conditions – has an arbitrary character. It is just a matter of certain brute causal facts. It is difficult to see why identifying correct judgment in this way is preferable to resting content with what an individual, as a matter of causal fact, happens to be disposed to do on a particular occasion. If in the latter case we leave out normativity, how in the former do we manage to bring it back in? We have something by reference to which we can criticize individual performance, it is true, but it is unclear why this should take precedence over the *other* brute fact in the situa- tion – what an individual is in fact inclined to do (prior to negotiation).

The alternative is that negotiation is a rational process. People offer *reasons* for or against certain proposals concerning what are to count as favorable conditions for the exercise of a particular judgmental inclination, and for what are to count as unfavorable conditions – conditions under which judgmental inclinations can be dismissed. Agreement results when all are convinced that the relevant reasons support a particular way of understanding such conditions.

This enables us to avoid the problem confronting the first view. We do not have to explain why a bargain, understood as the resultant of certain causal forces, should have normative import vis-à-vis individ- ual judgments. But the price of avoiding this problem is that we presuppose normativity in some form. If the negotiation of the correct employment of concepts is a process of tracking the force of reasons relevant to the identification of favorable and unfavorable conditions for the exercise of certain extrapolative inclinations, we are committed to acknowledging the existence of a form of normativity that is prior to and independent of negotiation.

We can employ the notion of proper functioning here. It is plausible that discriminating between favorable and unfavorable conditions for making judgments of various sorts is an aspect of the proper function- ing of animals of the kind we are. Thus, we can understand the negotiation of what constitutes favorable and unfavorable conditions for judgment as the joint exploration, by presumptively properly func- tioning judges, of what constitutes proper functioning in various kinds of cases.

Approaching proper conceptual functioning through the notion of favorable conditions for judgment seems especially apt in the case of observational judgments – judgements classifying observed items. For judgments of other kinds, proper functioning might be better charac- terized in inferential terms, as a proper grasp of the conceptual tran- sitions made possible by a judgmental practice (or nexus of practices). But this does not alter the basic conclusion we have reached about negotiation. In general, it is the joint exploration, by beings already sensitive to a certain kind of normativity, of appropriate participation in particular judgmental practices.

The idea that appropriate participation in judgmental practices is negotiated might suggest a two-stage process. First, the potential participants reason their way to an agreement on what constitutes proper functioning (for example, what constitutes favorable conditions for judgment). Then each proceeds to make particular judgments that can be characterized as properly made. But this cannot be right. If negotiation plays a role in the proper exercise of our conceptual capacities, it must be an ongoing process that *accompanies* the practice of judgment.

Regarding the judgments of others as interpersonal reasons enables us to view negotiation in this way. The fact that we can recognize others as employing concepts similar to ours, together with the fact that their judgmental performance provides interpersonal reasons, results in an ongoing process of mutual adjustment of our respective (independent) judgmental practices. To be sure, one should not modify one's judgmental practice simply because others proceed differently in a particular case. But the divergent practice of others always constitutes a reason to reexamine one's own. Thus, one always has reason to consider whether it would be appropriate to accept their way with the common concepts. Similarly, one's own practice provides them with a reason to reconsider what they are doing. This process of mutual reconsideration just *is* the process of "negotiation." It refines concepts as they diffuse through a population. In the previous discussion of the social check on judgmental practice, I said that it consists in an interplay between presumptively proper extrapolative inclinations and interpersonal reasons (which will be accepted by all properly functioning judges). We can now see that "negotiation" is just a shared sensitivity to these two dimensions of normativity.

On the view that I am proposing, then, negotiation plays a central role in the exercise of our conceptual and reason-grasping capacities, but this role is not that of providing a foundation for these capacities. Rather, negotiation is *internal* to the normativity that characterizes our lives as reasoning animals. This means that it does not constitute a third mechanism, between reasoning and bargaining, by which agreement can be reached. Rather, it is a species of reasoning that has an essentially social dimension, since it essentially involves interpersonal reasons.[41]

This way of understanding the negotiation of correct judgmental practice yields an important benefit. It enables us to view normativity as having a history. Of course, new concepts can be acquired and old concepts lost, and this constitutes an aspect of the history of our normative world. But on the present view, we can also regard the normativity associated with particular concepts as evolving internally. On the face of it, the idea that genuine normativity could have a history of this sort is puzzling, especially on a realist view of reasons. How can what is, in fact, the *correct* way of employing a certain concept at one time cease to be correct later? This puzzle can easily lead one to embrace a reduction of normativity to desire or convention, which are readily regarded as having histories. The only apparent line of resistance will involve saying that what is correct at the level of ultimate principle does not change, but that the ultimate principles require adherence to different lower-level principles in different circumstances.

The philosophy of Hegel may constitute an attempt to explain how genuine normativity can have a history.[42] But his view is best regarded as a retrospective interpretation of events, rather than a description of rational procedures by which historical agents "on the ground" can effect the transformation of the concepts, reasons, and values they accept. The idea that conceptual change reflects an internal process of negotiation concerning what constitutes proper functioning as animals whose conceptual capacities are acquired by socialization gives us a more down-to-earth way of understanding normativity as changing over time by means of a rational process. We do not have to suppose that such changes merely manifest the influence of various extra-rational contingencies.[43] Grounding normativity in the judgmental practices of properly functioning individuals allows us to accommodate normative change as a change in what constitutes appropriate participation in a judgmental practice brought about by an alternation in circumstances. Proper functioning is relative to an environment. So the sort of participation that manifests proper functioning may undergo alteration as features of the environment are altered. An especially important case is that in which our own prior actions have altered the environment.[44] And through the operation of interpersonal reasons, discoveries about what constitutes proper participation in a judgmental practice are disseminated to other participants, whose subsequent practice then confirms the appropriateness of the changes. It should be noted, however, that we may also find, as circumstances change, that the conceptual resources associated with a practice have had their day – that nothing can any longer be regarded as appropriate participation in that practice. That is, the loss of concepts and reasons can have an internal rationale, as well as being due to external causes.[45]

We should bear in mind, when considering the possibility that the standard of correctness embodied in a judgmental practice can evolve internally, that there is no necessary connection between this process and change in the practice itself, considered as a large-scale social phenomenon. Collective reasoning among a few advanced thinkers may distill into its final form a discovery about how changing circumstances alter what constitutes proper functioning in the employment of certain concepts well before that discovery becomes widely accepted, if it ever does. And, of course, some changes in general practices of judgment may simply reflect the influence of corrupting factors, thus constituting a departure from proper functioning with the associated concepts.

The idea of proper functioning – supplemented by the joint exploration, within groups of presumptively properly functioning judges, of what constitutes proper functioning in the particular judgmental contexts those groups face – gives us, then, a way that we can regard the normative world in which we live as evolving internally, through a process of collective reasoning. This picture does not require us to suppose that the changes represent progress, but neither is it incompatible with this interpretation. I shall have more to say about the possibility that reasoning can change the content of concepts in Chapter 7.

Chapter 6

Overcoming Malfunction

In Chapter 5, I argued that the goal of collective reasoning should be understood as the construction of a pool of reasons or criticized arguments germane to a question faced by a group. But I also said that there are two different ways of looking at this process. Collective reasoning is typically prompted by disagreement, but this is open to two different interpretations. Sometimes disagreement is attributable to a cognitive defect somewhere in the group – ignorance of relevant facts or failure to appreciate their rational significance – and sometimes it is not. In the first of these cases, cognitive cooperation can be understood as a shared effort to correct such defects. It involves (1) the presentation to the group as a whole of presumptive facts that the members think potentially relevant and (2) collective reasoning, taking the form of the construction of a pool of criticized arguments, aimed at determining which of these presumptive facts actually obtains and what their true significance is. As the process unfolds, mistakes that the members of the group might have been making are revealed, and – when the parties are reasoning in good faith – corrected. If ignorance and error are completely eliminated, the result will be agreement within the group. But unless agreement is necessary to achieve some further cooperative benefit, this is not the goal with which such cooperation is undertaken. The construction of a pool of criticized arguments is desirable from the standpoint of each because it provides a basis on which he or she can make a better justified judgment concerning the question being addressed.

Let us focus on collective reasoning. The view just described involves the assumption that there is a single correct way of understanding the rational significance of a given body of facts. This is plausible in the case of theoretical reasoning – for example, reasoning aimed at determining, on the basis of observed facts, further factual features of the world. It is plausible that there is a single correct way of understanding epistemic relevance and that failure to display it is indicative of cognitive malfunction.

But when a group faces a practical question, regarding what some individual or group should do, it is less clear that this way of interpreting the situation is appropriate. In the practical sphere, relevance is determined by values. So if we are to understand collective reasoning as overcoming malfunction, there must be one set of values from the standpoint of which the questions at issue are appropriately addressed. If all the members of the group happen to share this evaluative standpoint, they will be able to proceed directly to the construction of a pool of criticized arguments concerning what these values actually imply. But if the members of a group do not initially hold the same values, we can retain the elimination-of-malfunction model of collective reasoning only if we can suppose that reasoning is capable of creating an appreciation of the appropriate values in those who initially lack it.

In this chapter, I examine collective reasoning undertaken to overcome malfunction. I shall be concerned primarily with collective reasoning in the practical sphere, especially moral reasoning. The suggestion that there is a single set of practical values that all should acknowledge, so that disagreement indicates malfunction, is most plausible when moral issues are at stake.

I. THE STANDARD CASE

Before turning to moral reasoning, however, it will be useful to sketch in more detail some general characteristics of collective reasoning undertaken to overcome cognitive malfunction, characteristics found in theoretical as well as practical contexts. Crispin Wright provides a useful way of thinking about this process. He suggests that one feature of an assertoric practice that can lead us to give it a more realistic construal is *cognitive command*.[1] The idea is that assertions of a particular type are regarded as commanded by an independent subject matter, which brings with it a view of those making such assertions as representational devices of a certain sort. There is an input to the representational device, and an assertion is the output. Perceptual assertions are the clearest case. In discussing this idea, Wright notes the temptation to say that where there is cognitive command, there will eventually be convergence on one answer to a given question. If there is an independent subject matter, and we represent it correctly, our representations should agree. But he actually favors the opposite way of characterizing the phenomenon. The distinctive feature of cognitive command is that *disagreement* is understood as arising either from difference in "input" or from malfunction in the processing of it.

The present view of collective reasoning can be accommodated to this picture. The input consists of a body of evidence (that is, facts that have been construed as evidence), and the output is a judgment regarding what this evidence supports. Disagreement means either that the members are aware of different pieces of evidence, or are malfunctioning in their grasp of the significance of the assembled evidence. Cognitive cooperation consists partly of a pooling of evidence, which would eliminate disagreement arising in the first way, and partly of the exchange of arguments concerning its force. If done in good faith, this exchange will, ideally, result in the elimination of malfunction in the grasping of the rational significance of the evidence, and thus in agreement. But as I have emphasized, agreement is not the goal of the process.

The idea that those engaged in this process are representational devices fits most easily with a realist view, which understands the rational force of the evidence in terms of relations in an independent realm of reasons. Reasoners can then be regarded as registering these relations in a quasi-perceptual way. But it is also possible to view collective reasoning as involving cognitive command on a practice-based approach to reasons, at least if each party participates in the same practices. Then disagreement can be interpreted as indicating malfunction, somewhere in the group, in the extrapolation of these practices to the case at hand.

We should consider more fully how the construction of a common pool of reasons results in the overcoming of malfunction. We can see the connection by noting that the construction of a pool of reasons involves the exchange of arguments. To offer an argument concerning what the evidence supports is to present it for criticism by others. And in criticizing it, others regard it as manifesting malfunction. Thus, to the extent that others present cogent rebuttals, the result will be the purging from the individual offering the argument – and from the group, on the assumption that the process is public – of one form of malfunction. For completeness, it should be mentioned that we can also imagine a process of collective reasoning that is explicitly aimed at eliminating malfunction, with the construction of a shared pool of reasons as a by-product. Here, the members would take turns, each offering his reasoning to the group for criticism and receiving from the others the benefit of the reduction or elimination of malfunction. To the extent that all observe this process of serial criticism, the result will be a shared pool of criticized arguments. But the first way of understanding collective reasoning undertaken to overcome malfunction better reflects the actual collective reasoning we observe. Each offers his view on a question facing a group, not simply to find out what is wrong with it but to contribute a relevant consideration to an evolving pool of reasons and criticized arguments.

There is a further aspect of the process of overcoming malfunction through collective reasoning that deserves discussion. In Chapter 5, I distinguished two kinds of substantive reasons, primary and debunking. Some forms of cognitive malfunction are well understood, and we can assemble evidence that they obtain without considering what the primary reasons support in the case at hand. That is, we can assemble independent evidence that the reasoning of certain individuals has been corrupted, or that the methods they are employing are unreliable. This evidence is debunking. Often, however, the only basis we have for supposing that some people are malfunctioning cognitively is that we take it that there is a right answer to the question being considered, and we find disagreement about what it is. In such cases, the only way we have of identifying and eliminating malfunction is to consider what the relevant primary reasons truly require.

The points in this section are germane to the suggestion that the elusive notion of objectivity can be understood as "interpersonality" – that is, agreement within a group. To speak of objectivity is to import a standard of correctness for individual judgment that is "outside" the individual's own reasoning processes. On the face of it, it is unclear why the mere fact that everyone in a group agrees on something should be understood to constitute a standard with respect to which the views of the individual members can be evaluated. This becomes more plausible, however, if we suppose that it is really something else that is serving as the standard – not agreement per se, but a certain background of reasons, understood realistically or as grounded in practices.[2] Then we can say that what the group agrees on has normative force relative to each member because the agreement reflects an elimination or reduction of various forms of malfunction in the grasping of the force of the relevant reasons.

Similarly, even where there is no actual agreement, we can construct a standard for individual judgment by hypothesizing that at some time in the future, collective deliberation will eliminate malfunction in the grasping of the force of the relevant reasons, thus revealing their true implications. This move is characteristic of Peircian constructivism, as it us usually understood.[3] It should be noted that this presupposes that the reasons that are in play will remain the same over time. If the reasons change, it is more problematic to take what is accepted in the future as normative for us now. What is normative for us now is what is required by the reasons that are appropriately acknowledged now. Talk about what will be accepted at some future endpoint of inquiry can be regarded as expressing our commitment to the idea that there is something definite that the reasons acknowledged now support, which could be made manifest by the sort of collective reasoning that overcomes malfunction if it were continued long enough. The possibility that reasons can change over time was broached in Chapter 5 and will be explored further in Chapter 7.

II. THE MORAL CASE

Now let us turn to collective moral reasoning, viewed as a process that overcomes cognitive malfunction. As I have mentioned, this involves supposing that there is ultimately one set of moral values establishing the moral relevance of the factual features of the world. If we suppose further that morality claims the respect of all rational agents, we are committing ourselves to the idea that people can malfunction not only in reasoning from the values of morality but also through failure to acknowledge them in the first place. This would mean that if moral malfunctioning is to be fully overcome by collective reasoning, there must be arguments that can lead those who do not initially accept the values of morality to acknowledge them. Some kinds of rational malfunction may, however, be beyond repair by reasoning. I shall, then, focus on the case of actual moral disagreement – disagreement, among people who give morality a place in their lives, concerning how the requirements of morality are to be understood. Such disagreement will be interpreted as indicating malfunction in the grasping of a pregiven set of moral reasons or values. Then collective reasoning can be seen as a way of overcoming this malfunction, by constructing a pool of criticized arguments on which each can draw in making moral judgments.[4]

The primary role of moral reasoning is to resolve conflicts of interest, to identify the appropriate course to follow in situations where interests differ. On the view we are now exploring, the appropriate course is dictated by a single set of moral reasons. The complete elimination of malfunction through collective reasoning would result in agreement concerning what these reasons support, the sort of agreement that I earlier called a piecemeal consensus. This means that collective reasoning undertaken to overcome malfunction has the potential not just to give each a justified judgment regarding the appropriate resolution of a particular conflict of interest, but actually to eliminate the practical aspect of the conflict, the potential for struggle. If all those involved in the conflict participate in the process of collective reasoning, and a piecemeal consensus on the appropriate way of resolving it is produced, the parties will no longer be at odds. Their interests will still conflict, but their judgments concerning what they should do or allow will not conflict. This suggests that collective reasoning undertaken to overcome malfunction has a special role to play in the moral case. The nature of the problem that moral reasoning seeks to solve – the identification of the appropriate way to behave in situations where interests conflict – points to collective reasoning as the preferred form of reasoning by which to address it.

Of course, we are here speaking of the ideal scenario in which malfunction in the grasping of the import of a set of reasons is completely eliminated. Even after a common pool of reasons is constructed through collective reasoning, individuals may draw different conclusions from it. And this problem is, if anything, more acute in the moral case. Precisely because interests conflict, it will be difficult for the participants to obtain an unbiased appreciation of what the relevant moral reasons require. But the ubiquity of moral disagreement might also be explained in another way. We encounter so much moral disagreement that it may seem questionable that morality presents us with a single standard. Can the normal human condition really involve such extensive cognitive malfunction in addressing such frequently encountered problems? If this seems implausible, we will be sympathetic to the idea that there can be moral disagreement without malfunction because individuals can, without malfunction, hold different moral values.

It is a commonplace that moral reasoning is conducted as if there is a right answer to the questions being addressed, so that disagreement means either that there is ignorance of relevant facts or malfunction in the appreciation of their significance.[5] But we should not make too much of this datum. In the first place, it can be explained pragmatically, by supposing that while moral disagreement does not imply malfunction, communities can achieve various benefits, in particular the coordination of social interaction, by suppressing this fact – so that "I don't acknowledge reasons of that kind" is not an acceptable response to a moral claim.[6] And second, even in evaluative domains where it is usually conceded that there can be disagreement without malfunction – the aesthetic domain, for example – we find disputes that are conducted in a way that seems to reflect the conviction that there is a right answer to the question being considered.

These examples suggest that we cannot decide whether disagreement in a particular area is appropriately understood as representing malfunction simply by observing our linguistic practice. We must engage in metaphysical and epistemological investigation of the corresponding subject matters. The result might be a philosophical argument that there is a single standard in morality but not in aesthetics. My object here, however, is not to make a contribution to these debates but simply to explore the phenomenon of collective reasoning. Thus, I shall consider both the possibility that moral disagreement genuinely indicates cognitive malfunction and the possibility that it does not. This chapter focuses on the former case, the next on the latter. A point from the previous section perhaps warrants repetition here. Regarding morality as presenting us with a single set of values determining moral relevance is compatible with a practice-based view of reasons. We need only suppose that there is a single reason-constituting practice that is suitable to the conflict-resolving role of morality. This becomes more plausible when we consider that whole communities may be in conflict with one another, and thus that a practice that grounds reasons capable of resolving such conflicts must transcend particular communities.

If disagreement in moral matters reflects cognitive malfunction, collective reasoning can take the same form as in the standard case. The facts relevant to a moral question can be assembled, and their significance as reasons in support of one or the other conclusion assessed. This will involve the two sorts of substantive reasons I have mentioned, primary moral reasons and debunking reasons, as well as interpersonal reasons. But in the moral case, it is useful to distinguish two levels of moral reasoning.

First-order moral reasoning employs principles that identify morally relevant considerations. Collective reasoning at this level attempts to determine more accurately what action these principles support, all things considered. But even if all parties accept the same principles as relevant, such collective reasoning may hit a dead end. There is little that can be said explicitly at the first-order level in defense of an all-things-considered judgment. We seem restricted to inviting others to ponder the facts that we take to be significant, hoping that this will alter their perception of what is required, all things considered. Thus, although all the parties may share a background conviction that their disagreement involves malfunction, they may not be able to make much progress in identifying and eliminating it.

When this happens, moral reasoning can move to a higher level where the parties employ additional conceptual resources to determine which principles are genuine first-order moral principles and how conflicts among them are to be resolved. This is the level of moral theory, although one need not develop an explicit moral theory to engage in it. Second-order reasoning of this sort often involves adopting (an interpretation of) the moral point of view, understood as a conceptual standpoint especially suitable for the identification of genuine first-order principles. But a particular interpretation of the moral point of view must still be defended by second-order reasoning of some kind.

This distinction between two levels of moral reasoning opens up the possibility of a new role for collective reasoning in the moral realm. Earlier, I said that collective reasoning is the preferred form of moral reasoning. Collective moral reasoning does not merely enable each member of a group facing a conflict of interest to form a better-justified judgment regarding how the conflict is to be resolved. If piecemeal consensus is attained, concrete practical conflict among the parties will be eliminated. In making this point I was speaking of first-order moral reasoning. If the parties can agree about what is required by the moral principles that actually guide action, there will be no practical conflict. But the point can be extended to second-order reasoning. If the parties to a conflict move to the second level to resolve conflicting all-things-considered first-order judgments, and they reach a piecemeal consensus at the second level, this will translate into first-order agreement.

It might be suggested, however, that we can make a further claim about the role of collective reasoning at the second level: We must make use of the concept of collective reasoning in characterizing genuine first-order moral principles. The true principles of morality are those that would be the product of (a certain process of) collective reasoning. This would mean that the moral relevance of collective reasoning goes beyond the fact that, in favorable circumstances, it can produce agreement on what the relevant moral reasons require, thus eliminating concrete practical conflict. In addition, we need to employ the concept of collective reasoning to provide an account of what makes something a genuine first-order moral principle – what makes something a moral reason for action.

In the remainder of this chapter, I examine this idea in connection with the interpretation of collective reasoning that views the disagreement that prompts it as indicative of malfunction. That is, I consider whether collective reasoning of *this* sort is properly understood as playing an essential role in the characterization of the true principles of morality. The focus will be the moral theories of Jürgen Habermas and T. M. Scanlon.

On the whole, my conclusions will be negative. The main point can actually be made quickly. In general, collective reasoning undertaken to overcome malfunction presupposes a set of reasons, the grasping of which is facilitated by collective reasoning. Thus, collective reasoning that overcomes malfunction in the identification of the true principles of morality will presuppose a set of reasons germane to what the true principles are. But then the true principles can be characterized simply as the principles the adoption of which is supported by these reasons. The significance of collective reasoning will be entirely epistemic. It enables us to determine what the reasons germane to the acceptance of moral principles require and, thus, what these principles actually are. But what *makes* them genuine moral principles is their relation to the relevant reasons.[7] Still, it will deepen our understanding of collective reasoning in the moral case to work through the details with respect to the theories of Habermas and Scanlon.

III. THE MORAL POINT OF VIEW

The idea that collective reasoning plays an essential role in the characterization of the true principles of morality is closely connected with the idea that it plays an essential role in the characterization of the moral point of view. So it will be useful to begin by saying more about the place of the moral point of view in ordinary (noncollective) moral reasoning.

There are two different ways of understanding the moral point of view. One regards it constitutively. Adopting the moral point of view involves performing a thought experiment that generates first-order moral principles out of materials that either are not reasons at all or, if they are reasons, are not moral reasons. Of course, as I have noted, even on this interpretation, second-order reasoning will play some role because the particular interpretation of the moral point of view that is employed must be defended. But the relevant second-order reasons do not support the adoption of first-order moral principles directly; they support the employment of a certain procedure for generating first-order moral principles out of nonmoral materials.

The moral point of view can also, however, be viewed epistemically, as the vantage point from which various considerations germane to the identification of the true principles of morality are most fully revealed. On this way of looking at the moral point of view, first-order principles are established as genuine principles of morality by second-order reasons that support adopting them for the role of moral principles (principles that determine what is to be done in situations where interests conflict). These second-order reasons are themselves moral reasons of a sort; they are internal to the moral sphere. The moral point of view is simply the best standpoint for grasping their import.

Both possibilities can be illustrated in connection with the procedure of universalization. J. L. Mackie distinguishes three stages of universalization.[8] Stage One universalization is simply a matter of acknowledging the legitimacy of action by others on whatever principle (for a given kind of situation) one adopts for oneself. It is a requirement to judge like cases alike. Stage Two universalization is an expansion of the Golden Rule. It involves considering how one would like being on the receiving end of action in accordance with a particular principle. Stage Three universalization pushes this idea further by directing one to consider how one would like being on the receiving end if one had the desires and concerns of the people affected.

The core of universalization's claim to articulate the moral point of view lies in the idea that morality is fundamentally a matter of impartiality in the resolution of conflicts of interest. Viewed constitutively, as a procedure for constructing moral reasons out of nonmoral materials, universalization is basically a device for generating the requisite impartiality by securing an agent's *identification* with the interests of all those potentially affected. Having identified with these interests – made them her own – she then resolves conflicts among them by simply registering their respective motivational forces and allowing herself to be moved in the way determined by the resultant. The characteristic outcome is maximization of total aggregate satisfaction of all the interests in play. So the appropriate first-order principles are utilitarian.

The connection between universalization and identification can be seen in Mackie's stages. Stage Three universalization is explicitly formulated as a requirement to identify with the particular interests of others. And Stage Two universalization will effect such an identification if one's interests are of the same kind as the interests of others, so that putting oneself in their position will give one their specific concerns. Stage One universalization may seem at first sight to be a different idea, a simple formal requirement to judge like cases alike. But if I am in the same situation with respect to others that they are in with respect to me, to imagine their acting as I propose to act is to imagine myself on the receiving end of that action. So under certain circumstances, Stage One universalization is equivalent to Stage Two.

On the alternative, epistemic account of the moral point of view, it is the standpoint from which we can best appreciate the force of the second-order moral reasons germane to the identification of first-order moral principles, for example, reasons of fairness or need. Principles count as moral to the extent that they effect a fair resolution of conflicts of interest, or respect all the genuine needs at stake. On this way of understanding the moral point of view, first-order principles are constituted as moral, not by a procedure of identification that enables us to generate them out of nonmoral materials, but by the second-order reasons that support their adoption. That is, the requisite impartiality is introduced not by identification but by the presupposed reasons of fairness or need, which must simply be "tracked."

Nevertheless, we can view universalization of the familiar sort as contributing to this tracking by facilitating impartial assessment of the force of these reasons. Putting oneself in the position of others has an important role to play when we seek to grasp the import of the second-order reasons germane to the identification of first-order moral principles. If one thinks that reasons of fairness or need support the adoption of a certain principle, or a certain way of resolving conflicts between principles, one can check this by imagining oneself in the position of someone who will be negatively affected by the corresponding actions, with the object of determining whether this would change one's assessment of the force of the relevant second-order reasons.

The epistemic utility of this move reflects a fact mentioned earlier. One of the characteristic forms of rational malfunction is corruption by self-interested bias. In general, bias is a matter of reasoning on the basis of only a proper subset of the relevant reasons, or – when one could not keep all the relevant reasons in mind – reasoning on the basis of an unrepresentative sample.[9] Self-interested bias exists when self-interested motives are the cause of this distortion. It might be present in any case where one must assess the force of the reasons relevant to a question, but it is virtually guaranteed to be a threat when one must assess the force of reasons relevant to the adoption of moral principles, which have the function of resolving conflicts of interest. One's own interests will likely be affected in some way by the decision that is made. So it would not be too much of an exaggeration to say that when one is engaged in moral reasoning of any kind – either first-order or second-order – it is always appropriate to check for malfunction by imagining oneself in the position of those who will be negatively affected. This may involve acquiring a new bias, but it will serve to correct one's own self-interested bias. Thus, Stage Two universalization retains its claim to articulate the moral point of view when it is interpreted epistemically, as the point of view from which one is best able to see what the reasons germane to the identification of first-order moral principles require.

IV. HABERMAS

Now let us consider how the concept of collective reasoning might be understood as entering into the characterization of the true principles of morality. A proposal that seems to invite such an interpretation has been made by Jürgen Habermas. He has advocated a "dialogical" approach to ethics that posits a condition, which he calls (U), that any valid moral norm must satisfy:

> (U). *All* affected can accept the consequences and the side effects its *general* observance can be anticipated to have for the satisfaction of *everyone's* interests (and these consequences are preferred to those of known alternative possibilities for regulation).[10]

I take it that by a norm, Habermas means a principle, a conceptual entity that grounds reasons for action, rather than an observable regularity in the behavior of people in certain kinds of situations. This interpretation is consonant with the distinction he makes between discourses of application and discourses of justification.[11] Discourses of application seek to identify the course of action in a particular situation that is required by the totality of all the applicable moral principles. Discourses of justification establish what the valid moral principles are. This is basically the distinction between first-order and second-order moral reasoning mentioned earlier. (U) states a condition that is meant to be satisfied by discourses of justification only.

In the previous section, I distinguished between constitutive and epistemic interpretations of the moral point of view. Can (U) be understood constitutively, as articulating a condition the satisfaction of which constitutes impartiality? On its surface, (U) appears to involve a "socialization" of ordinary universalization, in particular, of Stages One and Three of Mackie's account. First, it requires that a principle be such that not just the agent, but all affected, can accept everyone's complying with it in a given situation. Second, this acceptance is to be based on a judgment by each that general compliance with the principle would be in everyone's interests. This latter feature seems to involve something like ordinary Stage Three universalization, with the difference that each must consider the effects not just of his own compliance with the principle but of everyone's. Each must reason as a kind of rule consequentialist.

If this interpretation of (U) is correct, it clearly has a constitutive element. As we have seen, Stage Three universalization involves identification with the interests of others, which constitutes impartiality. The result – in the context of (U) – would presumably be a kind of rule utilitarianism. But so far, nothing has been said about collective reasoning. Can it be regarded as playing an impartiality-constituting role within the framework of (U), so interpreted?

(U) stipulates that all must agree that general compliance with a certain principle would be in everyone's interests. On the interpretation we are now considering, this means that the Stage Three universalizations of all must agree. Presumably, this will not happen without the exchange of information concerning the interests of each. We may suppose that the monological Stage Three universalizations of different people will usually yield different results because of ignorance or error regarding what the interests of each are. The exchange of information about interests provides a way of removing this ignorance and error, thus producing the required agreement.

On the present interpretation of (U), then, agreement among individuals employing Stage Three universalization to generate principles will typically require the exchange of information about interests. But it does not follow that (U) gives collective reasoning a role in constituting morally required impartiality. Ultimately, Stage Three universalization is a matter of being moved in a certain way – causally influenced – by interests one has identified with. If people are moved in different ways, and they regard this as unacceptable, they can try exchanging information about interests in the hope that this will result in all being moved in the same way. But this would not be a process of reasoning, of assessing the force of a body of reasons.[12]

When (U) is viewed in this first way, then, the concept of collective reasoning is not employed, even implicitly, in characterizing the true requirements of morality. But this interpretation is probably not correct. In "Remarks on Discourse Ethics," Habermas provides this formulation of his view:

> [I]t follows from the normative content of these suppositions of rationality (openness, equal rights, truthfulness, and absence of coercion) that, insofar as one's sole aim is to justify norms, one must accept procedural conditions that implicitly amount to the recognition of a rule of argumentation, (U): "Every valid norm must satisfy the condition that the consequences and side effects of its *general* observance can be anticipated to have for the satisfaction of the interests of *each* could be freely accepted by *all* affected (and be preferred to those of known alternative possibilities for regulation)."[13]

Here, acceptance does not seem to be a matter of Stage Three universalization. Habermas's talk of *rationality* and a *rule of argumentation* strongly suggests that he has in mind reasoning to a judgment, that all can share, about what would be in the interests of each.

On this reading, moral principles are accepted for reasons. And if all are to accept the same principles, acceptance must presumably result from a process of collective reasoning employing reasons the force of which all can acknowledge. I cannot say that a given principle should be adopted because it will be in my interests.[14] I must, rather, advocate it on some ground that all could accept.

If the common ground is provided by the notion of what would be in the interests of each, the envisaged reasoning will presumably involve (1) considering what the true interests of each really are, and (2) invoking some principle or principles by means of which a conclusion about what the members of the group should do can be derived from considerations relating to the true interests of each. This might be the utilitarian principle of aggregation, but on the present reading – which makes no use of Stage Three universalization – a principle of fair distribution is more plausible. It is more likely to lead to agreement. An alternative would be to speak not of interests but of needs. When interests are at stake, considerations of fairness can block the utilitarian conclusion that a slight increase in the satisfaction of the interests of each member of a large group justifies major sacrifices for a few. If we focus on needs, we can achieve the same result by saying that important needs may not be frustrated for the sake of considerations that are either minor needs or not needs at all.

If we read (U) in this way, however, it seems to lose any constitutive aspect. Morally required impartiality is constituted by the reasons that are invoked in reaching a conclusion about what is required to satisfy the interests of each. The stipulation that there must be agreement leads to the exchange of arguments concerning what first-order principles these reasons require, rather than the mere exchange of information about interests. Thus, we can speak of genuine collective reasoning. But its role is purely epistemic. The moral point of view, as characterized by (U), is simply the standpoint from which the import of the relevant reasons can be correctly identified and assessed.

In particular, the case for (U), understood now as involving collective reasoning, is that talking with others can yield a more accurate grasp of the import of the relevant reasons (relating to fairness or needs) than imagining oneself in the situation of others and considering what force these reasons would then have. As was noted in the discussion of the moral point of view in the previous section, one of the characteristic forms of rational malfunction is the corruption of reasoning by self-interested bias. And this is virtually guaranteed to be a threat when one must assess the force of moral reasons, which are supposed to provide the basis for resolving conflicts of interest. So when one is engaged in moral reasoning, it is always appropriate to check for cognitive malfunction by considering what others who will be affected by one's decision would regard the relevant reasons as requiring. But then it seems that doing this by Stage Two universalization is merely a way of approximating something better – actually talking to people on the receiving end. One can deliberate with those who will be affected, letting them point out the way self-interest is biasing one's perception of the force of the relevant reasons. Of course, they will likely be biased as well, but it is plausible that the exchange of arguments will result in a reduction of self-interested bias, in the assessment of the force of the relevant reasons, throughout the group.

We should note a qualification, however. There are cases where morality requires us to make moral judgments without discussing them with those who will be affected by the resulting actions – because, for example, discussion would be embarrassing to them. So even in the best of all morally possible worlds, there will still be a role for the monological device of imagining oneself in the position of others, understood epistemically as a procedure for eliminating bias in the appreciation of the force of the relevant reasons.

From what we have seen so far, then, Habermas has not provided us with an example of a theory that makes essential use of the concept of collective reasoning in characterizing the true principles of morality. Either genuine collective reasoning plays no role at all, or it plays an epistemic, rather than a constitutive, role. It facilitates our grasp of the second-order reasons that ground the status of certain principles as genuine principles of morality. Since the principles of morality underlie social cooperation, Habermas's theory basically presents us with a variation on the situation, discussed in Chapter 5, where a group must resolve disagreement regarding what certain reasons support – disagreement that is attributable to malfunction – if it is to attain some further cooperative benefit. But to solidify these results, we should explore two further issues connected with Habermas's view.

First, it might be thought that I have been insufficiently sensitive to the fact that agents satisfying (U) are forced, by the requirement to reach agreement, to find common ground. From what I have said so far, the quest for common ground is simply a matter of clarifying the force of reasons already available to the parties. I suggested that these could be reasons of fairness or need. But, it might be held, Habermas envisages the *creation* of common ground through a process of collective reasoning. If this is right, the concept of collective reasoning would, after all, play an essential role in the characterization of the true principles of morality.

To assess this claim, we must consider how reasons could be created. One possibility is a nonrational or extrarational process – an unreasoned, "existential" commitment to take a feature of the world as a reason. This is something that an individual might do, but presumably it would be suggested that when a group needs to find a common basis for action, such a commitment must be collective. The idea that reasons of any kind can be created by an unreasoned commitment is not very attractive. Reasons have a normative dimension, and it is difficult to see how a mere existential leap can bring this into existence. For present purposes, however, the important point is that the process described is not a process of reasoning. So it provides no basis for the claim that the notion of collective reasoning must enter into the characterization of the true principles of morality.

It is more plausible to suppose that we always operate within a space of reasons to which we are initiated by socialization. Any creation of reasons is then a matter of modifying the set of pregiven reasons as rational considerations dictate. One way of understanding this process of modification is to attribute it to coherentist reasoning. Considerations of coherence relating to a pregiven set of reasons may force us to acknowledge that some further feature of the world should be viewed as a reason for action. Similarly, considerations of coherence can lead to our depriving a feature of the world of the status of a reason.

There is evidence in Habermas's writing that he accepts this picture. His theory of communicative action regards it as taking place against a background of culturally given interpretive patterns that he calls the *lifeworld*.[15] Although he does not, as far as I am aware, explicitly say that the lifeworld is the source of the reasons the force of which is grasped in deliberation, it is plausibly viewed in this way. Habermas views communicative action as reproducing the lifeworld, and since the ideal *outcome* of communicative action is intersubjective recognition of a validity claim – a claim about what the relevant reasons support – it apparently follows that the interpretations that constitute the *input* must also involve in some way the notion of support by reasons. The picture seems to be that as conditions change, the set of pregiven interpretations provided by the lifeworld, understood as grounding a set of reasons for action, starts to display an incoherence or lack of harmony that it is the goal of shared deliberation to repair.

Coherentist reasoning, then, provides a way that we can understand new reasons as being created. And this reasoning could be carried on collectively, by the exchange of arguments concerning what coherence requires. But in this process, the new reasons are created out of old reasons. Coherentist reasoning operates on reasons that already exist. New need-based reasons, for example, are created by correcting incoherence that has been detected in the previous understanding of what counts as a genuine need. So if coherentist reasoning underlies the generation of new reasons germane to identification of the true principles of morality, our previous conclusion is sustained. The true principles of morality are constituted as such by certain relations in the realm of reasons – in this case, relations of coherence. Collective reasoning merely has the epistemic role of bringing about an appreciation of these relations.

If this is right, the creation of new reasons can have a place within the sort of collective reasoning that we are exploring in this chapter, where initial disagreement is interpreted as indicating malfunction in the grasping of the force of a presupposed body of reasons. The creation of reasons is a consequence of sensitivity to relations of coherence in a presupposed body of reasons. Later in this chapter and in the next, I shall explore the possibility that when disagreement is *not* attributable to malfunction, collective reasoning may be able to produce agreement by transforming the content of the reasons grounding the initial disagreement. But this possibility does not seem to be germane to Habermas's project. He regards the participants in discourse as guided by the "force of the better argument." This suggests a picture according to which collective reasoning produces agreement by securing a shared perception of the import of a presupposed body of reasons.

The other feature of Habermas's view that requires discussion involves the possibility that the reasons that ground the status of a principle as a genuine principle of morality can only be grasped by a collective judgment. If we suppose, in addition, that a collective judgment must be produced by collective reasoning, there will be an intimate – if not exactly constitutive – connection between collective reasoning and any principle having the status of a genuine principle of morality. The second passage quoted from Habermas provides some reason to believe that this is what he has in mind. He says that certain presuppositions of rationality yield a rule of moral argumentation that requires, among other things, free acceptance by all parties of the conclusions that are reached. But for free acceptance by all to be a *rule* of moral argument – to be something the achievement of which constrains the deliberations of the parties – each must suspend judgment until something all can accept has been found. That is, deliberation must conclude in a collective judgment. Earlier I suggested that (U)'s requirement that all agree on moral principles could be regarded as an instance of the general case in which a group must agree on a cooperative scheme if it is to attain some further goal – if it is to benefit from cooperation in some further way. For that purpose, a piecemeal consensus will suffice.[16] But when Habermas describes the agreement of all as a rule of argument, he appears to be supposing that the nature of the reasons being considered is such that their force must be grasped in a collective judgment. A requirement of this sort to attain agreement would operate independently of whether the group needed to agree to realize some further benefit.

The claim that a collective judgment is required to identify the true principles of morality conflicts with the points made in the discussion of collective judgment in Chapter 5. It might be replied that judgments purporting to identify the true principles of morality constitute an exception. One possibility is that in this case, the relevant reasons are provided by the needs of each individual, and each has a kind of privileged access to what counts as a genuine need of hers. Thus, a justified conclusion regarding what is required by the needs of all can be established only by a collective judgment to which each brings her special insight.[17]

But this suggestion is dubious. The idea that each has privileged access to some of the reasons germane to the identification of the true principles of morality implicitly rejects the plausible thesis of the commonability of our concepts proposed by Philip Pettit.[18] This holds that each of the concepts employed by anyone is in principle accessible to everyone else, so that anybody can make correct judgments employing any concept. If this is right, A could be correct about what B's needs are, even if B disagrees. Thus, an individual could make a correct judgment about what is required by the needs of all without securing the agreement of everyone else.[19]

It does not appear, then, that Habermas's moral theory provides any basis for supposing that the notion of collective reasoning plays an essential role in the characterization of the true principles of morality. If there is a temptation to see something more at work here, it may be because Habermas can easily be interpreted as offering a constructivist account of moral truth that characterizes the genuine principles of morality as those that would be accepted at the endpoint of an idealized inquiry. His concept of discourse embodies certain idealizations.[20] But as we saw in Section I, the essential feature of this sort of constructivism is that truths are constituted by the reasons that justify their acceptance (that justify accepting the corresponding propositions). The device of a hypothetical endpoint simply provides a way of making vivid the distinction between what the relevant reasons really require and the beliefs we may have about this now.

I conclude, then, that the best interpretation of the role of collective reasoning in Habermas's account of the moral point of view – in the condition (U) – is the standard epistemic one identified earlier. A principle does not acquire the status of a true principle of morality by virtue of being the product of a certain process of collective reasoning. It acquires this status by standing in a particular relation to certain (second-order) reasons that justify its acceptance. The significance of the emphasis that Habermas places on collective reasoning (on dialogue) is best understood as deriving solely from the fact that collective reasoning enables the members of a group to acquire a better understanding of the force of the relevant reasons.

V. SCANLON

It might also be suggested that contractarian moral theories make essential use of the concept of collective reasoning in the characterization of the true requirements of morality. Theories of this sort give pride of place to agreement, rather than to the act of putting oneself in the position of others. And it is natural to suppose that this agreement is to be achieved by reasoning.[21]

We must be clear about what contractarian moral theories regard themselves as doing. In Chapter 5, we saw how what counts as correct participation in a practice of judgment is constantly negotiated. Presumably this holds true for moral reasoning as well. It is possible to construct a philosophical account of the place of morality in our lives, and of how moral reasoning ideally ought to proceed, that envisages ongoing negotiation. An example is the "expressive-collaborative model" developed by Margaret Urban Walker.[22] Standard contractarian theories, however, are not making the point that the moral dimension of our lives is constantly negotiated. They are intended as *contributions* to the ongoing process of negotiation, to the ongoing debate about what morality requires. They present arguments concerning what the true principles of morality are.

In general, contractarian theories view the moral order as an instance of mutually beneficial cooperation. In the first two chapters, I discussed how cooperation can be regarded as guided by reason. An aspect of this is how the members of a group can regard the choice of a cooperative scheme as guided by reason. Contractarian moral theories focus on this second aspect of rational cooperation. They view the task of identifying the true principles of morality as the task of deciding upon the moral order, understood as a cooperative scheme. Each contractarian theory involves a proposal concerning how to use the notion of agreement on a framework for the moral order to determine the true requirements of morality. Thus, each such theory constructs an account of the moral point of view in which the notion of agreement has a central place.

In our earlier discussion of universalization, I suggested that putting oneself in the position of others might either be a way of constituting morally required impartiality – through identification with their interests – or a procedure with an epistemic rationale. In the latter role, it reduces bias in one's assessment of the force of a presupposed set of reasons germane to the adoption of moral principles. Since contractarian moral theories give pride of place to agreement, they do not present us with the same alternatives. But we can still distinguish between theories that seek to generate morality without presupposing any moral materials, and those that presuppose moral materials.

An example of a theory that does not presuppose moral materials is that developed by David Gauthier.[23] It uses rational choice in a "strategic" situation – in particular, a bargaining game – to characterize the moral order. Rawls's ideal contractarianism is harder to classify.[24] The parties in the Original Position determine the correct principles of justice without doing any moral reasoning. And the veil of ignorance has the effect of forcing each to identify with others, which introduces something similar to constitutive universalization. But on balance, it seems that Rawls's theory is best understood as presenting a novel procedure for reasoning from antecedently established moral premises to a conclusion concerning the best way of understanding the moral order. In particular, choice in the original position provides a way of extracting conclusions regarding substantive fairness from premises regarding procedural fairness (which, it is hoped, will be less controversial). The reasoning involved here employs the method of reflective equilibrium, and it could be carried out collectively. People could exchange arguments regarding which account of the original position was really best and what would actually be chosen, given a particular account. But this would be reasoning on the standard model. It would be a matter of assembling a pool of criticized arguments on the basis of which each could make up his own mind.

A more interesting contractarian theory, for the purposes of an investigation of collective reasoning, is that offered by T. M. Scanlon. Scanlon defines moral wrongness as follows:

> [A]n act is wrong if its performance under the circumstances would be disallowed by any system of rules for the general regulation of behavior that no one could reasonably reject as a basis for informed, unforced general agreement.[25]

Scanlon intends this definition to apply only to the central core of morality, which he terms "what we owe to each other." This is the part most plausibly viewed as a cooperative scheme. Individuals may also acknowledge other concerns that can appropriately be regarded as moral, for example, environmental concerns, which fall outside the domain of moral wrongness so characterized.

The notion of what no one could reasonably reject plays a central role in Scanlon's definition of wrongness, and this might suggest that the concept of collective reasoning enters into the characterization of the true requirements of morality, as he understands them. In the remainder of this section, I consider this suggestion in more detail, focusing on how Scanlon's notion of what no one can reasonably reject is to be understood.

As we saw in Chapter 4, we can distinguish two notions of reasonableness. On the first, and most basic, notion, reasonableness is appropriate responsiveness to the relevant reasons. I called this "reasonableness-as-competence." But if we apply this notion of the reasonable to Scanlon's definition of wrongness, it comes out as virtually trivial. It says that an action is wrong if it would be disallowed by any system of rules that no one who was appropriately responsive to the relevant reasons could reject. But once we have gotten this far, it is hard to see what work the notion of reasonableness is doing. Why not just speak of what is required by the relevant reasons? For Scanlon, the situation to which the concept of what no one could reasonably reject applies is one in which people are making conflicting claims that have a moral character – for example, conflicting right-claims. But we could presumably regard these as prima facie reasons for doing or allowing certain things, and treat wrongness as what would be prohibited by these reasons all-things-considered. The real work would then be done by the reasons, rather than the notion of what no one could reasonably reject.

One point that might be made here is that Scanlon's formulation can be related to the epistemic interpretation of universalization discussed earlier. Even if the true principles of wrong action are determined by various reasons relevant to their acceptance, bias can lead to mistakes about what these reasons require. And asking oneself whether these principles could be reasonably rejected by others is a way of reducing this bias by looking at the relevant reasons from their points of view. If we take this epistemic view of reasonable rejection, we can make the same points about its relation to collective reasoning as were made earlier about the epistemic interpretation of universalization. Actually talking with people can often provide a more accurate grasp of what they could reasonably reject than asking this question on their behalf.

If this first interpretation is correct, Scanlon's incorporation of reasonable rejection into his definition of moral rightness – instead of simply speaking of what is required by the reasons germane to the identification of moral principles – could be explained as the result of his being misled by a cogent observation about moral motivation. What motivates us to be moral is not sympathy, or the natural social feelings of mankind, or respect for the deliverances of a part of ourselves that legislates for the rest, or any of the other familiar candidates. What motivates us to be moral is a desire to act in a way that is justifiable to others. This could mean doing what one knows that others will deem to be justified. But someone motivated in this way might also do something that others did not, antecedently, deem to be justified, if she thought she could convince them that it was justified (or could attribute any failure to convince them to mistakes on their part).

Scanlon can be seen as promoting this view of moral motivation into a theory of moral wrongness. If one wants to act in a way that can be justified to others, where this means in a way that they *should* accept as justified, then one wants to act in a way that they could not reasonably reject (on the "competence" interpretation of reasonableness). These are just two different ways of describing the same goal. But justification presupposes reasons that are already in place. So the idea of what I can justify is really the idea of what these reasons justify. And this means that the proposal boils down to the view that wrongness is a matter of acting contrary to what is required, all things considered, by the moral reasons legitimately in play in a given situation.[26]

Scanlon, however, explicitly rejects the suggestion that we could substitute talk of what is required by the reasons underlying people's claims for talk of reasonable rejection.[27] Apparently, then, there must be more to reasonableness, as he is employing the notion, than appropriate responsiveness to the relevant reasons. A natural suggestion is that it is a substantive moral notion, akin to what I have called reasonableness-as-fairness. If this is right, the connection with moral motivation described in the previous paragraph takes on a new layer. Strictly speaking, to want to act in a way that can be justified to others is equivalent to wanting to act in a way that they could not reasonably reject, in the sense of reasonableness-as-competence. But where conflicting claims are at stake, justification must involve the notion of fairness. So to act in a way that can be justified to others is, more particularly, to act in a way that they cannot reasonably reject as unreasonable – that they cannot competently reject as unfair to themselves or others.

Some features of Scanlon's discussion support this interpretation of his theory. He speaks of acting in a way that could not be reasonably rejected by others *similarly motivated,* by which he means people who themselves want their behavior to be justifiable to others. The core idea is that of *mutual accommodation* on the part of people who have concerns that underwrite conflicting claims. This is similar to making concessions, from what would best serve one's interests, as fairness requires.

To be sure, the notion of what could not be reasonably rejected can be seen as subtly different from fairness. It appears to be more suitable than the value of fairness to a situation in which the parties make claims grounded in independent sources of value, which others should recognize and respect.[28] As we have seen, the value of fairness seems most at home in situations where conflicting interests are at stake. Further, if fairness suggests the division of the benefits of cooperation, it is too narrow to capture all of what Scanlon has in mind. He wants to admit the possibility of claims that cannot be reasonably rejected, even though those making them have nothing to offer in return.[29]

But other features of Scanlon's discussion point to the conclusion that the notion of what cannot be reasonably rejected is, after all, fundamentally the notion of fairness (reasonableness-as-fairness). As he characterizes the ideal of acting on principles that others could not reasonably reject, it is grounded in the substantive value of a certain sort of relation with others – that in which each seeks to accommodate the reasonable concerns of others (those that do not involve excessive demands).[30] And a substantive value answering to this description will be very similar to the value of fairness. Moreover, this value works in the same way as fairness. It sets benefits against burdens.[31]

There is also another consideration that suggests that what can be reasonably rejected is ultimately a matter of fairness. Scanlon distinguishes between personal reasons that ground claims against others and impersonal values that constitute certain features of the world as desirable in their own right. The personal reasons are generic. They are reasons of a *kind* that would justify the rejection of certain rules, not reasons that particular people actually advance.[32] And they can have a moral content, invoking entitlements. But they do not comprise all the moral reasons anyone might accept. People may also acknowledge impersonal values, such as environmental values, that can be regarded as having moral force (although not falling under the concept of what we owe to each other). Scanlon argues that while values of the latter sort may be moral in a broad sense, only reasons of the former kind provide a basis for the reasonable rejection of principles that he associates with the core area of morality. Impersonal values figure in reasonable rejection only at one remove, because it is important to the people who acknowledge these values that they be able to live in accordance with them – that is, only by being transformed into personal reasons.[33] Thus, Scanlon seems to endorse something like the demotion of moral concerns to interests that, as we saw in Section II of Chapter 2 and Section III of Chapter 4, accompanies the employment of the notion of fairness to resolve moral disputes. Impersonal moral concerns are demoted to personal claims.

But in fact, we can go further than this. If conflicts grounded in competing personal claims are to be resolved as reasonableness-as-fairness dictates, it seems that these claims themselves will have to be demoted. They will have to take on the character of interests. So long as they retain a moral character – for example, as grounded in what those making them take to be rights – they could come into conflict with what reasonableness-as-fairness requires, and potentially outweigh it. Presumably this cannot be allowed if the notion of what cannot be rejected as unreasonable (in the sense of reasonableness-as-fairness) is to serve as the master value underwriting an account of moral rightness. So the personal claims this value puts into line must take on a character that enables them to be subordinated by the value of fairness.

To sum up, on this second interpretation of Scanlon's view, his assertion that we cannot reduce talk of what can be reasonably rejected to talk of what is required by the reasons underlying the claims people make is sustained. But this is because the operative notion of reasonableness is a further substantive value, akin to fairness, on the basis of which conflicts between claims are to be resolved. It determines the extent to which these claims may be acknowledged, given the claims of others. Establishing what cannot be reasonably rejected is not a matter of weighing against each other in a reasonable (as competent) fashion the moral reasons grounding the claims people can make. Rather, it is a matter of considering these claims as something like interests and determining what would be fair in light of them. Here again, any role for collective reasoning in Scanlon's moral theory will be purely epistemic. It will serve to reduce or eliminate malfunction in the grasping of what the master value of reasonableness-as-fairness requires.

There is, however, a third interpretation of Scanlon's theory that we should consider. Instead of demoting the moral concerns expressed in their conflicting claims to interests and reasoning their way to agreement on what would be a reasonable-as-fair way of resolving this conflict, the parties may be able to use the notion of what no one could reasonably reject to underwrite a *transformation* of the reasons that ground the initial claims, so that each claim is reasonable in light of the others.

An example may make this clearer. Suppose that the reasons underlying the initial claims are reasons of need. Need-based reasons are agent-neutral reasons that all should acknowledge. But even after shared deliberation that eliminates all the malfunctioning that can, given human limitations, be eliminated, the concept of a need – and the criteria of urgency it imports – may not be able to resolve the competing claims that people with different needs can plausibly make. Nevertheless, accommodation could be achieved if the understanding that each has of what constitutes a genuine need were transformed. And the notion of what someone seeking mutual accommodation could not reasonably reject (could not competently reject as unfair) may provide conceptual pressure sufficient to effect such a transformation. This would not be a matter of the destruction of these needs as agent-neutral reasons, their conversion into mere interests. Rather, the content of the agent-neutral reasons provided by certain needs would be altered to fit the requirements of "reasonableness." Scanlon occasionally says things that suggest that he may have something like this in mind, for example:

> There is no fixed list of "morally relevant considerations" or of reasons that are "morally excluded." The aim of justifiability to others moves us to work out a system of justification that meets its demands, and this leads to a continuing process of revising and refining our conception of the reasons that are relevant and those that are morally excluded in certain contexts.[34]

On this way of viewing the situation, there is a right answer to the question whether a particular way of transforming the reasons grounding the initial claims – a particular pattern of transformations – constitutes a reasonable accommodation. Thus, we still do not need to use the concept of collective reasoning to characterize the true requirements of morality. They will be constituted as such by certain relations in a space of reasons. The situation is analogous to that which obtains when coherentist reasoning is involved in the creation of common ground, as discussed earlier in connection with Habermas. The differences are (1) that we are dealing not with the creation and destruction of reasons, but with the reshaping of the content of reasons already on the scene, and (2) that a specific concept – that of reasonableness-as-fairness – provides a focus for the relations in the space of reasons that are grasped by reasoning.

But although the role played by collective reasoning will still be an epistemic one, discerning the appropriate pattern of transformation, this role will have an added dimension. The transformation of reasons is effected by a process of reasoning. I say more about how reasoning might accomplish such a transformation in the next chapter. Here, however, we can note that since reasonableness-as-fairness requires one person to transform the reasons grounding his claims only if the others do so as well, in cases of the sort we are considering, the reasoning that produces the requisite transformations will have to be jointly undertaken. And it is plausible that there will be an interplay between this process and the epistemic one of discovering the appropriate pattern of transformation. What constitutes the appropriate pattern may become clear to each of the participants only as an actual process of transformation unfolds.

On this final interpretation of Scanlon's theory, then, he still envisages a situation in which people regard themselves as able to make various claims against one another that have a moral character. These are not, however, to be resolved on the basis of what the associated moral reasons require, all things considered. Rather, they are to be resolved on the basis of what would be reasonable – what would constitute appropriate mutual accommodation. This means that we are operating with a substantive moral value akin to fairness. But we need not suppose that the claims are therefore converted into interests. It may be possible to modify the content of the conflicting claims in a reasonable-as-fair way. And although the concept of collective reasoning still plays no role in the characterization of the true requirements of morality – the pattern of transformation capable of bringing the different claims into a reasonable-as-fair alignment is determined by relations in the space of reasons – the discovery of this pattern will probably involve a dimension of social interaction going beyond that involved in ordinary shared deliberation.

It should be borne in mind, however, that if we regard reasonableness-as-fairness as the master value underlying the true requirements of morality, we are taking the disagreement arising from the conflicting initial claims to be disagreement *without malfunction*. If the initial disagreement could be attributed to cognitive malfunction, we could speak of what the reasons underlying the claims really require, all

things considered (which would be clear if malfunction were eliminated), and dispense with the notion of mutual accommodation. Since
in Scanlon's theory, the reasons underlying the initial claims are reasons of a kind that all acknowledge, the disagreement will apparently
involve what Rawls calls the burdens of judgment. It arises from the
fact that humans are inevitably susceptible to certain factors that make
the force of a given body of reasons appear different to different
people. In cases of this sort, we can speak of reasonable disagreement.
It is because the relative force of the applicable reasons is something
about which reasonable-as-competent people can disagree that it is
appropriate to seek a reasonable-as-fair resolution of the competing
claims.

Chapter 7

Reasoning to Agreement

In Chapter 6, we explored collective reasoning as a way of overcoming cognitive malfunction. Special attention was given to the possibility of viewing collective moral reasoning this way. In the present chapter, I examine the role of collective reasoning when initial disagreement within a group is not attributable to cognitive malfunction. The primary case is that in which a group could benefit from cooperation but must first agree on a cooperative scheme. Is it possible for people who disagree without malfunction about which cooperative scheme to adopt to reason their way to agreement?

I. PRACTICAL DISAGREEMENT

Practical disagreement is disagreement concerning what is to be done by an agent or group of agents. When it is attributable to cognitive malfunction, there is a single set of reasons germane to the question being addressed. Disagreement of this sort could be found when a group must choose a cooperative scheme. There is a single set of reasons relevant to the question of which scheme to adopt, and the initial disagreement means that some, at least, are malfunctioning in the grasping of these reasons. If collective reasoning succeeds in overcoming this sort of malfunction, at least to the extent necessary to create a piecemeal consensus on the appropriateness of a particular scheme, it will enable cooperation to go forward. This possibility was discussed in Section IV of Chapter 5. It also played a role in Chapter 6.

As I have said, however, here I shall be concerned with the case in which the initial disagreement that blocks cooperation – by preventing the adoption of a cooperative scheme – is not attributable to cognitive malfunction. There are three ways this might happen. The first is that there is a single set of relevant reasons, but because of inescapable human limitations (limitations not attributable to malfunction), there is disagreement concerning what these reasons support. This is the situation associated with Rawls's notion of the burdens of judgment. The second possibility is related to the first, a further burden of judgment not mentioned by Rawls. It may be that all the parties translate facts into reasons in the same way, but there are so many facts relevant to the question being considered that is it impossible for anyone to keep them all in mind. In such a case, there can be disagreement because each is focusing on different facts, yet exchanging factual information will not solve the problem because as new information is brought to mind, old information inevitably slips from view. Here, too, disagreement cannot be attributed to malfunction if malfunction is understood in terms of normal human capabilities.[1] The third possibility is that the parties can, without malfunction, base a decision about what to do, or what scheme to adopt, on different reasons or values. That is, there is no single set of reasons, germane to the choice the group faces, that all properly functioning agents will acknowledge. This case will be the focus of discussion in what follows, although much of what I have to say will apply to the others as well.

In Chapter 5, I briefly mentioned two ways that individuals can, without malfunction, acknowledge different reasons for action. One approach, broadly Humean in character, reduces value – and thus normativity – to motive. The behavioral signs of normativity are striving and avoidance. But we can accommodate these phenomena without supposing that they reflect the perception of relations in a space of reasons. Desires, including aversions, also provoke striving and avoidance. Since whether one has a particular desire or not is just a fact about oneself, it is only in connection with beliefs regarding how to obtain what one wants that genuine normativity plays a role in practical deliberation. These means–end beliefs can be criticized by reference to the appropriate standards for justified belief. But there are no independent normative standards for the practical realm. All striving other than striving to have justified beliefs is explained by the operation of ordinary desires.[2]

This sort of view leaves collective reasoning in the face of practical disagreement with a relatively circumscribed role. Each will acknowledge as reasons only facts germane to how she might better satisfy her wants. Shared deliberation will consist of one person trying to show the others that they can better satisfy their wants under the scheme she favors, followed by replies of the same sort. Agreement will result if some scheme is ultimately revealed as conducive to the wants of each. When it proceeds in this way, collective reasoning can be understood as eliminating initially mistaken views on the part of at least some members of the group concerning how they could best satisfy their wants. But it does not hold much promise of actually producing agreement. The parties may be correct in thinking that different schemes would best satisfy their wants.

If we wish to provide a larger role for collective reasoning in the face of disagreement, we must resist the reduction of normativity to facts about motivation. We must suppose that agents can have cognitive access to an independent space of reasons, or that reasons are grounded in practices (in a way that transcends mere facts about dispositions). The broadly Kantian theories with which Humean theories are often opposed provide one way of doing this. They hold that, in addition to desires and aversions of certain sorts, there are independent standards in light of which underived desires and aversions can be criticized – standards that establish certain states of affairs as appropriate to seek or avoid independently of whether doing so is a means to the satisfaction of some further desire.[3]

On this Kantian approach, practical disagreement, at least regarding moral matters, is normally treated as indicating cognitive malfunction. But it is possible to invoke standards of the kind that such views envisage without committing ourselves to the idea that disagreement means malfunction. In Chapter 5, I mentioned the pluralistic view usually ascribed to Isaiah Berlin. There are more values that are accessible to us – more standards whose claims we might accept – than can be given practical acknowledgment within the life of an actual individual or community. Thus, the normative lives of individuals and groups must be grounded in commitments to only some of these.[4] This possibility fits well with the hybrid view of reasons I presented in Chapter 5. According to this view, proper functioning for animals of the sort we are involves participating *appropriately* in certain social practices of reasoning and language use. This enables us to ground genuine normativity in practices. But, it is plausible to hold, we cannot participate in all of the available conceptual practices at once.

These observations deserve further elaboration. Evaluative notions, especially what Bernard Williams has called "thick" evaluative notions, often have a descriptive content.[5] The satisfaction of the value in question entails the existence in the world of a particular state of affairs. There seems to be no barrier in principle to an individual's mastering the descriptive content of any such evaluative notion – becoming able correctly to affirm or deny that it has been satisfied.[6] But this leaves out the action-guiding character of values. To acknowledge values as action guiding is to accept that value judgments have a different "direction of fit" from descriptive judgments. We do not try to fit such judgments to the world; we try to fit the world to such judgments. But fitting the world to some values precludes fitting it to others. So individuals can fully – that is, practically – acknowledge only some of them.

It is worth considering how a practice-based view of reasons could provide for the motivational force of judgments to the effect that one ought to do something. When reasoning about what to do is at issue, the relevant practices involve dispositions not just to make particular assertions in certain circumstances but to perform particular actions (of other sorts) in certain circumstances. And our ability to carry such practices forward in the mode of assertion – to make explicit practical judgments – may be intertwined with our ability to carry them forward in the mode of action. If so, the notion of appropriate participation in a practice, participation that displays proper functioning as a human being that has been socialized to a practice, could be regarded as introducing genuine normativity into both parts of this bipartite process of extrapolation. The result would be practical judgments that have "motivational content," to use Thomas Nagel's phrase.[7]

II. BARGAINING

If agreement is to be the goal of a process of reasoning when initial disagreement does not represent malfunction, there must be rational pressure to reach agreement – that is, a reason, which each member of a group can acknowledge, for not simply resting content with disagreement. We can understand this in terms of the framework set out in Chapters 1 and 2. The situation is one that offers the possibility of mutually beneficial cooperation. If the members of the group are cooperatively disposed, the realization of any of several cooperative schemes will produce an outcome that each would regard as preferable, from the standpoint of his values, to the noncooperative outcome. But for cooperation actually to take place, one of these jointly feasible schemes must be accepted by all as the scheme to be implemented. Various decision-making procedures, such as voting or a lottery, are available for this purpose. But on each occasion of their use, if not in the long run, they inevitably leave some people less satisfied than others. If the group could deliberate to agreement on one of the jointly feasible schemes, there would be no disparities of this kind.

The idea that people who disagree without malfunction can reason their way to agreement on a cooperative scheme when disagreement is not attributable to malfunction is, however, puzzling. Consider first the case where initial disagreement *is* attributable to malfunction. There is disagreement about which scheme to adopt, but there is a single set of reasons that is germane to the issue. Reasoning is most naturally thought of as a process that seeks to track the force of these reasons. That is, each seeks to determine what they require. If the parties proceed in good faith, the elimination of malfunction will result in agreement about this. But coming to agreement in any other way would apparently mean that some, at least, must acquiesce in a decision that they do not regard as reflecting the best answer to the question being addressed (which scheme to adopt). And it is difficult to see how such acquiescence could be viewed as what the relevant reasons require. If the parties initially disagree *without* malfunction, however, it seems that they will be in precisely this situation. Attaining agreement will require some to acquiesce in a scheme that they appropriately regard as unjustified.[8] How, then, can the process of attaining agreement be understood as a process of reasoning?

We can deepen our appreciation of this problem by contrasting reasoning with bargaining. Bargaining is also a response to the pressure for agreement. Each makes concessions, expressing a willingness to accept something less than his most preferred alternative, in the expectation that the others will do this as well. The eventual result is agreement on a common plan. There are theories of bargaining that seek to determine what constitutes rational behavior in a bargaining context, and what constitutes a rational bargain.[9] But rational bargaining seems to be antithetical to *reasoning*, understood as an attempt to track the force of a set of reasons germane to a question. Making "concessions" from the conclusion that one regards as best supported by the applicable reasons seems to involve a kind of rational failure. Of course, one may decide, when presented with new arguments, that a previously accepted position is mistaken. But this sort of concession is not the sort that would be involved in reaching agreement by bargaining. In bargaining, one would be expressing a willingness to accept a position different from what one regarded, *at that time*, as best supported by the applicable reasons.

We must be careful in our statement of this point, however. Consider a case in which an agent holds substantive values that he regards not merely as preferences but as identifiers of objectively valuable features of the world. Various contingencies may give him no alternative but to adopt a course of action that is seriously suboptimal in light of these values. But it would be a mistake to say that he is acting contrary to what he takes to be required by the relevant reasons. Reasons for action generate a ranking of possible outcomes, and acting on the basis of these reasons consists in choosing the highest ranked *attainable* outcome. One is not acting irrationally by acquiescing in an outcome that one regards as seriously suboptimal if the ideal is, as a matter of fact, unattainable.

Similar points apply to bargaining to a compromise. Acquiescing in what is less than ideal is not contrary to reason when what is ideal is unattainable. Thus, the sort of compromise that is least susceptible to the charge of some kind of rational failure is one arising from the actual distribution of bargaining power in the group. We can suppose that the group has a deadline by which it must take action or it will lose the possibility of benefiting from cooperation. This creates pressure on each to make concessions. But some are better able to resist this pressure than others, perhaps because the collapse of cooperation would be less costly for them. The result is a distribution of bargaining power that produces a certain result. If we can say that given this distribution, no other result is attainable, we can regard each as acting rationally in light of his values by accepting the resulting scheme.[10]

In genuine reasoning to agreement on a cooperative scheme, however, each would be led to the conclusion that a certain scheme was the appropriate one to implement, irrespective of the distribution of bargaining power. That is, we are envisaging a situation in which all accept that the choice of a certain scheme is appropriate, even though some may have the power to secure a different scheme. The question we face is how, when the initial disagreement is not attributable to malfunction, reasoning can achieve such a result. As far as I can see, there are two possibilities. We must suppose that there is a process, plausibly regarded as a reasoning process, that can produce agreement in a way that avoids the need for concessions from the values that underlie the initial disagreement. Or we must suppose that reasoning can transform these values so that they no longer conflict. I discuss an alternative of the former sort in the next section and then turn to the second approach.

III. COMBINING PERSPECTIVES

We are considering how the choice of a scheme might be accomplished by a process of collective reasoning when the parties disagree without malfunction (because they hold different values). The simplest way this might happen, already discussed in the earlier chapters, is that there are certain reasons, such as reasons of fairness, that all in the group acknowledge as relevant to the choice of a scheme. Reasoning concerning what fairness requires is reasoning undertaken to overcome malfunction. But it would provide a basis on which disagreement not attributable to malfunction could be resolved if the parties were willing to demote the evaluative concerns that underlie the initial disagreement to interests. Conflict between the initially clashing values would be eliminated by converting them into something else, interests, and then reconciling these interests as fairness requires. Still, this is not a wholly satisfactory result. It seems to mean that rational cooperation is incompatible with a rich sense of the evaluative dimension of life. Further, as we saw in Chapters 2 and 4, if some do not regard fairness as taking precedence over their evaluative concerns, they may judge that they have sufficient reason to subvert fair procedures for choosing a scheme.[11] It would be desirable, then, if we could find a way of proceeding that allowed us to avoid both demotion and subversion.

The problems associated with invoking fairness as the basis of agreement when the parties have evaluative concerns arise because the situation is understood as possessing a certain rational structure. The members of the group are taken to have, on the one hand, a shared value that supports the choice of a particular cooperative scheme, and on the other, further values, peculiar to each, that conflict with the shared value. This suggests that we should consider whether there is some way that a group that initially disagrees without malfunction can reason its way to agreement on a scheme without employing a shared value like fairness.

One possibility involves combining perspectives. The view I have called value pluralism (associated with Berlin) enables us to understand how people can be in evaluative disagreement without malfunction. There is a set of values accessible to all – either because they constitute objective evaluative facts, or because the practices grounding them are, in principle, accessible to everyone – but no individual life can be organized around commitments to all these values. As I mentioned earlier, we may understand this phenomenon to be a consequence of the fact that values provide reasons for action. The world is such that acting to promote one kind of value often precludes acting to promote another. This might be interpreted as having the consequence that people are always acting wrongly, in light of the total set of values. But another possibility is to suppose that only certain values, from the set of all those that are accessible in principle, actually provide each individual with reasons for action. Which these are is determined by her evaluative commitments. We can then say that while each person organizes her life around a (mere) partial view of the world of value, no malfunctioning is involved.

If we take this line, each individual can still be seen as conceding the legitimacy of values other than those to which she is committed. Each can regard these other values as *eligible*. Historical and anthropological investigation reveals that a great variety of evaluative postures are available to human beings. And it may be that with enough study, we can come to understand the evaluative thinking of anyone, at least in the sense of being able to predict how he will respond to new cases (in contrast to actually embracing his values, taking them as reasons for action ourselves).

Given this, a process in which each reveals how a cooperative

164

scheme looks from the standpoint of the values to which she is committed can have the effect of reminding the others of eligible values
that fall outside the commitments they have made. It might also create
for the first time an appreciation of the eligibility of certain values.
The notion of a *perspective*, or point of view, is useful in describing this
process. The values that actually provide an individual with reasons
for action constitute a perspective on the world of value. In the case of
ordinary perceptual judgments, it is possible to build a more complete
picture of an item by collecting and integrating the reports that different individuals make concerning how it looks from their points of
view. Perhaps we can do something similar in the evaluative domain.
Although each of us inevitably has a certain evaluative perspective,
we may be able, by collective reasoning, to integrate our evaluative
perspectives, thus constructing a more compete view of the values at
stake in a particular case.[12]

Of course, because of the practical limitations mentioned earlier, it
is unlikely that any individual will be able to organize her life around
a more comprehensive evaluative picture constructed in this way. Constructing a composite picture of the value of an item reminds each
person of other eligible values, but normally it will not provide a
composite basis for choice. The space that each has for practical commitments will already be fully occupied by the values she brings to
the process. But we should not be too pessimistic here. The action we
are concerned with is the choice of a cooperative scheme. So the
relevant practical limitation is not that confronting individual agents,
but that confronting the group. This means that if we can suppose that
a group is less constrained by practical limitations – if it can integrate
more values into its "life" – the combining of evaluative perspectives
by collective deliberation may create a common basis on which each
member can judge the implementation of a particular cooperative
scheme to be appropriate. This must, however, be done in a way that
respects the evaluative commitments that each group member has
already made. The goal would be to find a scheme that provides for
the promotion of other eligible values by the group as a whole without
forcing any member to compromise her evaluative commitments in
her own life. Each lives her own life in accordance with her personal
commitments, but accepts that the larger life of the group can be lived
on the basis of a more comprehensive set of values. Thus, the initial
disagreement about which scheme to adopt, which arises from each
using her personal commitments to ground a preference for a particular scheme governing the group's action, is overcome.

If this approach is feasible, the problems discussed earlier need not
arise. As we have seen, even if we can identify certain common values
– such as fairness – that are capable of guiding the members of a

group to agreement on which cooperative scheme to adopt, some may judge that other values they accept justify their use of bargaining power to secure the adoption of a different scheme. If each acts accordingly, the scheme actually adopted will be determined, in part, by the distribution of bargaining power, rather than by a process of reasoning. The present proposal has the potential to solve this problem because the looser practical limitations of the group allow the choice of a scheme to be made on a basis that all can regard as justified – namely, the full set of eligible values accepted within the group.

But this possibility takes us only so far. If many different values are held by the members of a group, there may be no way to accommodate them all, even within the less restrictive practical limitations facing the group as a whole. Or accommodating them may force some members to compromise the commitments that guide their personal lives. Thus, a choice will have to be made among different schemes on a basis that leaves out, or gives reduced representation to, some of the values in play. But then the problem we confronted earlier will reemerge. Each will still be forced – now by the practical limitations of the group for which the choice is being made – to endorse only a proper subset of all the eligible values held within the group. The group's larger capabilities may enable each to expand this set beyond the values with which she began, but the endorsement will still be partial, encompassing only some of the values accepted elsewhere in the group. And if each thus finds herself committed to a different subset of the eligible values, there will be no common basis on which a scheme can be chosen. Further, those who have greater bargaining power may again use this power to secure the choice of a scheme that is maximally in accord with the particular subset of values they view as appropriately guiding this choice – the values to which they are committed in their personal lives and certain other eligible values that they have accepted for the special case of choosing a scheme.

So far I have been understanding perspectives evaluatively. A perspective or point of view is constituted by the values an individual holds. It is possible, however, to give the notion a more epistemic construal. Postmodern epistemologies employ the concept of "socially situated knowledge," which is meant to capture the idea that the social scene looks different from different social standpoints, especially different standpoints in established social hierarchies. Still, introducing perspectives in this expanded sense would not alter the results just obtained.[13]

The paradigm of perspectival knowledge is ordinary perceptual knowledge. We have a perceived object and various possible perceptual standpoints on it. But each person accepts the same perceptual concepts, and the system of object and observers is located in a common (and commonly understood) spatial framework that guides the integration of the perceptual reports. So the pooling of these reports can, in principle, give each the same fuller picture of the perceived item. Cognitive cooperation of this sort belongs, then, with those examined in Chapter 6. It displays cognitive command. The exchange of perceptual information gives each the same "input," and any disagreement about the features of the perceived item that remains can be attributed to cognitive malfunction.

A more complicated case is that in which people occupying positions in a common (and commonly understood) spatial framework employ different perceptual concepts. Our concepts are determined partly by our interests, and so people with different interests may employ different concepts. Moreover, perceptual concepts need not pick out only simple qualities, such as greenness or squareness. All that is necessary is that the property in question be *observable*. Once one has developed a facility with a particular conceptual scheme, one may be able to observe a complex phenomenon, such as a tornado or a dance.

How are we to understand a situation in which different perceivers use different concepts to describe what they observe? One possibility is that we can give a debunking explanation of the judgments that others make with their concepts. The interests of others have led them to employ concepts that do not correspond to any properties actually possessed by the things comprising the world. Thus, judgments made with these concepts can be discounted. But it is also possible that judgments employing perceptual concepts different from ours genuinely capture truths. They are made true by features of the world, just as ours are. In this case, there will be no barrier in principle to forming a composite picture of the world out of all these true judgments. If there is a single world and each of these judgments is true of it, then it must be possible for them to be true together. We sometimes take advantage of this possibility when we describe something using words in a foreign language that have no precise equivalent in our own – as when a speaker of English asserts that someone possesses savoir faire.

This constitutes another situation in which disagreement means malfunction. People can hold different concepts without cognitive malfunction, but if these concepts describe facets of one world, there will be a right or wrong answer about whether any one of them is applicable to a given situation. And there will be no basis for any of the parties, operating with her particular concepts, to dissent from a composite description created by combining true judgments from different conceptual frameworks. The description will report facts about the world that go beyond those that each can report with her particular concepts, but provided that she has reason to regard them as true –

because, say, those making them seem to be normally functioning perceivers – she should accept the description. Or at least this is so if she understands the concepts others are employing. But failure to understand can be viewed as a kind of malfunction, one that could be overcome through study.[14] To be sure, the possibilities of such failure are so extensive, considered in the abstract, that we might want to resist attributing them to malfunction. Still, in a context where the members of a group holding different concepts could benefit by cooperation, the failure of each to grasp the truths that can be reported with concepts employed by the others is properly criticizable. It could block the rational choice of a cooperative scheme in much the same way that failure to grasp truths statable with shared concepts can.

When, however, we move beyond cases of the sort just described to the case of socially situated knowledge, we encounter problems. Different groups may employ not only different descriptive concepts but also different procedures of justification – different epistemologies. Thus, beliefs that are fully justified from one perspective will be deemed unjustified from others. Or at least that is the picture. An example would be a case in which the story a people tells about its origins contradicts the story others accept about this. Here there is no possibility of endorsing both claims if we suppose there is one world that makes such statements true. Thus, there is no possibility of organizing the affairs of the group on the basis of a composite description made up of both views – and others of the same sort. The most the group can do is try to frame the choice of cooperative schemes in a way that abstracts from the issues that divide it.

Of course, the postmodern notion of socially situated knowledge is meant to provide a way that conflicting views of this sort can all be "true." Postmodernism reflects the idea that there are no facts, only interpretations.[15] It is not the case that the different concepts in play can all be employed in judgments that are made true or false by a single world. Rather, the world that is "known" is *constituted* by the perspective held by each observer. "Reality" is different from each point of view, and thus it is appropriate to speak of "knowledges," rather than knowledge.

Disagreement arising from different socially situated "knowledges" does not, then, fit the model of cognitive command. The different perspectives are not perspectives on an independent reality that guides the coherent integration of all perspectival truths into a composite picture. Some perspectives may admit the idea of a common framework into which other perspectives can be fitted, but the way this framework is conceived will itself be a feature of the perspective in question, not shared by other perspectives. Of course, there is a standard question concerning such views. Is the claim that all knowledge is socially situated also the deliverance of a particular social point of view, or is it an objective truth? Either answer seems to weaken the postmodern position.[16]

But for our purposes, we need not take a stand on the coherence of postmodern epistemology. We need only consider what it implies for collective reasoning if it is right (or acceptable). I believe the same points made in connection with evaluative points of view apply to this case. "Knowledges" are like values; they provide the basis for a particular form of life. And from the postmodern perspective, disagreement between different "knowledges" is disagreement without malfunction. Although an individual can occupy several points of view – be both Native American and female, for example – it is not plausible that a single life can be lived from all such points of view simultaneously. An individual must, to put it redundantly, have a *partial* perspective.

It is plausible that a group's life is less limited and, thus, that it can adopt cooperative schemes on a basis that integrates a range of "knowledges" that are eligible, in the sense employed earlier. But it seems likely that a particular group's life will not be able to accommodate an active commitment to all "knowledges." As in the case of evaluative perspectives, for the purpose of choosing a cooperative scheme, the members of the relevant group may be able to expand their personal commitments to encompass some further "knowledges," but the practical limitations of the group's life will usually force each member to exclude others. This means that individuals or subgroups will again have sufficient reason to use bargaining power to secure a cooperative scheme maximally congenial from their (expanded) points of view. And any agreement that results will not be the product of collective reasoning.

To be sure, we can introduce fairness and speak of a fair reconciliation of the claims of different socially situated points of view. This would be determined by collective reasoning understood as overcoming malfunction with respect to a shared conception of fairness. But then we would face all the problems noted in our earlier discussion of the use of the value of fairness to guide the choice of a cooperative scheme. If we treat "knowledges" as interests to be compromised as fairness requires, we are viewing their claims as important only because they are important *to* someone. And if those holding them resist this dilution of their significance, on the ground that compromise means acquiescing in "falsehood," then we are in the same situation as when fairness is employed in conjunction with other moral values. Fairness must compete with "truth," and may be defeated by it – in which case individuals or subgroups will have good reason to use bargaining power to secure an unfair scheme.

It might be thought that this is also the situation of those who reject postmodernism. They are unwilling to compromise truth as fairness (to those who accept opposing procedures of justification) requires. But it would be more accurate to say that they view the case at issue as one in which the initial disagreement is attributable to malfunction. Some of the concepts in play are not adequate to the epistemic task, or some of the procedures of justification do not reflect genuine relations of warrant, and thus those employing them display cognitive malfunction. This means that fairness to opposing views does not have a legitimate role.[17]

IV. COHERENTIST REASONING

In the discussion of Scanlon's view at the end of Chapter 6, I suggested that a group that initially disagrees without malfunction might be able to reason its way to agreement on a cooperative scheme if collective reasoning is able to transform the reasons underlying the initial disagreement. In the remainder of this chapter, I explore this possibility.

The first alternative of this sort to consider involves coherentist reasoning. As we saw in Chapter 6, coherentist reasoning opens up the possibility of creating and destroying reasons. Considerations of coherence relating to a pregiven set of reasons may force us to acknowledge that some further feature of the world should be treated as a reason for action. Similarly, considerations of coherence can lead to our depriving a feature of the world of the status of a reason. At first sight, however, it does not appear that this possibility would be of much help with our present problem. Coherentist reasoning operates with a set of reasons that is already on the scene. It presupposes that this set displays a certain incoherence, which we seek to eliminate. This suggests that to the extent coherentist reasoning produces agreement, it should be understood as doing so by overcoming malfunction in the grasping of pregiven rational facts. This is how I presented it in the discussion of Habermas in Chapter 6.

In the case we are now considering, by contrast, the initial disagreement is not attributable to cognitive malfunction. This need not mean that the theory each holds of the relations between the reasons she acknowledges is fully coherent. But it does seem to mean that the elimination of any such incoherence could not be expected to produce agreement. Reasons might be created or destroyed. But in the end, each would still acknowledge certain reasons or values not shared by others, and some might conclude that all things considered, they were justified in using bargaining power to secure a result more in accord with their values.

Still, we should not give up on coherence too easily. There may be a way of using it to greater effect in resolving disagreement that does not involve malfunction. What I have in mind is the theory of "holistic dialectic" recently proposed by Henry Richardson.[18] In Chapter 1, I briefly sketched Richardson's notion of the specification of norms (or principles).[19] He suggests that we can reconcile the claims of competing principles that are relevant to a practical decision by specifying them – reducing the scope of their application – so that they do not actually yield conflicting advice in the case at hand. Specification is saved from being just as ad hoc as intuitive balancing by the fact that in specifying norms, we are understood to be constructing a practical theory the development of which is appropriately governed by considerations of coherence.

In his book, Richardson embellishes this view in several ways. The most noteworthy addition concerns the notion of an end, understood as that for the sake of which something is done. The "for the sake of" relation structures our concerns, and thus practical reasoning must work with it. Richardson devotes much space to defending the view that practical reasoning need not only be *from* ends. We can also reason our way *to* ends. This is true of final ends, ends that we pursue for their own sake even though they can also be pursued for the sake of other ends (of which they might, for example, be constituent parts). But it is also true of ultimate ends, ends that are both final and not themselves pursued for the sake of any other ends. In reasoning our way to ends, the leading role is again played by the notion of the coherence of an evolving practical theory.

One problem that Richardson discusses is whether the picture he has sketched is workable in the case of an individual who is "bicultural," and whose final ends thus appear to resist coherent resolution. To develop a way of handling this case, he considers *interpersonal* reasoning among people who come from different cultural traditions and who initially disagree.

For our purposes, of course, the primary interest of Richardson's argument concerns what he says about the interpersonal, rather than the intrapersonal, case. How can agents seeking coherent practical theories of different sets of ends be led by such reasoning to agreement? Richardson's solution is subtle. It has three main parts. The first is to note that there must be limits to the depth of disagreement. However different the reasons acknowledged by the parties, there must be a common question, to which each seeks an answer. The answers will be different, and it is in this that the disagreement lies. But the views held by the parties cannot disagree so much that they do not even generate the same question.[20] We may take it that this condition is met by the cases we are concerned with. The shared question is which of the candidate cooperative schemes to adopt.

The second main point that Richardson makes is that while the coherentist reasoning involved in holistic dialectic must proceed from something the competing views have in common, this need not be their final ends. Deliberative holism admits many routes by which justificatory force can be transmitted. Richardson mentions, in addition to specification, abstraction (which makes norms less specific, enhancing the possibility of agreement on them), distinction (which allows different answers concerning what a norm requires in different contexts), and analogy (the opposite of distinction, assimilating apparently different contexts).[21] These tools make it possible to build agreement on an end, such as that governing the choice of a cooperative scheme, from agreement on "lower" as well as "higher" elements.[22]

As I have just indicated, agreement on the choice of a cooperative scheme will presumably involve agreement on ends of some kind. But Richardson's third point is that these need not be final ends. Instead, we can make use of the Rawlsian notion of overlapping consensus.[23] Richardson distinguishes an overlapping consensus from mere agreement about what to do. It involves agreement, at some intermediate level, on *values*. This gives the agreement the kind of strength that Rawls claims for an overlapping consensus, in contrast to a modus vivendi.[24] For our purposes, however, the importance of this point lies in the fact that parties facing the need to agree on a cooperative scheme can be led by holistic (coherentist) reasoning to such agreement – by being led to agreement on certain *intermediate* ends or values associated with the scheme – while remaining in disagreement at the higher level of their final ends. Still, it should be noted that the fashioning of the shared intermediate ends may involve a "softening" of final ends that are initially expressed by "hardened" principles thought to be beyond revision.[25]

The foregoing summary does not do justice to the complexities of Richardson's discussion, but I believe that it is sufficient to show that his proposal has the right structure to provide a solution to the problem we have been considering. The initial disagreement concerning which cooperative scheme to adopt need not arise from malfunction. Each of the parties has different final ends, which could easily justify different schemes. But this disagreement prevents the group, and thus each member, from realizing the benefits of cooperation. Or at least this is so if they are cooperatively disposed, and thus accept a principle like the PCR that is capable of justifying participation in a scheme that has been chosen. The result is that there is a certain incoherence in the practical posture of each. On Richardson's view, if they can find any common ground at all, they may be able, by coherentist reasoning, to develop it into agreement on an intermediate end sufficient to underwrite the choice of one of the feasible schemes. And if this happens, nobody will be justified by her ultimate ends in using bargaining power to secure a cooperative scheme different from that supported by the common basis of choice (the shared intermediate end). The adoption by each party of the intermediate end supporting the choice of a particular cooperative scheme is the result of coherentist reasoning within her total set of concerns. So it represents for each the final answer about what posture to assume toward the choice – in contrast to a mere prima facie reason for accepting the choice that could be outweighed by other considerations.

One feature of this process deserves emphasis. The initial disagreement is not attributable to cognitive malfunction. But if the views of the group manifest the conceptual potential to yield an overlapping consensus on an intermediate end that will enable cooperation to go forward, there is a sense in which the members are malfunctioning if they do not succeed in actualizing this potential. This is what we should expect. If there is reasoning capable of guiding to agreement a group that initially disagrees without malfunction, there must be room for the idea that failure actually to agree can be attributed to malfunction (in a different respect).

I do not, however, believe that we can rest content with holistic dialectic, as described by Richardson. First, as he acknowledges, it will not always be sufficient to produce agreement.[26] But beyond that, there is a certain vagueness about how it works. For one thing, it is unclear what role fairness plays in the coherentist reasoning that produces agreement. If it plays a role, the issues considered earlier relating to the reduction of moral concerns to interests may return. Related to this is Richardson's idea that the process he describes may involve a "softening" of final ends that are originally expressed in hardened principles. How is this to be understood? It, too, may involve the demotion of values to interests. And if it involves instead a transformation of the content of an abiding end, we are accepting a view of ends according to which they are not individuated solely by their specific content, so that a difference in content means a different end. Rather, ends are plastic; they can be bent or squeezed in such a way that their content changes, while their identity as the ends they are is maintained. These issues are explored further in the next section.

V. THE PLASTICITY OF REASONS

It is tempting to think of the relation between reasoning and reasons by using the metaphor of a track. In reasoning, we follow a track constituted by the relevant reasons. To leave the track is to malfunction as a reasoner. In this chapter, we have been concerned with the case in which initial disagreement cannot be attributed to malfunction. Each is successfully following the track constituted by the reasons he accepts. Invoking fairness to explain how a group in such a situation might be able to reason its way to agreement means positing a further track, common to all, that leads to agreement. But as we have seen, this requires the parties to choose between two tracks, and depending on the circumstances, either choice could be appropriate.

This metaphor, however, suggests another way of thinking about how reasoning might lead to agreement among people who initially disagree without malfunction. Perhaps reasoning can bend the track. If so, we could regard collective reasoning as a process that bends the tracks that all are following in such a way that each, staying on his track, is led to agreement with the others concerning which coopera-tive scheme to adopt.

The idea that reasons can be bent goes most naturally with a prac-tice-based view (including the hybrid view I introduced in Chapter 5, which makes use of the notion of proper functioning on the part of persons socialized to certain practices). It is difficult to see how reason-ing could bend reasons if they are understood as abstract entities residing in a timeless realm. But the suggestion that the practices in which reasons are grounded can change over time is relatively easy to comprehend. Still, we must be clear about what is being proposed. Practices can be altered by external forces. Historical contingencies of various kinds can cause the dispositions underlying practices to change.[27] What we are looking for, however, is something that can modify these practices *from within* and can, thus, be understood as a process of reasoning. If the result is agreement, we can then regard people who initially disagree without malfunction as having been led to agreement by a process of reasoning.

One way to understand how the bending of reasons might be ac-complished is to suppose that rule following is not always automatic, but can involve active consideration of how new cases are to be assim-ilated to a rule. Charles Larmore's discussion of the role of judgment in moral reasoning provides a way of illustrating this possibility.[28] Larmore distinguishes judgment from mere rule following. He says that judgment plays an especially important role in the determination of what would constitute behavior in accordance with the moral vir-tues. Judgment is needed to recognize that a situation calls for the exercise of a virtue, and also to determine what would be "fitting" in light of that virtue.[29] In ordinary rule following, the right way of assimilating a case to our concepts often stands out. An item that we encounter is clearly a box, for example. It is only at the vague edges that we have any hesitation. But Larmore suggests that in moral cases involving the virtues, it can be less clear what the relevant rules require – less clear how to "go on." This does not mean that there is no fitting way to proceed. It rather means that an effort must be made to find it. This effort takes the form of carefully examining all the facts of a case, in the hope of finally feeling comfortable with a particular way of employing the concept at issue.

When this process is successful, the facts that ultimately provide a basis for assimilating the case to a rule are the reasons that justify employing the associated concept. We can also speak of reasons in connection with the easy cases – for example, reasons why something is a box. But there is a difference when judgment plays a role. In the easy cases, facts are constituted as reasons by the rule. The "impetus" of past practice highlights certain features of a new case, which then become the basis for assimilating it to the rule. In moral cases involving the virtues, by contrast, the impetus of past practice encounters obstacles, and there must be an active search for a way of looking at the case that reveals how it can be brought under the rule. This means that there is a sense in which the rule is constituted by the reasons, instead of the other way around.[30] The rule is constituted, in part, by the way of looking at the new case that enables it to be extended to that case. Thus, the reasons shape the projection of the rule. But they still count as reasons of the sort at issue – reasons for taking a certain course of action to be courageous, for example – because they connect the new case with the previous practice.

This picture readily lends itself to the idea that the process of reasoning can bend reasons. In finding a way to apply a concept to a new case, we may alter its content. The concept will be extrapolated to future cases in a way that differs from the way it would have been extrapolated had the case in question not been encountered. Since the alteration is ultimately controlled by what seems a fitting extension of a preexisting rule, we can speak of a rule as undergoing a transformation, rather than as being replaced by a new rule. And since everything boils down to appropriate participation in a judgmental practice – to functioning properly as a participant in that practice – we can regard the alteration as something dictated by reason, rather than as caused by extranormative factors.

Although the process that Larmore describes may be especially characteristic of the exercise of the virtues, there seems to be no reason that it must be restricted to this context. The key idea is that some feature of the case makes impossible the "mechanical" extrapolation of a previous practice. But this can happen even with rules the employment of which has not in the past required much in the way of judgment, if new circumstances create obstacles to straightforward extrapolation. Applying a concept in the face of these obstacles may involve an active search for a way of viewing the case that allows the rule to be applied to it. And this could have the effect of altering the content of the rule.

There is a connection between the possibility that reasons could be bent in this way and the suggestion, made in Chapter 5, that the hybrid view of reasons and concepts enables us to regard normativity as having a history. The proper functioning that the hybrid view invokes is relative to an environment. Thus, as circumstances change, perhaps as a consequence of previous actions of ours, what manifests proper functioning in beings socialized to certain practices of judgment could change as well. The social dimension of the process – the fact that what changes is a practice shared by the members of a group – is provided by interpersonal reasons that justify reconsidering one's own performance when others disagree, and thus introduce an element of coordination. But although this process can be regarded as involving the sort of bending of reasons we have been examining, as described in Chapter 5, it belongs with cases in which disagreement is attributable to malfunction. The concepts at issue are common to all the members of the group, and as the judgments that manifest proper functioning on the part of beings employing these concepts change, those who fail to register the change fall into malfunction.

The question we are now considering, however, is how the bending of reasons might play a role in facilitating agreement on a cooperative scheme in a group of people who initially disagree *without* malfunction about which scheme to adopt. Here the obstacle to straightforward extrapolation is provided by the fact that if the members of the group proceed in this way, they will not be able to realize the benefits of cooperation. We may suppose that each member of the group is cooperatively disposed, in the sense of being prepared to follow the dictates of the PCR. But the reason this provides to behave cooperatively will be activated only if all (or most) come to accept a particular jointly feasible scheme as the one to be implemented. And this provides the basis for considering how far the reasons that underlie the disagreement can be bent.

A possible example is the transformation of religious values so that they come to endorse freedom of religion. In his account of political liberalism, Rawls speaks of an overlapping consensus among different comprehensive moral and religious doctrines.[31] Each can support, from its own point of view, various political and civil liberties. But if we are in this situation now with respect to a variety of religious doctrines, it is because religious values have undergone a transformation over the past 500 years. Confronted with the costs of noncooperation – of conflict – the adherents of each doctrine found it problematic to employ their values in the way that would have been suitable under conditions of religious homogeneity. And in groping for a satisfactory mode of extrapolation, they modified their values so that they ceased to underwrite the suppression of other religions and instead supported, or were at least compatible with, religious toleration. The adherents of different religious doctrines were thus ultimately able to agree on a general scheme of social cooperation that provided for freedom of religion.

It should be noted that considerations of fairness may play a role in this process. The extrapolative practice of each may be influenced not only by the perceived need to avoid the noncooperative outcome but also by the perceived need to find a fair basis for cooperation. In bringing the value of fairness to bear, the parties would ordinarily be treating their moral concerns as interests of a certain sort. But we now have a way of avoiding this conclusion. The constraint of fairness could guide the bending of these values, so that in their ultimate form they do not underwrite demands that would be unfair, and thus do not need to be demoted to interests to be reconciled with fairness.

This process should be spelled out more fully. Values are considerations that identify states of the world thought to be important in their own right. But as I have repeatedly noted, fairness governs the resolution of conflicting interests, understood as considerations the satisfaction of which is important primarily because it satisfies those advancing them. So if fairness is to guide the bending of values, they must be viewed in this way. But viewing a concern as an interest need not mean relaxing the underlying evaluative commitment. One's commitment is threatened only when fairness directs a compromise that one's values cannot justify. And on the bending hypothesis we are considering, one does not actually make any compromise unless it can be provided with a rationale from the standpoint of the values at issue – unless it can be regarded as licensed by an appropriate bending of these values. So while one must view one's values as interests to get some idea of what fairness requires, one does not, in the end, accord them the status of interests.

Once we accept that values can be bent, squeezed, or softened, it is tempting to bring back into the picture the notion of reasonable rejection employed by Scanlon's moral theory. Even when mutual accommodation is at issue, the term "reasonable" has a slightly different ring from the term "fair." It is more suggestive of a *process* of accommodation. So it may be preferable to describe the bending of values that we have been considering as taking place under the pressure of the concept of reasonableness (as fairness). In Chapter 6, I noted that Scanlon seems to envisage a transformation of the content of various moral claims that is guided by this concept.

I have said that interpersonal reasons exert (defeasible) pressure toward uniformity in judgmental practice. This process has a natural place when disagreement is interpreted as indicating cognitive malfunction in the group. The new moves of some are perceived as appropriate by others and copied by them, or criticism of some moves sets off a pattern of mutual adjustment that eventually attains an equilibrium. The negotiation of judgmental practices under the pressure of interpersonal reasons can, however, also play a role when disagreement is not attributable to malfunction, yet values must be bent if there is to be convergence on a cooperative scheme. In the first place, there will be negotiation within subgroups of people holding the same or similar values concerning how they might be appropriately bent to make them more compatible with the values held by others. But there may also be negotiation among subgroups, each pointing out to the others certain ways that the requisite bending might be accomplished. This will be possible to the extent that the members of one subgroup are capable of understanding the concepts employed by other subgroups. And, of course, if a shared conception of fairness guides the bending, it is especially likely that intergroup negotiation of appropriate bending will take place.

We have been discussing how the content of the reasons that underlie disagreement without malfunction (about which cooperative scheme to adopt) might be altered by a process of reasoning. It should be emphasized, however, that if we are to understand this alteration as a rational process, there must be a place for the notion of correctness. We must be able to distinguish appropriate from inappropriate patterns of bending. And disagreement about what is appropriate in this way *would* be attributable to malfunction. This parallels a point made earlier in connection with Richardson's view.

I have mentioned the role that fairness can play in the bending of reasons. One might raise the question whether this value, too, could be bent by collective reasoning. The process of value change described in Chapter 5 – value change as a result of an alteration, brought about by changing circumstances, in what manifests proper functioning on the part of beings socialized to a certain concept – could transform the content of the concept of fairness. In this case, those who failed to register the change would fall into malfunction. But there may also be a place for bending when disagreement about what fairness requires is not attributable to malfunction – because, for example, the burdens of judgment are playing a role, or people are employing different conceptions of fairness – but agreement on a scheme is necessary if cooperation is to go forward. In such a situation, collective reasoning may be able to effect a bending of the operative understandings of fairness. In Chapter 4, I mentioned that some of the most contentious political disagreements seem to be grounded in conflicting conceptions of fairness. So the possibility that conceptions of fairness can be bent would enhance the social importance of the phenomenon of bending.

We should not exaggerate the potential of bending for attaining agreement on a cooperative scheme. Its effects can be quite pronounced over time. But there may be limits to what bending can accomplish when people who disagree without malfunction must come quickly to agreement on a cooperative scheme if they are to realize the benefits of cooperation. Usually, only a limited amount of bending will be possible on a given occasion.

There is, however, an alternative process that may be able to take the place of bending in cases of this sort. When fairness conflicts with other moral values, these values might outweigh it, with the result that an individual would have sufficient moral reason to use bargaining power to secure an unfair scheme that promotes these values more effectively. But suppose this does not happen. Suppose all the members of the group at issue regard fairness as taking precedence over the other values they hold, and are thus prepared to accept the demotion of the concerns grounded in these values to interests (to be compromised as fairness requires). In this case, fairness does not bend the values but, rather, breaks them, turning them into something different. But there may be a way that, having been broken by being reduced to compromisable interests, the concerns of the parties can be restored to the status of genuine values, albeit in a modified form that makes them no threat to fairness. This would involve the resumption by each party of a practice of judgment covering cases of the kind at issue, but employing evaluative concepts that, while related to the old, were compatible with the requirements of fairness. That is, the new values would be designed to ensure that they did not call for anything different from what the parties would get if the concerns grounded in these values were treated as interests and a fair resolution of their claims determined.

Negotiation, reflecting sensitivity to interpersonal reasons, would have a natural role to play in this process of revitalizing values that have been demoted to interests because fairness prevails over them. It would confirm the status of the new values as genuinely normative considerations. This negotiation could take place within the subgroup of people holding the values at issue. But the input of other subgroups might be regarded as relevant as well, especially when finding values that are compatible with fairness is a desideratum.

As I have said, this quicker process does not involve the bending of reasons by a process of reasoning. Reasons are first broken and then resurrected in a new form. A case could thus be made that when a particular reason undergoes a change of content in this manner, it does not retain its identity. The continuity of practice that permits this way of looking at the matter is absent. Rather, what we have is the replacement of one reason or value with a different one that we refer to by the same name, perhaps because of certain similarities. But this would still give us a way of avoiding the conclusion that if fairness – or reasonableness-as-fairness – guides the choice of a cooperative scheme, it becomes the only genuine moral value on the scene (the others having been reduced to mere interests).

It may be useful at this juncture to make two observations of a summary nature. The first concerns the implications of the discussion of the previous three chapters for the conclusions about deliberative democracy reached in Chapter 4. Nothing that we have discovered alters the results of that chapter. Over time, the plasticity of reasons could allow a considerable narrowing of political disagreement that is not attributable to cognitive malfunction. But in most cases where an issue has been proposed for democratic resolution, a decision will be necessary before the processes described are able to secure complete agreement on a scheme. So even given the plasticity of reasons, voting will normally be required. There is no reason, however, why these processes cannot continue after a vote.

The discussion of the last three chapters also has implications for democratic decision making in the case where disagreement reflects cognitive malfunction. It is important to note that many issues proposed for democratic resolution may not have this character. But if they do, collective reasoning has the potential to overcome the malfunction. Still, the best outcome that can normally be hoped for, especially in large groups, is that in the time the group has to make a decision, malfunction – and thus disagreement – will be reduced but not completely eliminated. So in cases of this sort as well, voting will usually be necessary. In the discussion of the epistemic virtues of democracy in Chapter 4, I argued that all we can say when a disagreement that is attributable to cognitive malfunction is resolved by a vote is that the members of the minority may be able to regard the decision as less wrong (in the sense of being closer to their view) than it would have been in the absence of deliberation. We can now bolster this conclusion with the results of Chapter 5. The fact that a majority holds an opposing view constitutes an interpersonal reason for the members of the minority to suppose that they may be wrong. But as we saw in Chapter 5, if the integrity of the system of interpersonal reasons is to be maintained, this can only be taken as a reason for them to reconsider, not as a reason to change their minds. And if after reexamining the relevant substantive reasons, a member of the minority decides to retain his position, the most he will be able to conclude is that shared deliberation has made the majority's view less wrong than it would otherwise have been.[32]

Second, we should bring together the various points made in this book about the employment of the value of fairness to underwrite cooperation when it is threatened by the centrifugal tendency of the other values, especially moral values, held within a group. When what is at issue is whether to make one's assigned contribution to a cooperative scheme, the PCR provides a way of justifying this that allows the parties to accord their values the same significance that they have when they are promoted in accordance with individual rationality (the PIR). In making their assigned contributions, the parties can regard themselves as advancing the good as they see it, in contrast to merely satisfying interests of theirs.

No such device, however, is available in connection with the second aspect of rational cooperation, the choice among the cooperative schemes that are jointly feasible under the PCR. When there is disagreement regarding which scheme to adopt, the rationality of the group's choice is often secured by shared (or overlapping) substantive or procedural values that justify a way of resolving this disagreement. The characteristic moral virtue of cooperative schemes is fairness, and so it is natural to invoke it in this connection. But the parties may also have moral reasons for preferring particular schemes. If fairness prevails over these competing values, they (or the concerns they ground) will acquire the status of interests, the satisfaction of which is important primarily because it satisfies those holding them. Alternatively, the parties may judge that the moral values grounding their other concerns outweigh fairness, and thus reject the demotion of these concerns to interests. In this case, they will take themselves to be justified in trying to use bargaining power to secure the choice of a scheme more to their liking, even if this means subverting a fair decision procedure.[33] It seems, then, that the choice of a cooperative scheme can be seen as guided by reason – and, thus, cooperation as a whole seen as fully guided by reason – only at the cost of diluting the evaluative dimension of the lives of the cooperators.

We have now added a new element to this picture. In addition to the alternatives of demoting moral concerns to interests or subverting a fair procedure, there is the possibility of reshaping moral concerns so that they do not compete with fairness. This can be accomplished by a relatively slow process of bending and also, perhaps, by a faster process that involves the demotion of values to interests and then their revitalization in a new form that is compatible with the requirements of fairness.

It is not clear that the ultimate hegemony of fairness is to be preferred. People who are not prepared to allow fairness to bend, soften, or demote their moral concerns command our respect. We often call them, with approval, "principled." But people who are prepared to relax their principles to some extent in order to achieve cooperation on a basis all can accept also command our respect. We call them, with approval, "reasonable." I have no argument that one of these postures

181

is, in the end, more appropriate than the other. The world contains people of both types. For present purposes, the important point is that reasonable people will sometimes be able to realize the benefits of cooperation when principled people cannot (because they are unable to settle on a particular scheme). And if we admit the plasticity or revitalization of values, reasonable people need not regard themselves, when effecting the choice of a cooperative scheme, as living in a world in which fairness, or reasonableness-as-fairness, is the only genuine moral value. Other moral values can be shaped to fit the requirements of reasonableness-as-fairness.

It should be emphasized, however, that we are here assuming that the initial disagreement is not attributable to cognitive malfunction. When disagreement means that somebody is malfunctioning, and one is able to reaffirm one's position after reconsideration, a principled refusal to bend may be in order. One's unmodified values will then give one a reason to try to reverse a choice underwritten by reasonableness-as-fairness. The question of the proper interpretation of the moral disagreements that arise in cooperative contexts is thus an important one.

Chapter 8

The Rationality of Collective Reasoning

In the previous three chapters, we have been considering how collective reasoning can benefit those who participate in it. I have mentioned two main ways this can happen. When disagreement in a group about the correct answer to some question is attributable to cognitive malfunction, collective reasoning can reduce or eliminate the malfunction. And when disagreement that is not attributable to cognitive malfunction prevents the members of a group from choosing a cooperative scheme, collective reasoning may enable them to modify their views to the extent necessary to effect a choice.

We should not, however, lose sight of the fact that collective reasoning is a form of mutually beneficial cooperation. I have identified two respects in which cooperation can be understood as guided by reason. Participation in a cooperative scheme, even when one could do better by defecting, is sometimes in accordance with reason. And if they share certain procedural or substantive values – or if the values they hold overlap in the case at hand – the cooperatively disposed members of a group may all be able to regard the choice of a scheme as guided by reason. In this concluding chapter, I consider these two aspects of rational cooperation in the particular case of collective reasoning.

One issue is of special interest. I have defended the claim that collective reasoning should be understood as a cooperative effort to construct a pool of reasons or criticized arguments on which each member of a group can draw in making judgments. But the process exhibits a striking contrast with the sort of mutually beneficial cooperation discussed in the earlier chapters. Typically, contribution means incurring costs, which are then compensated for by the benefit produced by the aggregate contributions. Since it is possible to receive the benefit without incurring the costs, individual rationality (the PIR) usually dictates noncontribution. There is a free rider problem. Thus, some further principle must be invoked to justify contribution, and I have argued that the PCR is the best candidate. But specifically cooperative dispositions do not usually seem to be required for participation in collective reasoning. People *want* to contribute. If there is a constraint operating, it is one that prevents individuals from making too much of a contribution – from hogging the discussion. Further, those who do not contribute are not normally criticized as free riders. Before discussing this peculiarity, however, something should be said about the way a choice among different cooperative schemes can be understood as playing a role in collective reasoning.

I. SCHEMES OF COLLECTIVE REASONING

When mutually beneficial cooperation is a possibility, there will often be a number of jointly feasible schemes, one of which must be selected. Presumably, this is also true of the construction of a pool of reasons or arguments. It could be carried out in different ways, with different results. There are, to be sure, some differences from the standard case. Contributions cannot be assigned, because only as discussion unfolds will it become clear what an individual might contribute, and often it will be clear only to him or her. But at a different level, a common choice, by the members of the group, among alternative cooperative schemes – alternative patterns of action capable of producing a common pool of reasons – can still be seen as playing a role.

This fact is partly obscured by the peculiarity just mentioned. We typically exploit the willingness of people to contribute to the discussion of questions that interest them. Thus, the construction of a pool of reasons is the outcome of what might be called the "flow of discussion." One person offers an argument; someone who has something to add, in defense or rebuttal, makes a further contribution; and so on. The process ends when no one has anything more to say, or when discussion is closed off by some deadline. In this case, the precise way in which the pool of criticized arguments that constitutes the final product is constructed will be heavily influenced by contingencies relating to how the process began and what each feels prompted to say in response to previous contributions. Is there any reason to think that some alternative to the natural flow of discussion would constitute a preferable way to construct a shared pool of reasons?

The suggestion that there is not might be defended as follows. All the participants are interested in answering a particular question. And the most that can be hoped for in the way of constructing a pool of reasons is that all the relevant reasons known to anyone in the group will be presented. But – especially when discussion ends when no one has anything more to say – it can be expected that the natural flow of discussion will achieve this result. What others have already said may prompt people to thoughts that they would not otherwise have had. So the manner in which the pool is constructed will depend on the flow of discussion. But at least if time pressures are not severe, and thus people who have already spoken can speak again if something that is said prompts new thoughts, the different possible flows should all result in (approximately) the same pool.[1]

If this is right, there is little reason to worry about how contingencies that govern the flow of discussion might influence the construction of a pool of reasons or criticized arguments. But there is a tacit assumption at work here that needs to be exposed. We are assuming that everyone who wants to speak has the opportunity to do so, and can say all that he or she thinks worthy of being said. This may be unrealistic unless there is some active management of the process. One possibility would be a "conductor" who calls on people who want to make contributions (together with the convention of compliance with the conductor's directions). Alternatively, the members of the group could pay attention not only to opportunities for making contributions themselves but also to whether others are getting opportunities, with the result that the unmanaged flow of discussion involves explicit invitations to others to speak. Such a procedure might reflect the acceptance by the members of certain moral reasons, but it could also be given a cognitive rationale. If all do not get a chance to say what they think important, the creation of a comprehensive pool of reasons and criticized arguments may be compromised.

We must, then, qualify our initial proposal. So long as all get a chance to speak, there seems to be little reason to suppose that an alternative to the natural flow of discussion would be preferable as a way of constructing a pool of reasons. But there is a further issue that needs to be considered. The process of responding to the contributions of others can be either more adversarial or more collaborative, and this, too, might be thought to have a bearing on the ultimate composition of the pool. The choice among these two options can be regarded as a choice among cooperative schemes. It should be emphasized, however, that we are assuming that the goal of collective reasoning is the creation of a common pool of reasons, of which criticized arguments will form an important part. So even the more collaborative mode will involve the criticism of arguments presented. This is essential if collective reasoning is to result in judgments that are better justified than they would otherwise have been. The more collaborative mode just approaches the task of criticism in a more cooperative spirit.

In the adversarial procedure for constructing a common pool of reasons, the parties have conflicting views concerning which judgments are warranted, and seek to support them as best they can with arguments. This involves attacking opposing arguments. Often the parties remain in disagreement at the end of the process. But this does not mean that they do not benefit from the construction of the pool. What they regard as justified may be different after the pool is constructed. Or the next time they take up the issue, some may want to defend different positions. Here we are considering the process as one that benefits the participants. But it can also take place in front of an audience, in which case it is usually termed "debate." Debate results in the construction of a pool of reasons and criticized arguments on the basis of which the audience can make independent judgments.

How should we understand the adversarial procedure? One possibility is that it is a regrettable concession to human weakness. When the members of a group face a question the answer to which can have an impact on their interests – when interests will be affected differently depending on how the question is answered – they will favor different answers. We might add to this picture a further feature of human nature. Even when interests will be little affected by how a particular question is answered, different people might have different views about it. And all have an interest in appearing to their fellows to be epistemically competent. So once anyone ventures an opinion, she has a self-interested reason for defending it. If she is shown to be wrong, her epistemic prestige will suffer. Thus, even casual discussions of some point that attracts the attention of the members of a group can acquire an adversarial element.

We may be able, however, to put the adversarial procedure in a more favorable light. The discovery of reasons for or against a particular position takes work. Gathering evidence takes time and effort, and so does thinking up arguments concerning what the evidence supports. Thus, the question arises as to what motivation people have to do these things. A disinterested concern for the truth is one possibility. But it may be that people who are not disinterested will in fact work harder, albeit to prove that their preferred positions are right. This suggests that an adversarial mode of collective reasoning might actually uncover more of the relevant facts and more thoroughly explore their relevance than disinterested inquiry. In this case, the human weakness that underlies adversarial procedures would have the beneficial consequence of generating a more comprehensive pool of criticized arguments.

Still, if the adversarial procedure is indeed to produce a good result, it cannot involve a "no holds barred" struggle to convince others by any means necessary. This might involve the use by some of various forms of social power to suppress the expression of opposing views altogether. If an adversarial process is to achieve cognitive goals, it must be viewed as a competition constrained by rules. An example would be a rule giving each a chance to speak. This is connected with the points made earlier about how the flow of discussion may have to be actively managed – either by a conductor or by the participants themselves – if a comprehensive pool of reasons is to be constructed.

A related point also deserves mention. The construction of a shared pool of reasons by the exchange of arguments will be most effective – will produce the most useful pool – if the parties are prepared to concede the force of the arguments brought against them. Arguments are sets of propositions presented as supporting, with the force of reason, a conclusion. So if a useful pool is to be constructed, the clash of arguments must unfold in a way that reflects a genuine responsiveness by each party to the reasons offered by the others. If the parties simply resort to rhetoric, failing to acknowledge the apparent rational force of opposing arguments, the resulting pool will not be as helpful an indicator of where the weight of reason actually lies.[2]

The alternative to the adversarial approach is explicitly collaborative reasoning. As I have mentioned, this too involves the presentation of arguments, understood as sequences of propositions presumptively supporting a certain conclusion, including arguments criticizing previously offered arguments. But it is not an adversarial process. In adversarial reasoning, the situation of the parties is asymmetrical. Each has a commitment to a certain view, and is looking for ways to strengthen it and weaken opposing views. In collaborative reasoning, by contrast, the situation is symmetrical. Each is disinterested – or more accurately, each is interested only in determining which answer to the question being considered is best justified by the relevant reasons. Each party is thus equally concerned to discover the strengths and weakness of each argument offered. To be sure, the parties may have initial views about the matter being considered, but this merely gives the process of offering and considering arguments a place to start. The parties then respond with further arguments in support or defense of the initial offering. But each adopts a posture of maximal sensitivity to both the strong and the weak points of every argument, whether his own or that of others. Thus, the phenomenon is not adversarial.

The issues concerning the desirability of constructing a pool of arguments in this collaborative way parallel those that arise in connection with an adversarial process. If defending an interested position is effective in harnessing rational energies, so that a more comprehensive pool of reasons is constructed, this would count against the collaborative mode of collective reasoning. Still, collaborative reasoning may have compensating advantages. If the pool of reasons is constructed by an adversarial process, people who enjoy, or at least are not bothered by, conflict and struggle will have a disproportionate influence on the composition of the pool. But there is no reason to suppose that these people will possess all the relevant reasons. Some of those who do not enjoy conflict may be in a position to make very important contributions. By contrast, the choice of a more collaborative procedure would presumably not have the effect of silencing those who would be comfortable with an adversarial process (although they might have to exert some willpower to play by the collaborative rules). So there is also some reason to suppose that a collaborative approach would result in a more comprehensive pool of arguments. It should be emphasized, however, that although the process is collaborative, the participants must still be prepared to suffer the experience of having proposals they have made revealed as incorrect.

The foregoing discussion of how issues relating to the common choice of a cooperative scheme can be viewed as playing a role in collective reasoning has presupposed that the choice is appropriately made on instrumental grounds. All the members of the group have the same view of the cooperative product: a maximally comprehensive pool of relevant reasons or criticized arguments on the basis of which they can make up their own minds. The choice between the adversarial and collaborative modes of collective reasoning involves a decision about how this result might best be achieved. This need not be a question that has to be answered once and for all. For some sorts of issues, the adversarial approach might yield better results, and for others the collaborative approach.

We should note that moral considerations may also be relevant to the choice of modes of collective reasoning. First, even if the adversarial mode is preferable on instrumental grounds (given the cognitive goal of making better justified judgments), it might be thought that the ends do not justify the means. That is, it might be thought that it matters how we treat each other in the course of constructing a pool of reasons, and thus we should observe the more courteous procedures of collaborative reasoning, even if this will result in a less comprehensive pool. Second, moral considerations can enter into the choice of topic for collective investigation. There may be a greater number of issues that the members of a group would like to see discussed collectively – so that a pool of criticized arguments germane to them can be constructed – than can actually be considered. In this case, they face the problem of the creation of an agenda, and conflicts about this might have to be resolved on moral grounds, such as fairness.

If we expand our focus to encompass a whole society, however, the issue of the agenda becomes less pressing. A society can contain a sphere of organizations and associations, each of which is devoted to the consideration of a particular question or set of questions. Each of these entities will continuously produce a stream of arguments relevant to the questions it addresses, and these streams will converge to create a large pool of reasons available to the whole society.[3] Organizations and associations of this sort may take different sides on certain issues in which the public is interested, or they may profess to be impartial investigators. Either way, they will usually respond to one another's arguments. So there will be a division of epistemic labor that ensures that virtually every question any member of the larger society wants investigated collectively will be investigated collectively.

We should mention a consequence of society-wide (or worldwide) efforts to construct a pool of criticized arguments through a division of rational labor. While there is a clear sense in which a common pool of criticized arguments germane to a variety of issues is produced, it will usually be impossible for any individual to be aware of all these arguments. Our attention must inevitably be selective. On most issues, we can keep in mind only some contributions, and some responses to them. And even those who make a profession of contributing, and thus know most of the contributions relevant to certain questions, will be largely ignorant of the full range of contributions to other questions on which they wish to form an opinion. So it is to be expected that individuals who seek to draw on the common pool to reach conclusions about issues of concern to them will disagree – not as a result of cognitive malfunction, but because inputs will inevitably differ. The possibility of this sort of disagreement without malfunction was mentioned in Section I of Chapter 7.

II. THE REASON TO REASON

Now let us consider what justifies the individual members of a group in contributing to a process of collective reasoning. In the first part of this book, we saw that cooperation often requires general acceptance of a principle justifying contribution to a cooperative scheme when it is possible to benefit as a free rider. Do individuals need to acknowledge such a principle to be justified in participating in a process of collective reasoning?

I have suggested that the cooperative product in the case of collective reasoning should be understood as a common pool of reasons or criticized arguments on the basis of which each can make a (better) justified judgment regarding the answer to some question. But when we try to fit cooperation to answer a question of any kind into the picture presented in the first part of the book, we encounter some difficulties.

Cooperative behavior can arise in the context of a coordination problem. In this sort of case, defection by anyone will prevent the cooperative benefit from being produced. Collective reasoning does not appear to have this structure. The pool of arguments constructed by the group's efforts is typically available even to those who contribute nothing to it. Does collective reasoning then have the structure of a multiperson prisoner's dilemma? In prisoner's dilemma situations, the PIR dictates free riding, and some explicitly cooperative reason must be acknowledged if the benefits of cooperation are to be realized. In Chapter 1, I argued that the PCR provides the best formulation of the reason to contribute. Since the good produced by collective reasoning is an incremental public good within the relevant group, one would expect to find a free-rider problem here as well. But as I mentioned earlier, it is a striking fact about collective reasoning that this is not usually the case. Usually, most members of the group want to contribute. We can make this point in terms of the value of fairness. If there is a problem of unfairness associated with collective reasoning, it does not take the form of some exploiting the cooperative dispositions of others. Rather, it takes the form of some denying others the opportunity to contribute.

How, then, are we to understand the reason to participate in a process of collective reasoning? I shall divide the discussion of this problem, focusing first on the case where disagreement is attributable to cognitive malfunction, then on the case where it is not.

Before proceeding, however, it may be useful to make a further observation that will bring the problem we are considering into sharper focus. For collective reasoning to take place at all, it must be possible for each group member to make a contribution that is available to the others. In small face-to-face groups, this condition is easily satisfied. Each speaker will be heard by all, and the securing of opportunities for each to speak can be handled informally. In larger groups, it will be necessary to institute rules of order to ensure that each can make a contribution that is available to all. But rules of order cannot solve the problem in whole societies. At that level, ensuring that each individual – or more plausibly, a representative of each view – can make a contribution that is available to all requires equal access to various media of communication.

The maintenance of certain rules of order, and the instituting of procedures to ensure equal access to media of communication, themselves involve rational cooperation. Presumably, this, too, can be viewed as cooperation to produce the benefit of a shared pool of reasons on the basis of which a decision can be made. But these forms of cooperation fit the paradigm discussed in the earlier chapters. They involve overcoming a multiperson prisoner's dilemma. Thus, I shall not say anything about them here. I shall assume that suitable rules or procedures governing access to opportunities for speaking and to means of communication are in place, and focus on the nature of the reason that people have to take advantage of these opportunities – to contribute to the evolving pool of criticized arguments.

III. REASONING TO OVERCOME MALFUNCTION

It is tempting to explain the disposition to participate by invoking a fundamental human desire to say what one thinks about any issue that arises in a group of which one is a member. But people seem to differ in the extent to which they possess such a desire, and there may be cultural factors at work as well. I shall try to be more precise about the reasons that are potentially involved, while keeping in mind the possibility that cultural factors play a role.

The first point to notice is that collective reasoning, as I have characterized it, is undertaken to answer a question facing a group. It is thus to be distinguished from conversation, which has no external goal of this sort. People enter into conversations simply to establish and maintain a certain sort of social contact. The desire for this sort of contact can play a role in collective reasoning as well. But it will help to focus our investigation to suppose that it does not. What we wish to know, then, is what reason someone who simply wants to be able to make a better justified judgment about some question has to participate in a collective effort to assemble a pool of criticized arguments germane to that question.

When disagreement is attributable to cognitive malfunction, this is normally reduced or eliminated as each corrects his view in light of the evolving pool. But as I mentioned in Chapter 6, we can imagine a form of cooperation that is explicitly aimed at eliminating malfunction in the members of a group. In this case, cooperation takes the form of the sequential examination of the views of each member by the remainder. At each juncture, the whole group cooperates to detect malfunction in the reasoning of the individual currently being "treated." The designated individual shares with the group his view about what the relevant reasons require, and the others respond with critical arguments. Since the views of each can undergo further change when he takes the role of examiner, the process may have to be repeated.

What reasons are there for the participants to contribute to such a scheme? We can distinguish participation by the person whose views are being examined from participation by the others. The examinee cannot receive the benefit of having his view examined unless he offers it to the others. But importantly, it will usually not be enough for him simply to describe his view and then sit back to receive the benefit of criticism. He may not fully understand how what is said bears on his view unless he offers responsive arguments at each point where he feels the criticism is not fully successful. So the PIR can justify the examinee in contributing arguments himself. Only by contributing can he receive the full benefit of the contributions of others.

How do things look from the standpoint of the examiners? To the extent that they lack a desire to benefit the examinee, the PIR will not justify their contributing. Their reason for contributing must be specifically cooperative, a reason deriving from the fact that those not being examined must take the role of examiners if the cooperative benefit is to be produced. Similarly, those who have already been examined will have no reason under the PIR to participate further, and specifically cooperative reasons will be required if they are to do so.

We should, however, note a feature of this case that can reduce the need for specifically cooperative reasons to contribute. We have seen that the full receipt of the benefits of examination often requires active engagement – the exchange of arguments – with the examiners. But this engagement will have as a side effect the provision to the examiners of a critical perspective on *their* views. That is, there is a certain artificiality about the scheme proposed. The examination of anyone's views is likely to confer the benefit of examination, to a certain extent, on the examiners as well. But to receive the full benefit, they must contribute responsive arguments. So there will be personal benefits to be derived from joining the examiners after all. Still, this will be less true for those whose views have already been examined. They can expect a smaller gain from continued participation. So in this respect at least, the scheme of sequential examination will probably require the general acknowledgement in the group of some specifically cooperative reason for participating.

Now let us turn to the typical case in which collective reasoning simply involves the gradual construction of a pool of criticized arguments. This benefits each because it enables her to make a better justified judgment concerning the issue at hand. It seems that each could get the benefit of such a pool without contributing, in which case we would have a free-rider problem. Yet this is not what we usually observe. We can explain this in the same way that we explained contribution to the process of sequential examination. Often one cannot fully *receive* the benefit provided by a pool of criticized arguments without contributing oneself by offering responsive arguments. For example, one may not understand how the pool relates to other considerations one acknowledges unless one throws these considerations into the pool to see what happens to them.

This point is related to the observation made in Chapter 5 about the way that one benefits from a shared pool of reasons. There I said that the benefit is not simply conferred on one, as it is in the case of some other public goods, such as clean air. One must do something to appropriate it. To obtain the benefit of better justified judgment, one must actually make a judgment on the basis of the evolving pool. Now we can add that the appropriation of the benefit has a further dimension. To receive the full benefit of a group's efforts to assemble a pool of criticized arguments, one must understand how they relate to other considerations one may regard as relevant. But one can get a much better idea of this if one adds these considerations to the pool and then participates in the resulting discussion.

Here, then, we have one possible explanation for the fact that collective reasoning does not usually present a free-rider problem. When collective reasoning is undertaken to construct a common pool of criticized arguments, each will have an explicitly cooperative reason for contributing, provided by the PCR. But the case will not have the feel of a prisoner's dilemma because the PIR supports contributing as well. Each must contribute (do something that constitutes a contribution) if he is to receive the full benefit of the common pool of reasons.[4]

There is, however, more to be said about the reasons that justify participation in collective reasoning when disagreement is attributable to cognitive malfunction. The fact of disagreement also plays a role. By hypothesis, we are considering a situation in which there is disagreement regarding the correct answer to a question facing a group, and this disagreement is taken by all as indicating malfunction somewhere in the group (or perhaps acceptance of different facts). But differences in the way an individual might respond to disagreement can have a bearing on the reason each has for participating in a process of collective reasoning.

One possibility is that each takes the disagreement of others to be an interpersonal reason for reconsidering her own view, and thus suspends judgment, or at least relaxes her commitment to her view, until she has heard what they have to say. In this case, there is a clear sense in which each expects to benefit from collective reasoning. Each believes that she will be in a position to make a better justified judgment regarding the question being addressed after the pooling of the considerations all think relevant. The reasons to contribute are those identified previously. Each will have an explicitly cooperative reason, provided by the PCR, for contributing. But the PIR will also justify contribution because each will have to contribute if she is to receive the full benefit of the common pool of reasons.

But there is also another possibility. An individual may have so much confidence in her view that the reason for doubt provided by the disagreement of others does not lead her to suspend judgment until she has heard what others have to say. Perhaps she has already reconsidered her position, and expects to learn nothing new from further discussion. Nevertheless, she finds the fact that others disagree a kind of irritant, and she would be more comfortable if she could make it disappear.[5] She thus reacts to disagreement from others by *defending* her view, by presenting arguments designed to get them to come around to her view. But by responding in this way, she contributes to the construction of a shared pool of criticized arguments. Thus, an individual who is confident about the correct answer to the question at issue but is motivated to eliminate the irritant of disagreement can be led – inadvertently, so to speak – to participate in collective reasoning. And by participating, she receives the full benefit of the cooperative product, in the way we have been considering. She acquires a better grasp of the force of the pool.

This inadvertence deserves special mention. We can imagine a group of self-confident people all of whom are motivated solely by the desire to eliminate the irritant of disagreement. In this case, each will be led by a self-regarding reason to engage in what, in this context, is cooperative behavior – to offer her view to others and to criticize their resistance to it. That is, collective reasoning of this sort will display the form of an invisible-hand process. A self-regarding reason leads each to act in a way which, when combined with the actions of others similarly motivated, produces a cooperative benefit.[6]

These two ways that disagreement can give rise to a reason to contribute are related to the collaborative and adversarial cooperative schemes discussed in Section I. It should be mentioned, however, that an individual's response to the disagreement of others can take an extreme form that leaves her with no reason at all to contribute to the process of collective reasoning. This will happen if she concludes that she is surrounded by fools. She thus does not regard their disagreement as providing a presumptive reason for thinking she is wrong and does not suppose that she would gain anything from hearing what they have to say. As a consequence, the reason for participating that derives from the fact that this is necessary to receive the full benefit of the arguments offered lies dormant. There is, so far as this individual is concerned, no benefit to be received. Indeed, not even the PCR will suffice to justify contribution. And since an individual in this situation will not be irritated by the disagreement of others, which she simply dismisses, the invisible-hand process just described will not operate either. Only moral reasons, such as a desire to minister to the benighted, will be able to justify her joining with the others in shared deliberation.

IV. THE DESIRE FOR RECOGNITION

I began by noting that collective reasoning does not seem to be characterized by the problems usually associated with multiperson prisoner's dilemmas. We have now identified some features of collective reasoning that have the potential to explain this. The first is that one cannot get the full benefit of the critical arguments offered by others without offering one's own view for their consideration and participating in the ensuing discussion. The second is that the disagreement of others can be perceived as an irritant that leads us to defend our views, even though we are confident that they are correct, with the result that a common pool of criticized arguments becomes available to the group by an invisible-hand process.

Both these reasons for contributing ultimately derive from the goal of making a judgment that is as well supported as possible (which includes eliminating the reason to reconsider created by the disagreement of others). But there is also another motive that can play a role in underwriting collective reasoning. This additional motive derives from the desire to maintain a certain sort of status in a group of which one is a member. When one's proposals are rebutted in a way that one is forced, as a competent reasoner, to acknowledge, one does not typically feel unambivalently grateful for the favor that others have done by pointing out one's mistakes. One also has a sense of having been defeated. If one is functioning properly as a reasoner, one will acknowledge the force of the rebuttal and modify one's beliefs. But the fact that one feels defeated suggests a further feature of our orientation toward justified judgment. We want to have justified judgments, but we also want to be acknowledged by others as competent reasoners. We want *recognition* as competent reasoners. When our views are rebutted, we are in a position to make better justified judgments, but the desire for recognition is frustrated.

The desire for recognition adds a further dimension to the possibility of providing the public good of collective reasoning with an invisible-hand process. The desire to be recognized as cognitively competent will lead the members of a group to defend the views they initially express and to attack opposing views. And in doing so, each will contribute to the creation of the public good associated with collective reasoning: a pool of criticized arguments.

The desire for recognition may provide, in those who possess it, a stronger motive for participation than the desire to have justified judgments. But precisely for this reason, it also presents a danger. Since the good at issue (recognition) is not directly tied to making justified judgments, acting to obtain it can frustrate the latter goal. The desire to be recognized as a competent reasoner may lead one to retain a particular view when the accumulated evidence indicates that it should be abandoned. To be sure, there are limits to this. If one's tenaciousness is too extreme, one will in fact create the impression of being incompetent, and thus lose the status in question. But there are intermediate cases in which (rational) pursuit of recognition as competent can cause an individual to maintain a view when a dispassionate consideration of the accumulated evidence would result in its abandonment.[7]

We should be clear about the significance that this defect of the desire for recognition has from the standpoint of the ultimate goal of collective reasoning – justified judgment. The threat to this goal posed by the desire for recognition is most serious for the person who is led into error by it. It need not have any detrimental effect on the ability of others to benefit from his participation. The cooperative product is, after all, a pool of criticized arguments germane to some question that a group faces, and the arguments of someone who is incapable of conceding defeat may still constitute contributions. To be sure, if the group has an independent reason to agree – if it is trying to decide upon a cooperative scheme by which some further benefit can be obtained – the judgment-distorting effects of the desire for recognition may be detrimental to the realization of a benefit obtainable by collective reasoning. But when there is no further reason to agree, as in a discussion group, the desire for recognition need not impede the general receipt of the benefits of cooperation (unless it leads to the hogging of discussion).

There is, however, a further aspect of the desire for recognition as a competent reasoner that is genuinely counterproductive from the standpoint of amassing a shared pool of criticized arguments. The desire for recognition may lead some to express and defend their views. But it may also lead others to suppress theirs. That is, the fear of embarrassment if one is shown to be wrong – the fear of being revealed as incompetent – may lead one to forgo offering one's view on a matter. This problem is actually exacerbated by the general possession, within a group, of the desire for recognition. Those who are motivated by this desire will often attack opposing views. Such attacks, when they are successful, can make the incompetence of others painfully obvious. So the inhibiting effect of fear of exposure as an incompetent reasoner may be greater when all in a group are motivated by a desire to be recognized as competent. Of course, this consequence of the desire for recognition can be detrimental to cognitive cooperation. While it may prevent the group from wasting time with some defective arguments, it may also keep arguments that would constitute valuable additions to the pool from being offered.

The desire for recognition is not the only status desire that can affect contribution to the enterprise of collective reasoning. There is also the opposite desire, the desire not to put oneself forward, not to be perceived as presuming to have a better understanding of some matter than others. We have seen that the desire for recognition supplements the invisible-hand potential inherent in a situation where people think they are right but find the disagreement of others an irritant. The status desire we are now considering, however, has no invisible-hand potential. It rather creates an additional cost associated with participation in collective reasoning – the status cost incurred in putting oneself forward – thus making cooperation more problematic. Given the extra cost of contributing, the benefit each receives from the shared pool must be greater than it otherwise would be if the PCR is to justify contribution. And the same holds for the reason the PIR provides for contributing, deriving from the fact that the benefit one receives from the pool of reasons that others have assembled will be greater if one tests one's understanding of its significance by making a contribution. The benefit one can receive in this way must be large enough to outweigh the status cost of speaking up. It should also be mentioned that the desire not to put oneself forward can corrupt judgment, just as the desire for recognition can. It can blind one to the force of reasons in one's possession that would require *others* to modify their views.

Ultimately, we may be dealing with cultural variables here. People in our culture are encouraged to express and defend their beliefs. This means that positive status is conferred on people who do so effectively. This positive status is what those who have a desire for recognition seek. But encouraging these behaviors has costs. It can result in distorted judgments concerning what the relevant reasons support, and can inhibit participation by people who might have something to offer. Similar points apply to the desire not to put oneself forward. I do not have enough anthropological knowledge to identify any particular cultures in which people are encouraged not to put themselves forward. But if there are such cultures, individuals will have a corresponding status desire. They will want the status one receives by blending in. This motive can be detrimental to cognitive cooperation as well. By adding to the costs of collective reasoning, it can render infeasible some projects of collective reasoning that would otherwise be feasible. And even when it does not prevent cooperation from going forward, it can have the effect of inhibiting the expression of relevant arguments, especially those that threaten to upset widely held beliefs.

It should be mentioned that simply speaking of collective reasoning, understood as a form of mutually beneficial cooperation, may betray a cultural bias. It means assuming that each member of a group wants to be able to make a better justified judgment about some question the group faces. This is why a common pool of criticized arguments constitutes a public good. So if there are cultures whose members do not have such personal cognitive goals, we will not be able to describe any shared deliberation that might take place in them as collective reasoning.

It is interesting to consider what the rational structure of shared deliberation would be if it did not involve collective reasoning in our sense. Let us suppose that the desire not to put oneself forward takes the more specific form of the desire not to inflict the irritant of disagreement on others. This is plausible since one suspects that people so motivated would not be reluctant to put themselves forward to express agreement. If a group of people who are so motivated face a question, they will clearly prefer to arrive at a consensus regarding its correct answer. That way, in the end, no one will be inflicting the irritant of disagreement on anyone else.

But if they view the question as one that has a correct answer, they must somehow consider the reasons germane to the answer, and this will require that some members of the group make and criticize proposals concerning what these reasons support. So to achieve a *rationally justified* consensus – which we are now supposing is the group's goal – the parties must overcome the desire each has not to inflict the irritant of disagreement on others. The considerations at issue here could have a moral character. The goal of achieving rationally justified consensus could be regarded as having moral value, and the desire not to put oneself forward could reflect an agent-relative moral concern – perhaps a concern not to be personally responsible for causing pain to others.

If we suppose that the good of a justified consensus can be approached incrementally, as more and more contributions are made and a shared sense of what the evidence requires begins to emerge, the situation will have the form of a standard multiperson prisoner's dilemma. The contributions that the members make by offering reasons do not, considered individually, have enough value to offset the cost to each of contributing. But the PCR may be able to justify each in contributing. This will happen if the collective product, a *justified* consensus, is viewed by each as having a value great enough to outweigh the cost he incurs by putting himself forward (and thereby inflicting disagreement on others who have presented opposing arguments). Each would prefer to ride free on the contributions of others, but if all act accordingly, a justified consensus will not be produced. So in a cooperative spirit, each bears the cost of putting himself forward. The parties may be able to reduce the moral costs of contributing by adopting tactics designed to minimize the irritation caused by disagreement. But there will be no self-interested reason for contributing that derives from the fact that one cannot, as an individual, receive the full benefit of the pool reasons without contributing. By hypothesis, the members do not have the personal goal of making justified judgments. They do not have this goal as individuals.[8]

We should note the implications of these observations concerning the role of status desires in collective reasoning for the choice between adversarial and collaborative ways of proceeding. The desire to be perceived as a competent reasoner can be useful, as a supplement to other cooperative motivations, in the case where the process is adversarial. But it would be incorrect to say that the desire not to put oneself forward will be similarly useful when a more collaborative form of collective reasoning has been implemented. Collaborative reasoning still involves mutually beneficial cooperation. The cooperative product is a shared pool of criticized arguments on the basis of which each can make up his or her own mind – can make an individual judgment. And cooperation will be most successful if each is happy to put forward arguments, even though this means rejecting what someone else has said. What makes the process collaborative is simply that the parties are not tied to particular positions but, rather, pursue the truth in a disinterested way. As we have just seen, the desire not to put oneself forward has its natural place in conjunction with a different form of cognitive cooperation, cooperation in which the parties do not have personal cognitive goals but, rather, wish to arrive at a consensus. And if the consensus is to be one that is well supported by the applicable reasons, this desire does not facilitate the attainment of the goal, but creates a further cost of contribution.

V. LIKE-MINDED GROUPS

Now let us turn to another sort of collective action problem that can arise in connection with cooperative efforts to eliminate cognitive malfunctioning. So far we have been implicitly assuming that each member of the group at issue has a unique understanding of the way the relevant reasons combine to support a particular conclusion. This means that if the group is to realize the full cognitive benefit of collective reasoning, each must contribute. And as we have seen, each will usually have to offer her own understanding of the import of the evolving pool if she is to benefit fully from it.

We can, however, imagine cases which lack these features. It may be that there are subgroups whose members all hold the same view of the force of the relevant reasons. In such a case, the receipt by each member of a subgroup of the benefits of collective reasoning requires only that one of them offer the subgroup's view for public examination. This will allow all to see how the common pool bears on this view. Similarly, what is required if the larger group is to receive the full benefit of collective reasoning is that one member of each subgroup present responsive arguments in a public forum. But then the full benefit of collective reasoning can be provided to the larger body by a small group of active contributors. What reasons are there for individuals in this situation to become active contributors?

If we accept the fundamental motive for contributing that we identified earlier – that it is necessary to receive the full benefit of the cooperative product – one might suppose that each would want to be one of the active contributors. But especially in large groups, serving as a subgroup's spokesperson can involve making an effort that is, in various ways, quite costly. Still, the problem of securing contribution is not a collective-action problem of the most familiar sort, in which individual rationality gives each a reason to ride free no matter how many others are contributing. We can suppose that each would be willing to undertake the task of reasoning for the subgroup to which she belonged if no one else stepped forward. Since each of the holders of a view will be able to receive the full benefit of collective reasoning only if that view is offered for examination by the larger group, each will have a self-regarding reason to present and defend that group's view if no one else is willing to.[9]

Further, in this case, too, motivational resources are available that go beyond the desire to form judgments that are maximally supported by the evidence. Typically, those who serve as spokespersons are not reluctant to do so. Indeed, there is often a competition for this position. This can be explained by invoking a variant of the desire for recognition. The desire for recognition as a competent reasoner is a desire for a status good. But serving as a spokesperson for a group holding a certain view also involves possessing a status that many people value. It makes one important within the subgroup and also in the larger body. Typically, there will be enough people seeking this status to ensure that someone in every subgroup is willing to undertake the task of articulating and defending the group's view.

There is also another feature of such cases that requires mention. We have been making the assumption that the subgroups of like-minded people are completely homogeneous in values and in ability to make the subgroup's case in a larger forum. Both assumptions are unrealistic. There will be some disagreement even within subgroups of largely like-minded people, and there will be differences in ability to reason publicly on behalf of the group. The first of these facts has the consequence that subgroups can benefit from internal collective reasoning, as well as from the exchange of views with other subgroups. The full range of reasons to participate that we discussed earlier will be applicable here. Moreover, in the course of these intragroup deliberations, it may become clear that some are more effective at articulating the group's perspective than others. And once this has happened, it will be difficult for these people to avoid serving as spokespersons.

The possibility that we are now considering – the nesting of collective reasoning in a large group, so that there is collective reasoning within more or less like-minded subgroups, followed by collective reasoning by their spokespeople – plays an important role when whole societies could benefit from collective reasoning. We see it in the familiar structure if intermediate associations and advocacy groups in our own society. Collective reasoning in the larger group is carried out by well-qualified spokespeople, against the background of collective reasoning within each subgroup (in which the spokespeople play a leading role). There is thus a division of rational labor. But in general, specifically cooperative reasons, such as that provided by the PCR, are not needed to underwrite this pattern of activity.

VI. CHOOSING SCHEMES

Now let us turn to the case where collective reasoning is undertaken to facilitate some further cooperative venture by effecting the choice of a cooperative scheme on the basis of which that venture can proceed. This could be a matter of eliminating disagreement arising from cognitive malfunction. Normally, the goal of such reasoning is simply the amassing of a pool of criticized arguments. But if the members must agree on a cooperative scheme, they could impose upon themselves a requirement of integral consensus, or each could keep trying to convince the others of his position in the hope that a piecemeal consensus on what is justified by the relevant reasons will eventually emerge.

The case of reasoning to the choice of a scheme with which we have been mainly concerned, however, is that in which the initial disagreement is not attributable to malfunction, because people can legitimately hold different values. In Chapter 7, we examined various ways that a group of this sort might be able to reason to agreement on a scheme. One lesson of that investigation was that the value of fairness will often play some role in such reasoning. Fairness is the characteristic moral virtue of cooperative schemes. So it appropriately guides the effort to identify a scheme on the basis of which a further cooperative benefit is to be distributed. It should be borne in mind that although the initial disagreement is not attributable to malfunction, any disagreement about what fairness requires may be so attributable, so that reasoning about what would be fair is reasoning undertaken to overcome malfunction. As we have seen, actually effecting the choice of a cooperative scheme on the basis of fairness is threatened by the fact that other values held by the members may be taken to outweigh it. But let us suppose initially that this threat is blunted because the parties are prepared to demote their other values to interests. We can, then, understand them as reasoning about what fairness requires.

Here the members of the group will have all the motives for contributing to the process of collective reasoning that were identified earlier when we considered the case of reasoning to overcome malfunction: the desire to assimilate fully the offerings of others, the desire for recognition, and so on. In addition, when the question being addressed concerns the selection of a scheme that will divide cooperative benefits, some may accept moral reasons for engaging in deliberation with people from whom they expect no cognitive benefit – from whom they expect to learn nothing about fairness. The value of fairness, applied to the procedure of deliberation itself, provides a moral reason for at least giving such people the opportunity to influence one's thinking. But when a group is deliberating about the choice of a cooperative scheme to guide some further venture, a *nonmoral* reason for participating that is unrelated to receiving the cognitive benefit of collective reasoning comes to the fore. When the cooperative scheme that is chosen is put into effect, each member of the group will receive a certain benefit from *it*. But how great this benefit is will depend on the scheme that is chosen. Thus, each will want to contribute to any process of collective reasoning undertaken to effect the choice of a scheme because this may enable her to secure an outcome that is more favorable from her point of view. Of course, if the parties are reasoning about what fairness requires, each will have to couch her case in these terms. But there will usually be disagreement, and each may plausibly suppose that if she does not participate, a mistake that redounds to her disadvantage will be made.

Let us look at this case in more detail. Independent interests, including those provided by values treated as interests under pressure from fairness, can produce distorted judgments of what fairness requires, but they also make people especially sensitive to any genuine unfairness to them. So when all participate, it is reasonable to expect that the heightened sensitivity to unfairness that each brings to the process will remain, while the distorting effects are identified and removed by collective reasoning concerning what is truly fair. But in addition, by participating, each will be able to ensure that her interests are as fully respected as they can be, consistent with fairness. Thus, when a group is trying to determine what would constitute a fair scheme on the basis of which to organize some further cooperative venture, each will have a self-interested reason to contribute that goes beyond those that operate when disagreement is taken to indicate malfunction (and each merely seeks a better justified judgment).

Similar points can be made about the case where collective reasoning leads to agreement by bending the evaluative commitments with which the parties start. The perception that certain potential benefits of cooperation are being lost leads each to extend her values to new cases in a way that alters their content, so that ultimately the values held by each are compatible with the choice of a particular cooperative scheme. An understanding of what fairness requires may play a role in this process. We also considered a short-term possibility, in which the parties are prepared to demote their values to interests and compromise them as fairness requires, but then reconstitute these values in a new, accommodating form. In both these cases, a desire to be sure that the cooperative scheme ultimately put into effect requires as little bending or breaking of one's own concerns as possible (consistent with fairness) provides a personal reason to contribute to the process of collective reasoning that results in the selection of that scheme.

To conclude, then, there are several reasons for contributing to the process of collective reasoning that operate independently of the reason provided by the PCR. These reasons reflect the fundamental distinction between the case where collective reasoning is undertaken to establish a scheme by which some further cooperative benefit can be achieved, and the case where the benefit produced is simply the cognitive one of being able to form a better-justified judgment.

When a cooperative enterprise will determine the extent to which the parties' interests, or the values they hold, are satisfied, these interests or values give each a reason to participate in any process of reasoning that will determine which scheme governs that enterprise. In this way, each ensures that the chosen scheme will promote his values or interests as effectively as possible, within the constraints provided by any overarching standard, such as fairness, that may apply to the choice. This reason for participating will also play a role when a group does not have the prospect of reasoning all the way to the choice of a scheme – that is, to a consensus on which scheme would be best – and thus must employ a procedure such as voting. The prospect of being able to influence the votes of others provides ample self-regarding justification for participating in the deliberation that precedes voting. It should also be mentioned that in both these cases, some may accept moral reasons for giving others the opportunity to influence them.

Cases where collective reasoning is undertaken simply to achieve the cognitive benefit of better-justified judgment, as exemplified by a discussion group, are perhaps less common. But they are fundamental for an analysis of collective reasoning as a form of mutually beneficial cooperation. The cooperative product is a pool of reasons or criticized arguments on the basis of which each can more fully attain a personal cognitive goal: (better) justified judgment. And extracting the full benefit from the pool usually requires one to perform actions that constitute a contribution to it.

Notes

CHAPTER 1. THE REASON TO CONTRIBUTE

1 For an argument that the term "irrationality" should be restricted to failure to meet the privative standard, see T. M. Scanlon, *What We Owe to Each Other* (Cambridge, MA: Harvard University Press, 1998), pp. 25–30.

2 In *The Authority of Reason* (Cambridge: Cambridge University Press, 1998), chap. 7, Jean Hampton argues that strictly construed, expected utility theory is solely a predictive theory, and that reading it normatively, as a theory of instrumental reason, requires developing a (noninstrumental) theory of the good.

3 For a discussion of these issues, see John Broome, *Weighing Goods* (Oxford: Blackwell, 1991).

4 The numbers indicate the desirability of an outcome, given an agent's principles of value. There is no assumption that they are interpersonally comparable. It is customary to characterize games by using numbers that provide only ordinal information, indicating how the players rank the different outcomes. This has the virtue of providing a definition of each kind of game, while the matrices I employ rather illustrate particular cases of each kind. But I think the points that I want to make are more easily grasped if we indicate not only rankings but also gains and losses to each player (in light of her principles of value).

5 An account can be found in James D. Morrow, *Game Theory for Political Scientists* (Princeton, NJ: Princeton University Press, 1994), chap. 4.

6 See Amartya Sen, "Isolation, Assurance, and the Social Rate of Discount," *Quarterly Journal of Economics* 80 (1967), pp. 112–124.

7 Outcome *X* is Pareto superior to outcome *Y* if *X* is such that one party is better off and none are worse off. *X* is strongly Pareto superior to *Y* if *X* is such that everyone is better off. An outcome is Pareto optimal if there is no way to make anyone better off without making someone else worse off. In the prisoner's dilemma, the cooperative outcome is Pareto optimal and strongly Pareto superior to the outcome in which both behave uncooperatively. For an account of dominance, dominant strategy equilibria,

and Pareto dominance (which I have called Pareto superiority), see Morrow, *Game Theory for Political Scientists,* chap 4.

8 For a discussion of chicken games, see Michael Taylor, *The Possibility of Cooperation* (Cambridge: Cambridge University Press, 1987), chap. 2.

9 For an account of the multiperson prisoner's dilemma, see Russell Hardin, "Collective Action as an Agreeable n-Prisoner's Dilemma," *Behavioral Science* 16 (1971), pp. 472–481.

10 For a helpful discussion of the defining features of a public good, see Taylor, *The Possibility of Cooperation,* pp. 5–8.

11 I take the distinction that follows from Jean Hampton, *Hobbes and the Social Contract Tradition* (Cambridge: Cambridge University Press, 1986), p. 177.

12 The example is from Jean-Jacques Rousseau, *Discourse on the Origin of Inequality,* Part II, Para. 9, in D. Cress, trans., *The Basic Political Writings* (Indianapolis, IN: Hackett, 1987), p. 62.

13 Hampton's solution involves the identification of a subgroup just large enough to cross the threshold. She shows that if such a minimally sufficient subgroup can somehow be singled out, each of its members will find it individually rational to make his contribution, and she argues that the problem of singling out one of the minimally sufficient subgroups is an impure coordination problem. See her *Hobbes and the Social Contract Tradition,* esp. chap. 6, and "Free-Rider Problems in the Production of Public Goods," *Economics and Philosophy* 3 (1987), pp. 245–273.

14 See Taylor, *The Possibility of Cooperation,* pp. 40–43.

15 The principal problem that confronts attempts to reconcile individual rationality with contributing to mutually beneficial cooperative schemes is incompleteness – failure to capture all the cooperative behavior that seems, intuitively, to be required. The most prominent recent attempt is the argument of David Gauthier in *Morals by Agreement* (Oxford: Clarendon Press, 1986). The critical consensus appears to be that even if one grants that it is rational to act on any disposition that it is rational to adopt, the disposition that it is individually rational to adopt would sometimes call for exploitation of the cooperative behavior of others. Another strategy that I believe suffers from incompleteness is Robert Nozick's method of calculating a "decision value" for an action that combines causal expected utility, evidential expected utility, and symbolic utility (See *The Nature of Rationality* [Princeton, NJ: Princeton University Press, 1993], chap. 2). Nozick's proposal is developed in connection with the two-person prisoner's dilemma, and seems more problematic in the multiperson case, where free riding is the issue. Here many others are already contributing, and the conditional probability that they will defect if one does seems low, whether calculated on the basis of causal influence or on the basis of a judgment that the reasoning that one finds convincing will also convince them. And if symbolic utility is a function of what one expresses by acting in a certain way, the symbolic disutility of defection may be less when it can be kept hidden from others.

16 See Philip Pettit, "Free Riding and Foul Dealing," *Journal of Philosophy* 83 (1986), pp. 361–379. The formal results in game theory that address the

possibility of securing cooperation by threatening to punish defection are
known collectively as the "folk theorem." See, Morrow, *Game Theory for
Political Scientists*, chap. 9, for an account. The Hobbesian strategy for
using threats to secure cooperation involves positing a punisher who is
not himself one of the potential cooperators, but has an interest in their
cooperation. It is natural to wonder whether this device can be dispensed
with – whether the potential cooperators can secure cooperation by
threatening each other with punishment for noncooperation. In the purest
case, the punishment will simply be the denial of cooperation in the
future. The folk theorems identify various ways that cooperative outcomes
in situations displaying the basic form of the prisoner's dilemma can be
Nash equilibria when the parties adopt strategies that provide for the
punishment of defection by denial of future cooperation. Morrow notes,
however, that defection from such a strategy may nevertheless be rational
(p. 278). In *Game Theory: A Critical Introduction* (London: Routledge, 1995),
chap. 6, Shaun P. Hargreaves Heap and Yanis Varoufakis point out that
since many different combinations of strategies constitute Nash equilibria
for the purposes of the folk theorem, these formal results do not by
themselves tell agents what to do when they face iterated prisoner's dilemmas. The best strategy for an agent to follow depends on what strategy
the others are following.

17 Norman Daniels, *Justice and Justification: Reflective Equilibrium in Theory
and Practice* (Cambridge and New York: Cambridge University Press,
1996), esp. chaps. 2 and 4.

18 Daniels, *Justice and Justification*, chap 4.

19 The *locus classicus* is H. L. A. Hart, "Are There Any Natural Rights,"
Philosophical Review 64 (1955), 175–191. The label "principle of fairness"
appears to be due to John Rawls. See *A Theory of Justice* (Cambridge,
MA: Harvard University Press, 1971), pp. 108–114. The stipulation that
the benefits must be voluntarily accepted is the most contested part of
the principle of fairness. My argument here does not depend on this
feature.

20 For an account of the unfairness involved in free riding, see Garrett
Cullity, "Moral Free Riding," *Philosophy and Public Affairs* 24 (Winter,
1995). Cullity does not consider the problem that I discuss here.

21 In *Weighing Goods*, John Broome says: "To understand fairness we must
start by dividing the reasons why a person should get a commodity into
two classes, *claims* and other reasons. By a claim to a commodity, I mean
a duty owed to the candidate herself that she should have it. Many
reasons are not claims. . . . Claims, and not other reasons, are the object of
fairness. Fairness is concerned only with mediating between the claims of
different people. If there are reasons why a person should have a commodity, but she does not get it, no unfairness is done her unless she has a
claim to it" (pp. 194–195). This is not entirely clear, however. If a claim
implying a duty in others is denied, the holder of the claim is, ipso facto,
treated unfairly. But the notion of *mediating* between claims implies that
after fairness does its work, one may not get everything one has claimed.
It is hard to reconcile this with the idea that others have a duty to provide

what is claimed. The point might be better made by saying that fairness mediates between legitimate (that is, permissible) interests, but there are also other moral reasons that have implications for the satisfaction of interests, and the outweighing of these reasons need not involve unfairness.

22 If the benefit produced by the combination *equals* that which could be achieved in the noncooperative outcome, acting cooperatively is not dictated by the PCR, but neither is it excluded. As I mentioned earlier, uncertain outcomes can be accommodated by correlating each combination of actions to which the PCR directs our attention with a set of possible outcomes that can be assigned a probability distribution. But for the sake of simplicity, I shall assume that the outcomes of combinations are certain.

23 I am assuming that the agent considers whether there is sufficient reason to form an "all out" belief that enough others will contribute – in contrast to assigning probabilities to various degrees of participation by others.

24 In *The Limits of Government* (Boulder, CO: Westview Press, 1991), David Schmidtz provides a discussion of rational cooperation that emphasizes the importance of solving the assurance problem, and explores the possibility that human psychology may be such that solving it suffices to produce cooperative behavior. His preferred mechanism for effecting a solution is a certain kind of contract between potential cooperators. But most actual cooperation proceeds on the basis of other ways of solving the assurance problem.

25 This condition should, perhaps, be stated more cautiously. The PCR takes precedence over the PIR in any situation in which it is possible to effect a Pareto improvement over the outcome produced by general conformity to the PIR.

26 It may be useful to consider another case of this sort, suggested to me by David Copp. Suppose that A has been assigned a contribution to a cooperative scheme having the following features. All of the other cooperators enjoy making their contributions. Their values are such that defection has no appeal to them, and thus they have sufficient reason under the PIR to contribute. By contrast, A does not enjoy contributing. Yet it seems that the PCR could direct him to contribute. The benefit produced when everyone does his assigned part may exceed the best result that A could obtain with the resources at issue if no one contributed. And this is counterintuitive. But if A cares about fairness, the PCR can accommodate the intuition that contribution is not required. Given that the others enjoy making their contributions and he does not enjoy making his, the distribution of burdens that would result if he contributed would be unfair. And he might regard the noncooperative outcome, in which the scheme did not exist at all, as lacking this unfairness.

27 The other main form of universalization involves identifying all those who will be affected by what one proposes to do and then considering whether one could endorse this treatment were one in their positions (where this could involve either taking one's own concerns into their positions or adopting their concerns as a part of putting oneself in their

positions). For discussion, see J. L Mackie, *Ethics: Inventing Right and Wrong* (Harmondsworth, Eng.: Penguin, 1977), chap. 4.

28 Similar points apply to the question of how the PCR compares with the recent interpretations of Kant's Categorical Imperative offered by Onora Nell [Onora O'Neill] and Christine Korsgaard. (See Onora Nell, *Acting on Principle* [New York: Columbia University Press, 1976], and Christine Korsgaard, "Kant's Formula of Universal Law," in her *Creating the Kingdom of Ends* [Cambridge: Cambridge University Press, 1996], pp. 77–105.) These interpretations stress the fact that the Categorical Imperative speaks of acting on a maxim that one can *at the same time* will to be a universal law. They thus regard it as highlighting the sort of immorality that involves making an exception for oneself – that is, acting in a way that depends for its success on others not doing the same thing. This seems to make the Categorical Imperative especially suitable for underwriting contribution to mutually beneficial cooperative schemes. If my maxim is, "I will enjoy the public goods provided by the state without paying taxes," I will clearly fall into a kind of irrationality, involving something like contradiction, if at the same time I intend that everyone adopt this maxim. Everyone's behaving in this way would prevent me from obtaining what I intend to obtain. I have nothing to say about the adequacy of this proposal as an interpretation of Kant's ethics. But I believe that the PCR is preferable as a way of characterizing the requirement to contribute to mutually beneficial cooperative schemes. The Categorical Imperative (so characterized) takes no account of how many other contributions will actually be made. Thus, it could require one to make a contribution whose cost exceeded the benefit produced by the scheme. Indeed, it could require a contribution when no one else was prepared to contribute.

29 For a proposal that grounds the requirement to contribute to cooperative schemes in a moral requirement of reciprocity, see Robert Sugden, "Reciprocity: The Supply of Public Goods Through Voluntary Contributions," *Economic Journal* 94 (1984), pp. 772–787. Sugden's approach is similar to mine in that the requirement to contribute is activated only if enough others are contributing or will contribute. However, he regards the notion of reciprocity not only as providing a reason to contribute but also as determining how much each should contribute. The PCR does not work this way. It simply establishes whether one has sufficient reason to make a particular, assigned contribution. I discuss independent contribution in Chapter 2, Section III. In *The Cement of Society* (Cambridge: Cambridge University Press, 1989), Jon Elster identifies a "norm of fairness" that can lead to cooperative behavior. This, too, supports contribution only if enough others are contributing or will contribute. But unlike the PCR, the threshold is not provided by the point where the benefits produced exceed the cost to the contributor, but rather by the point at which the contributor feels that not chipping in would be unfair. Of course, my argument that reliance on the principle of fairness can lead to suboptimal outcomes when agents have moral reasons for defecting would apply both to Elster's norm of fairness and to Sugden's principle of reciprocity.

30 Compare Amartya Sen, "Rational Fools," in F. Hahn and M. Hollis, eds.,

Philosophy and Economic Theory (Oxford: Oxford University Press, 1979), pp. 87–109. Sen uses a ranking of preference rankings to elucidate the phenomenon of commitment (which involves choosing an action that one believes will afford one a lower level of personal welfare than some alternative).

31 "Specifying Norms as a Way to Resolve Concrete Ethical Problems," *Philosophy and Public Affairs* 19 (1990), pp. 279–310. Richardson presents a more comprehensive version of his theory of practical reasoning in *Practical Reasoning about Final Ends* (Cambridge: Cambridge University Press, 1994).

32 *Value in Ethics and Economics* (Cambridge, MA: Harvard University Press, 1993).

33 Similar points concerning incommensurability apply to my argument against the principle of fairness. My claim that promoting the value of fairness within the framework of the PIR can lead to suboptimal outcomes made use of the idea that considerations of fairness can be outweighed by other moral considerations, which implies that fairness is commensurable with these other considerations. I think we often feel comfortable judging that from the moral point of view, what can be gained by perpetrating modest unfairness outweighs the moral cost, or vice versa. But if incommensurabilities are thought to obtain here, they can be handled in the way I have described. Just as there is no reason to suppose that fairness will always outweigh competing moral values, there is no reason to suppose that doing what fairness requires will always be expressively preferable to doing what the competing values require. And if there is no basis at all for choice when fairness conflicts with other values, there is no reason to suppose that the course fairness requires (contribution) will always be taken. Thus, the inferiority of the principle of fairness to the PCR as a formulation of the reason to contribute remains, even if fairness is regarded as incommensurable with other values.

CHAPTER 2. COOPERATIVE STRUCTURES

1 For brief overview, see Shaun P. Hargreaves Heap and Yanis Varoufakis, *Game Theory: A Critical Introduction* (London: Routledge, 1995), chap. 4.

2 I shall not consider the case in which the PCR gives some members of the group no reason to contribute to any scheme. One way to deal with this possibility is to use the notion of a jointly feasible scheme to define a cooperating group. That is, we can understand the relevant group to consist of those individuals for whom there is at least one jointly feasible scheme.

3 The distinction between substantive and procedural values that I employ in discussing the choice of a cooperative scheme should not be confused with the distinction between substantive and formal principles that I employed in discussing the difference between the PCR and the principle of fairness in Chapter 1. The procedural and substantive values of Chapter 2 are both grounded in principles of value that are substantive in the sense of Chapter 1.

4 David Copp, *Morality Normativity and Society* (New York: Oxford University Press, 1995), p. 159.

5 This point also applies to the resolution of conflicts by appeal to substantive fairness. Members holding different conceptions of fairness could agree that a particular resolution was substantively fair.

6 Gauthier characterizes a constrained maximizer as an agent who "seeks in some situations to maximize her utility, given not the strategies but the utilities of those with whom she interacts" (*Morals by Agreement*, p. 167). The situations he has in mind are those in which the agent has an opportunity to do her part in a joint strategy to which it would be rational to agree (one that is nearly optimal and fair). Another notion that seems intended to do some of the work of the PCR is the "limited conditional good will" employed by Kurt Baier in *The Rational and the Moral Order* (Chicago: Open Court, 1995), pp. 186–193. Good will, however, is a straightforwardly moral notion.

7 These points are emphasized by Elster in *The Cement of Society*. See also the discussion of asymmetries in collective action in Russell Hardin, *Collective Action* (Baltimore: Johns Hopkins University Press, 1982), chap. 5.

8 For an alternative view of collective agents, see S. L. Hurley, *Natural Reasons* (Oxford: Oxford University Press, 1989), pp. 145–159. Hurley presents an account of collective rationality that regards the choice of a unit of agency as playing a central role in it. As she puts it, "Collective action does not calculate consequences from a fixed unit of agency; rather it involves first identifying those willing to act collectively, and then *together* doing what is best given what the non-co-operators do (or are likely to do)" (*Natural Reasons*, p. 146). Hurley accommodates the rationality of an individual's participating in a cooperative scheme through the idea of self-determination. She regards the choice among the various agents, individual or collective, accessible to a bodily individuated person in a particular situation as an aspect of personal self-determination. But she offers no explicit account of when it is appropriate for a person to identify with a collective agent. Supplementing her view with the PCR fills this gap. An individual guided by the PCR will decide whether to identify with a given collective agent by determining whether the net benefit derived from cooperation to create that collective agent exceeds the benefit he could obtain in the noncooperative outcome, where this may include the benefit obtainable by identifying with a different collective agent.

9 The reasoning here can be fitted more precisely into the framework provided by the PCR as follows. Each compares cooperation on the basis of the scheme on which she proposes to act with the noncooperative outcome. In the case of a listener-sponsored radio station, we may suppose that the noncooperative outcome (where the station does not exist) displays no unfairness. In general, an individual who cares about fairness will want to contribute to a scheme that similarly displays no unfairness. But in a case of independent contribution, she can always remedy any unfairness (to her, at least) that she perceives in the scheme (the pattern of contributions) that actually supports the station by adjusting her con-

tribution. The cooperative and noncooperative outcomes will then be equivalent from the standpoint of fairness, and the decision to contribute can be made on the basis of the fact that the individual judges the benefit provided by the station to exceed the cost of her (fair) contribution.

10 The issues discussed in this section are treated in the relevant literature under the heading of "reciprocity." The idea is that acceptance of the moral value of reciprocity by the members of a group can make possible the provision of public goods through independent contributions. I mentioned Robert Sugden's "Reciprocity: The Supply of Public Goods through Voluntary Contributions" in Section V of Chapter 1. Sugden notes the assurance problem but also describes a further respect in which independent contribution threatens to yield suboptimal outcomes. He shows that as he has defined reciprocity, if a group of reciprocally motivated people is heterogeneous, in the sense that its members differ in their preferences for a given public good, the good will be undersupplied: "Roughly speaking, the problem for the heterogeneous community is that those people with the strongest preferences for the public good will not contribute as much as *they* would like everyone to contribute – because the others (quite justifiably) will not reciprocate" (p. 783). He regards this consequence of his analysis as confirming it, since voluntary production of public goods is usually suboptimal. The point I would wish to make, however, is that employment of a common choice mechanism to select a scheme for the group can yield outcomes that are Pareto improvements over the outcome of independent contribution. One way it can do this is by directing those who value the public good more to contribute more. Reciprocity is also discussed by David Schmidtz in *The Limits of Government*, pp. 138–152.

11 It is noteworthy that most cooperative ventures that rely on independent contributions seek to provide their cooperators with some of the benefits of a choice mechanism by suggesting a particular amount to contribute – often described as the cost of a membership – calibrated to ensure that if all those who can be expected to contribute act accordingly, the full benefit of the good at issue (for example, twenty-four-hour operation, a comprehensive library of recordings, and so on) can be provided.

12 Derek Parfit, *Reasons and Persons* (Oxford: Clarendon Press, 1986).

13 See Parfit's *Reasons and Persons*, chap. 3. For an argument that the problem posed by cases where each action makes no discernable contribution to a bad outcome does not require this solution – which means that beneficence needs only individual rationality – see Michael Otsuka, "The Paradox of Group Beneficence," *Philosophy and Public Affairs* 20 (1991), pp. 132–149.

14 See, for example, Michael Bratman, "Shared Cooperative Activity," *Philosophical Review* 101 (1992), pp. 327–341, and "Shared Intention," *Ethics* 104 (1993), pp. 97–113; Raimo Toumela, "We Will Do It: An Analysis of Group-Intentions," *Philosophy and Phenomenological Research* 51 (1991), pp. 249–277; Margaret Gilbert, "What Is It for Us to Intend?" in G. Holmstrom-Hintikka and R. Toumela, eds., *Contemporary Action Theory* (Dordrecht: Kluwer, 1997), pp. 65–85; and J. David Velleman, "How to Share an Intention," *Philosophy and Phenomenological Research* 57 (1997), pp. 29–50.

15 The term "collective intention" is, perhaps, more suitable for the individualistic approaches, but I shall ignore this subtlety here, and use the term
interchangeably with "shared intention."

16 See Bratman's *Intention, Plans, and Practical Reason* (Cambridge, MA: Harvard University Press, 1987).

17 Bratman discusses these processes in "Shared Intention" and "Shared
Cooperative Activity." So far in this chapter, I have spoken of an *established* choice mechanism, a *common* choice mechanism, and now a *formal*
choice mechanism. I have used each of these terms to mark a contrast that
is germane in the context. A formal choice mechanism is one that involves
explicit choice. The contrast is with an informal mechanism based on
mutual adjustment. A common choice mechanism is a single mechanism
that each member of a group accepts as the mechanism by which a
scheme is to be chosen. The contrast is with the independent choice, by
each member, of the scheme on the basis of which she will contribute. An
established choice mechanism is a procedure that is adopted in the expectation that it will be employed to make a number of different choices. Of
course, a given choice mechanism may have more than one of these
properties.

18 I believe this analysis can be applied to the other accounts of shared
intention as well. Toumela's theory, according to which a collective intention must be built up out of intentions individuals have regarding their
own behavior, fits especially well with the PCR. A member of a group
who accepts the PCR might adopt an intention to contribute to a particular cooperative scheme if he believes that enough others will contribute to
produce an outcome that is preferable, in light of his values, to the noncooperative outcome. Such a belief could take many forms. But one possibility is that he believes that there is a mutual belief, within a sufficiently
large subgroup, that all the members of this subgroup accept the PCR and
regard the condition it sets for contribution as satisfied – where to speak
of a mutual belief is to say that each believes this, believes that the others
believe it, and so on. In this case, the agent will have what Toumela calls
a "we-intention." Further, if the agent's belief is true, the others he believes to be cooperatively disposed will also have we-intentions. And this
suffices to ascribe a collective intention to the group, and to characterize
the ensuing actions as constituting the intentional joint realization of a
cooperative scheme. (My point here is only that a belief that others accept
the PCR and regard the condition it states as satisfied is sufficient for a
we-intention. Agents who operate only with the PIR could also have we-
intentions. Still, the scope for we-intention is extended by the PCR.)

19 Another important form of authority is the authority of expertise. I discuss the distinction between subordinating authority and the authority of
expertise in *Authority and Democracy: A General Theory of Government and
Management,* (Princeton, NJ: Princeton University Press, 1994), chaps. 2
and 4.

20 See Joseph Raz, "Reasons for Action, Decisions, and Norms," in Raz, ed.,
Practical Reasoning (Oxford: Oxford University Press, 1978), pp. 128–143.

21 For a discussion of preemption, see Raz, *The Morality of Freedom* (Oxford,

Clarendon Press, 1986), chap. 3. I discuss Razian preemption in *Authority and Democracy*, pp. 27–33.

22 I do not mean to suggest that the existence of de facto subordinating authority requires that the subordinates hold a political theory. A simple habit of deference will suffice. But if preemption is central to authority, this habit must have a certain structure. The reasons it provides must be regarded as excluding and taking the place of the competing reasons.

23 I shall not address the differences that might exist between a widespread habit the existence of which is common knowledge, a convention, and a norm. Common knowledge of a habit suffices to solve the assurance problem. For an account of norms that regards punishment for deviation, by guilt feelings or the actions of others, as a necessary feature of a norm, see Elster, *The Cement of Society*, chap. 3.

24 De facto authority can also provide the assurances required to make ordinary coordination, underwritten by the PIR, possible.

25 I have stated a necessary, rather than a sufficient, condition for the legitimacy of coercion, because I do not wish to imply that any contribution to a cooperative scheme that is in fact justified by the PCR can be legitimately coerced. There may be moral considerations that further constrain how coercive power can be deployed. This issue is treated in greater detail in Chapter 3.

26 Some elements of the account of promising that follows are taken from my "Promising and Coordination," *American Philosophical Quarterly* 26 (1989), pp. 239–247.

27 Jean Hampton calls cases like this "contingent-move 'PD-like' games." In a standard prisoner's-dilemma, the moves of the players are independent. By contrast, when there is a first performer and a second performer, the move of the second performer is contingent on his knowledge of what the first performer has done. But the preferences of the parties for the various possible combinations of moves are the same as in the prisoner's dilemma. Both rank contribution by both as the second-best outcome and contribution by neither the third best. Unilateral defection is ranked first by the defector and last by the contributor. See *Hobbes and the Social Contract Tradition* (Cambridge: Cambridge University Press, 1986), pp. 227–228.

28 "When a man says *he promises anything*, he in effect expresses a *resolution* of performing it; and along with that, by making use of this *form of words* subjects himself to the penalty of never being trusted again in case of failure." David Hume, *A Treatise of Human Nature*, L. A. Selby-Bigge, ed., 2d ed. (Oxford: Clarendon Press, 1978), p. 522.

29 For an account of promising that builds upon moral requirements arising from the creation of expectations and the disappointment of reliance, see T. M. Scanlon, *What We Owe to Each Other*, pp. 295–317. Scanlon emphasizes that these moral considerations have force independently of any social practice of promising.

30 Since the PCR preempts the PIR, an agent who makes a legitimate promise will have a reason to keep it that preempts any reason provided by the PIR for breaking it. We might suppose that the motive associated with explicit promising also has this character – that it works in such a way

that the disposition that an agent acquires by making a promise is regarded by her as the source of a preemptive reason for acting as she has
promised. This would extend the parallel with authority. A possible objection is provided by the fact that promises can be outweighed, which
argues against understanding them as creating motivation that has a preemptive structure. But on the account offered here, we can say that cases
where it seems that a promise has been outweighed are actually cases
where the conditions for mutual cooperation no longer exist, yet reasons
connected with the induction of reliance are present, and these are outweighed.

31 We can suppose the dispositions associated with promising to be qualified
in other ways as well, in accordance with the standard understanding of
the conditions under which one need not keep a promise. Many of these
conditions can be derived from the PCR, however – for example, the
condition that one need not keep a promise when doing so would be
detrimental to the promisee, or when it would involve serious costs that
one did not anticipate.

32 It should also be mentioned that there will often be a prudential reason
to keep a promise that is not legitimate, in the sense that keeping it is not
underwritten by the PCR. Keeping it may increase the confidence of
others in the motivational efficacy of the promising mechanism in one's
own case, and thus make future promises more readily acceptable.

33 There is a connection between the account that I have offered of promising
and authority and Hume's notion of an artificial virtue (see Hume's *Treatise*, Bk. III, Part II, Sect. I). On my view, the motivational dispositions
underlying promising and authority are artificially inculcated, and are
then rendered legitimate by the role they play in facilitating mutually
beneficial cooperation. But sentiments of approbation elicited by the production of these benefits play no role in my account. Promising and
authority are worthy of esteem because they serve to activate *reasons* to
cooperate provided by the PCR (or the PIR, in the case of ordinary
coordination) that would otherwise have lain dormant.

CHAPTER 3. STATES AND GOVERNMENTS

1 See Quentin Skinner, *Liberty Before Liberalism* (Cambridge: Cambridge
University Press, 1998), pp. 4–5.

2 In *An Essay on the Modern State* (Cambridge: Cambridge University Press,
1998), Christopher Morris emphasizes the recent origin of the state as a
political form. See especially the excellent historical discussion in Chapter
2. Morris's intention is to loosen the grip of the state on our imagination
by drawing our attention to its historical contingency. But his discussion
also has the effect of making the idea that states could be deliberately
created more plausible.

3 A. John Simmons, *Moral Principles and Political Obligations* (Princeton, NJ:
Princeton University Press, 1979), pp. 31–35.

4 *Moral Principles and Political Obligations*, pp. 194–195. Simmons takes the
term from R. P. Wolff.

5 On the account I have just provided, then, there is a close connection between the legitimacy of political authority and the existence of sufficient reason to obey the law. This reason is not, however, provided by a substantive moral consideration. So legitimate authority is not grounded in political obligation.

6 I thus agree with Hume that legitimate authority (in his terms, "allegiance") and promising are equally fundamental, and in particular that we need not suppose that legitimate authority is grounded in a promise: "I maintain that though the duty of allegiance be at first grafted on the obligation of promises and be for some time supported by that obligation, yet it quickly takes root of itself and has an original obligation and authority, independent of all contracts." (*A Treatise of Human Nature* [Clarendon Press, 1978], p. 542).

In *Authority and Democracy* I present an argument that the authority of the mangers of corporations should be understood as grounded in their cooperation facilitating role, rather than in a promise to comply with managerial directives in return for pay. This argument views promising in the traditional way, as a device for creating moral obligations. I believe that the argument can be reformulated in terms of the account of promising I have defended here (according to which it is a way of solving the assurance problem confronting cooperatively disposed people when they must form new groups), but I shall not attempt to present the details.

7 It must be acknowledged that a judgment about the injustice of the state of nature will be difficult to make because it is unclear exactly what the social situation would be if all political cooperation collapsed. But what we are attempting to determine is how the existence, or nonexistence, of a requirement to obey unjust laws is to be understood. The corresponding epistemic problem is a separate matter.

8 Such efforts might sometimes include civil disobedience. This means disobeying particular laws, but in a way that involves accepting the legal order as a whole (by making no effort to evade the legal consequences of disobedience).

9 As I have mentioned in earlier chapters, in directing one to compare the outcome of a particular scheme with the best that could be achieved in the noncooperative outcome, the PCR allows one to consider what one could accomplish by joining a different cooperative scheme. The point in the text is that if the members of a group of people who care about justice are displaying piecemeal compliance with the law, they will probably find it appropriate to institute holistic compliance if they have the option.

10 A recent example is David Copp's "The Idea of a Legitimate State," *Philosophy and Public Affairs* 28 (Winter 1999) pp. 3–45. Copp argues, against philosophical anarchists, that states can possess a right to compliance with "morally innocent laws." This implies that they have no right to compliance with morally pernicious laws.

11 Leslie Green, *The Authority of the State* (Oxford: Clarendon Press, 1998), p. 243.

12 *An Essay on the Modern State*, p. 216. Morris cites Green and Simmons.

13 I am assuming that those who do not regard the government as exercising

legitimate authority would constitute a minority, and thus would not be able to block the use of coercion against them by voting it down.

14 Strictly speaking, this claim is too strong. We need to bear in mind the points about holistic compliance in the previous section. The voluntary cooperators will be people who believe that the legal order as a whole – including those parts that provide for the enforcement of the law generally – is preferable to the situation that would obtain in its absence.

In "Justification and Legitimacy" (*Ethics* 109 [1999], pp. 739–771), John Simmons argues that we must distinguish the moral virtues of a state – which might justify supporting it in various ways – from the obligation to participate in it. This distinction resembles in some respects the distinction I have drawn between legitimate government and legitimate authority. There are important differences, however. Simmons grounds legitimate authority in explicit consent, while I ground it in the PCR. And for him, justified states are those that might deserve our support, while as I characterize legitimate government, the issue is whether the people in control of the coercive apparatus of the state take themselves to be justified in coercing compliance with the law. The most important difference, however, is that Simmons regards his distinction as marking two dimensions of the moral evaluation of states (from our standpoint as moral theorists). By contrast, I am concerned with what agents who accept the PCR have sufficient reason to do, given the particular values they hold.

For a defense of the use of coercion by a democracy, see Jane Mansbridge, "Using Power/Fighting Power: The Polity" (in S. Benhabib ed., *Democracy and Difference* [Princeton, NJ: Princeton University Press, 1996], pp. 46–66). Mansbridge argues, however, that democratic societies should be aware of the residue of injustice inevitably left by coercion and encourage political structures that keep this residue before the public mind.

15 "The search for legitimacy can be thought of as an attempt to realize some of the values of voluntary participation, in a system of institutions that is unavoidably compulsory. . . . To show that they all have sufficient reason to accept it is as close as we can come to making this involuntary condition voluntary." Thomas Nagel, *Equality and Partiality* (Oxford: Oxford University Press, 1991), p. 36.

16 John Rawls, *Political Liberalism* (New York: Columbia University Press, 1993), p. 137.

17 See Rawls, *Political Liberalism*, p. 36

18 The claim that unreasonableness is a rational defect in a pluralistic society can be questioned. As will be discussed more fully in Chapter 4, there are two senses of reasonableness: competent operation with relevant reasons, and a kind of fairness. Failure to be reasonable in the first sense clearly involves a rational defect, but it is reasonableness is the second sense that underlies Rawlsian public reason. And especially when "unreasonableness" arises from regarding other moral values as outweighing fairness, there is room for doubt whether it constitutes a rational defect.

19 A more restrained account of public reason is offered by Gerald Gaus in his *Justificatory Liberalism* (Oxford: Oxford University Press, 1996). Gaus understands public reason in terms of the idea, mentioned earlier, that

people can be coerced into doing what they are implicitly committed to by the values they actually hold. Public values are those that everyone in the society actually holds. When certain further conditions are satisfied, those in control of the coercive apparatus of the state may employ coercion to secure compliance with laws that in fact have the support of these values, even if the people coerced cannot be brought to accept that this is so. Like Rawls, Gaus employs the notion of reasonableness in this connection. It is a condition of the legitimacy of government that those in control of the coercive apparatus of the state make reasonable decisions in light of the common public values. But what is at issue here is simply competent application of these values, not the introduction of a further positive value, akin to fairness, to be employed in reconciling competing claims grounded in other moral values.

20 Rawls, *A Theory of Justice*, p. 282.

21 See *Political Liberalism*, pp. 133–158. Rawls says that "the values of the political are very great values and hence not easily overridden" (p. 139) and that "political values normally outweigh whatever values oppose them, at least under the reasonably favorable conditions that make a constitutional democracy possible" (p. 155). He makes the same point in terms of public values at p. 218.

22 Here I am speaking of the injustice associated with noncompliance with the law as such. Of course, some laws direct us to avoid actions that are unjust in themselves, and the violation of these laws may bring serious injustice into the world.

23 In *Political Liberalism* (pp. 141–142), Rawls seems to introduce a consideration that goes beyond the great weight of public values. He says that stability is secured in part by the fact that people growing up in a just society develop an effective sense of justice. But if this means that they come to acknowledge a duty of justice (independent of public values) to comply with the law, the argument of Chapter 1 is again applicable. Substantive moral values cannot reliably justify contribution to cooperative schemes when the parties have moral reasons for defecting. We need something like the PCR.

24 For a discussion of these points, see Allen Buchanan, *Secession: The Morality of Political Divorce from Fort Sumter to Lithuania and Quebec* (Boulder, CO: Westview, 1991), esp. chaps. 2 and 3. Buchanan offers a moral theory of secession, which attempts to establish the basis on which it can (actually) be morally justified. As I have repeatedly indicated, however, the approach I am taking is concerned with what people who hold different moral values can regard themselves as having sufficient reason, under the PCR, to do.

25 Buchanan suggests that Lincoln may have regarded preserving the union has having moral importance because the fate of democracy in the world depended on the success of the American experiment. See *Secession*, p. 97.

CHAPTER 4. DEMOCRACY

1 For discussion of this point, see Brian Barry, "Is Democracy Special?" in P. Laslett and J. Fishkin, eds., *Philosophy, Politics, and Society*, 5th series (New Haven: Yale University Press, 1979), esp. pp. 176–177. Barry considers the case in which the probability that each is in the majority on a particular vote is proportional to the size of the majority on that vote. For example, if a 60 percent majority is obtained, each has a .6 probability of being in the majority.

2 I explore this point in *Authority and Democracy*, pp. 137–141. See also David Estlund, "Beyond Fairness and Deliberation: The Epistemic Dimension of Democratic Authority," in James Bohman and William Rehg, eds., *Deliberative Democracy: Essays on Reason and Politics* (Cambridge, MA: MIT Press, 1997), pp. 173–204

3 See John Rawls, *A Theory of Justice* (Cambridge, MA: Harvard University Press, 1971), pp. 83–90.

4 Joshua Cohen, "Deliberation and Democratic Legitimacy," in A. Hamlin and P. Pettit, eds., *The Good Polity* (Oxford: Blackwell, 1989), p. 17.

5 Ibid., p. 22.

6 Ibid., p. 23.

7 For a discussion of democracy as a method of political decision making that affords each equal opportunity for political influence, see, Jack Knight and James Johnson, "What Sort of Democracy Does Deliberative Democracy Require?" in Bohman and Rehg, *Deliberative Democracy*, pp. 279–319, and James Bohman, "Deliberative Democracy and Effective Social Freedom: Capabilities, Resources, and Opportunities," in Bohman and Rehg, pp. 321–348.

8 Equal opportunity for political influence through the presentation of arguments in the public forum is thus precisely analogous to the paradigm cases of equal opportunity. In these, there is something to be distributed – desirable jobs, say – and we determine which of the applicants will be successful by means of a fair competition on the basis of what are taken to be relevant criteria. It is the fairness of the competition that establishes equality of *opportunity*. When there is equal opportunity for political influence, each competes for influence by presenting arguments. Those who actually "receive" influence are those who win the competition by convincing a majority. Here again, opportunity is equal if the competition is fair. Ensuring equal access to education, information, and the means of communication contributes to the fairness of this competition. But it remains the case that some arguments will lose.

9 Rawls, *Political Liberalism*, p. 217.

10 I take this second way of formulating the constraint underlying public reasoning from Joshua Cohen, "Procedure and Substance in Deliberative Democracy," in Seyla Benhabib, ed., *Democracy and Difference* (Princeton, NJ: Princeton University Press, 1996), p. 100.

11 This appears to be Rawls's view. See *Political Liberalism*, pp. 227–230.

12 See Ibid., pp. 231–40.

13 Amy Gutmann and Dennis Thompson, *Democracy and Disagreement* (Cambridge, MA: Harvard University Press, 1996), pp. 84–85.

14 Gutmann and Thompson's point about economizing on moral disagreement seems to be that there may be several equally satisfactory rationales for what one favors, but some are more accommodating to opposing positions than others, in the sense that these positions become less objectionable. Choosing the most accommodating rationale promotes mutual respect, and also reduces the distance that must be bridged to reach agreement. It is important to note, however, that choosing the more accommodating rationale is not a matter of proceeding deliberatively, in the sense of tracing the implications of the reasons underlying one's convictions, but rather of making adjustments to one's position for the sake of reaching agreement. Gutmann and Thompson's point is that sometimes one can make such adjustments without compromising one's convictions. But if the members of a group cannot get all the way to agreement in this way, achieving the benefits of cooperation will ultimately require concessions that involve compromising personal convictions. The problem then becomes identifying a morally appropriate pattern of concessions – for example, a fair pattern – and deliberation will focus on this question.

15 *Democracy and Disagreement*, pp. 52–53. In "Reconciliation through the Public Use of Reason: Remarks on John Rawls's Political Liberalism" (*Journal of Philosophy* 92 [1995]), Jürgen Habermas makes a distinction between two senses of reasonableness that is similar to the one I have drawn.

16 Rawls, *Political Liberalism*, p. 49. As we saw in Chapters 1 and 3, the values of fairness or justice are not able by themselves to justify routine participation in a cooperative scheme, even given assurances that others will do likewise, when individuals have moral reasons for defecting. These values must be supplemented with the PCR. But people who are cooperatively disposed, in the sense captured by the PCR, can be termed reasonable. This constitutes a third sense of reasonableness.

17 See Rawls, *Political Liberalism*, p. 164.

18 See, for example, Thomas Christiano, *The Rule of the Many* (Boulder, CO: Westview Press, 1996), p. 72–93.

19 It might be thought that the Rawlsian device of an overlapping consensus (see *Political Liberalism*, Lecture IV) enables citizens to avoid the demotion of their comprehensive doctrines, at least, to interests. But this is not so. The device of an overlapping consensus is intended to secure the stability of a liberal society. Stability is threatened by the fact that the different comprehensive moral doctrines held by the members can provide reasons to behave uncooperatively. An overlapping consensus of reasonable comprehensive doctrines obtains when each such doctrine can endorse, from its own standpoint, the political conception of justice that guides the common life of the society. As we have seen, if we add the PCR to this picture, we can block the threat to stability posed by morally motivated defection. But it does not appear that an overlapping consensus can prevent the demotion of moral concerns to interests that takes place when the value of fairness (or reasonableness-as-fairness) is invoked to justify a decision procedure. Rawls repeatedly emphasizes that in a well-ordered

liberal society, conflicts between the political conception of justice and reasonable comprehensive doctrines are reduced. (See, for example, *Political Liberalism*, p. 157.) But he seems to have in mind the fact that citizens will be free to live their personal lives in accordance with their doctrines. When it comes to making political decisions involving the choice of policies (cooperative schemes), conflicts between the political conception (employed to justify a decision procedure) and the comprehensive doctrines will still be a possibility.

20 See, for example, Jon Elster, "Introduction" (p. 1), and Adam Przeworski, "Deliberation and Ideological Domination" (p. 140), both in Jon Elster, ed., *Deliberative Democracy* (Cambridge: Cambridge University Press, 1998).

21 I discuss the distinction between subordinating and expert authority in *Authority and Democracy*, chaps. 2 and 4.

22 David Estlund, "Making Truth Safe for Democracy," in D. Copp, J. Hampton, and J. Roemer, eds., *The Idea of Democracy* (Cambridge: Cambridge University Press, 1993). See also my discussion of expert authority in *Authority and Democracy*.

23 For an accessible explanation of how the jury theorem works, see David Estlund, "Beyond Fairness and Deliberation: The Epistemic Dimension of Democratic Authority," in Bohman and Rehg, *Deliberative Democracy*, pp. 173–204, note 21.

24 This picture, according to which the legitimacy of voting, as a way of exercising subordinating authority, is established on a nonepistemic basis, but deliberation provides additional epistemic benefits, is one way of interpreting the "epistemic proceduralism" defended by David Estlund. See his "Beyond Fairness and Deliberation," in Bohman and Rehg. S. L. Hurley also defends democracy on epistemic grounds in *Natural Reasons* (Oxford: Oxford University Press, 1989). Her claim is that democracy fosters a division of epistemic labor that makes it likely that views that can be debunked (as formed in a way that does not track the truth) will be rejected. But she regards the case for a democratic division of epistemic labor, in which *all* participate, as based partly on the value of autonomy. And in one place (p. 354) she writes as if she believes that to introduce autonomy, as an independent value, is to introduce fairness. So the proposal we are investigating (the third alternative) may not be seriously at variance with hers either.

25 In "Toward a Deliberative Model of Democratic Legitimacy," (in S. Benhabib, ed., *Democracy and Difference* [Princeton, NJ: Princeton University Press, 1996], pp. 67–94), Seyla Benhabib argues that the deliberative model provides a way of elucidating (in the sense of vindicating) various democratic practices, including majority rule. With respect to majority rule, she says, "if a large number of people see certain matters a certain way as a result of following rational procedures of deliberation and decision making, then such a conclusion has a presumptive claim to being rational until shown to be otherwise" (p. 72). By "rational" she appears to mean "the most rational of the alternatives" – that is, the presumptively right answer. One point to be made in reply is that the minority will often

constitute a large number of people as well. So the claim must be strengthened to assert that there is a presumption that the *larger* group is right (even though it may be only slightly larger). In cases of this sort – the norm in most democratic polities – a more plausible interpretation would be that if all have deliberated in good faith, the issue is one about which reasonable people can disagree. But even if we waive this difficulty, the majority view cannot acquire, in the way Benhabib proposes, a status that makes it appropriate for those in the minority to defer to it. She stresses the presumptive character of the result, emphasizing that further deliberation may enable the minority to overturn it. But a stronger point is actually in order. For those in the minority, the majority view has *already* been shown not to be rational (been shown to be contrary to reason). The very same process of deliberation that convinced the majority of its view has convinced the minority that this view is wrong. So the method of majority rule cannot be legitimated in the way Benhabib suggests – at least if legitimation involves justifying compliance with the majority position to those in the minority.

26 There is a connection between this point and Hurley's view, mentioned in note 24. She observes that shared deliberation can have epistemic virtues, even when we remain unsure of what the truth is, by virtue of its ability to debunk views, showing them to be the product of influences that would cause them to be held even if they were not true. A set of conflicting judgments about an issue facing a group may survive attempts to debunk them in this way, in which case we could have greater confidence that they represented reasonable disagreement.

27 Jürgen Habermas's theory – according to which (roughly) reason influences political decision making to the extent that political will formation through formal decision making by the government takes place against the background of deliberative opinion formation in an autonomous public sphere – is, I think, compatible with these observations. Presumably, the influence of reason manifests itself in an epistemic improvement. But the claim seems only to be that political will formation, which citizens must have *nonepistemic* reasons to accept, can be regarded as more in accord with reason when it takes place in such a context than not. And for those in the minority, "more in accord with reason" can only mean "less wrong than it would otherwise be." For Habermas's view, see, "Popular Sovereignty as Procedure," in *Between Facts and Norms*, W. Rehg, trans. (Cambridge, MA: MIT Press, 1996), pp. 463–490, and "Three Normative Models of Democracy," in S. Benhabib, ed., *Democracy and Difference*, pp. 21–30.

CHAPTER 5. COLLECTIVE REASONING

1 In *Change in View* (Cambridge, MA: MIT Press, 1986), Gilbert Harman describes reasoning as a psychological process that results in a change in belief or intention. Reasoning, as I have characterized it, can be regarded as satisfying this description. Coming to regard a judgment as justified involves an alteration of one's previous psychological state. I am focusing,

however, on a proper part of the general phenomenon of changes in view (in belief or intention) warranted by sound principles of revision – namely, the generation of judgments by the self-conscious identification of facts that count as reasons and the self-conscious assessment of their rational force. Collective reasoning involves doing this cooperatively. In *The Nature of Rationality* (Princeton, NJ: Princeton University Press, 1993), Robert Nozick suggests that the processes of thought by which we distill a question out of an inchoate situation, and locate promising lines of attack, go beyond reasoning understood as the marshaling of reasons (see pp. 163–172). These activities, too, can be carried out collectively, by the exchange of ideas (if not reasons), but for the issues I want to explore, it will suffice to focus on the collective marshaling of reasons in response to a definite question.

2 For a statement of this way of understanding justification, see Laurence Bonjour, *The Structure of Empirical Knowledge* (Cambridge, MA: Harvard University Press, 1985), pp. 7–8. In *Knowledge in a Social World* (Oxford: Clarendon Press, 1999), Alvin Goldman argues that the appropriate standard for epistemic assessment of social practices is their tendency to produce true beliefs. He says that this enables us to make useful distinctions. There may be cases where an epistemic practice produces a belief that an individual is not justified in holding because of other beliefs that he has. But if we evaluate practices on the basis of their tendency to produce true beliefs, we can regard the *practice* as epistemically unexceptionable, despite the fact that the belief is not justified. (Ibid., p. 156). Goldman, however, looks at practices from the outside, evaluating them as epistemic instruments. (He makes this explicit at p. 283.) On a given occasion, by contrast, those actually engaged in collective reasoning will have no basis for distinguishing between judgments that seem justified on the basis of all the evidence relevant to the question they are considering (including the evidence of their senses) and judgments that are true. So Goldman's observation that justification can diverge from truth does not appear to identify an epistemic shortcoming that a group engaged in collective reasoning can actually address. I shall have more to say about Goldman's project later in this chapter.

3 Here I am drawing on Crispin Wright's characterization of what he calls "cognitive command" in *Truth and Objectivity* (Cambridge, MA: Harvard University Press. 1992), esp, chap. 3. Wright speaks of an assertoric practice as displaying cognitive command when disagreement is attributed either to difference in "input" or to malfunction. By assuming that the parties disagree about the rational import of a given body of facts, I am assuming sameness of input, with the result that disagreement must be attributed to malfunction in capturing the rational import of these facts.

4 See Rawls, *Political Liberalism*, pp. 54–58.

5 For Rawls's view of pluralism, see Ibid., p. 36.

6 For discussion of this point, see Bernard Williams, "The Truth in Relativism," in his *Moral Luck* (Cambridge: Cambridge University Press, 1981), pp. 132–143, and S. L. Hurley, *Natural Reasons* (Oxford: Oxford University Press, 1989), chap. 3.

7   I take the term from Bernard Williams, "Internal and External Reasons," in his *Moral Luck* pp. 102–113.

8   "The world that we encounter in ordinary experience is one in which we are faced with choices between ends equally ultimate, and claims equally absolute, the realization of some of which must inevitably involve the sacrifice of others." (Isaiah Berlin, "Two Concepts of Liberty," in *Four Essays on Liberty* [New York: Oxford University Press, 1970], p. 168.) He also speaks of "the necessity of choosing between absolute claims" (p. 169). Berlin's view about the nature of these claims is not completely clear, however. He also says that pluralism involves surrendering the idea that our values have "eternal validity," or reside in an "objective heaven" (p. 172). This suggests that what counts as an ultimate end, making an absolute claim, is different in different historical circumstances. In Section V of this chapter, I explore the possibility that genuine normativity – going beyond mere desire – could change over time. If some such view is tenable, Berlin can be understood as pointing out that the values accessible to us *at any point in time* are too numerous to be integrated into the life of a single individual or community.

9   Philip Pettit has provided a useful characterization of judgment. He says that "there is an important contrast between [an agent's] coming to believe that q after intentionally checking the evidence and its coming unthinkingly to believe that q." In the former case, the agent makes a judgment. See *The Common Mind: An Essay on Psychology, Society, and Politics* (New York: Oxford University Press, 1993), p. 59.

10 That is, it has the standard feature of a public good, nonexclusivity, and also displays a further feature, not possessed by all public goods: nonrival consumption. In Chapter 1, public goods were defined in terms of nonexclusivity and indivisibility (which is a broader notion than nonrival consumption).

11 Two works addressing the case of individuals are Gilbert Harman, *Change in View* and Robert Nozick, *The Nature of Rationality*, pp. 75–93. Harman views practical reasoning as revising intentions, but here I take it to be a process that produces judgments regarding what the applicable reasons for action require.

12 See Goldman's discussion of argumentation in *Knowledge in a Social World* chap. 5. I have suggested that cognitive cooperation involves not just the pooling of arguments, but also the pooling of presumptive facts thought to be potentially relevant to the question being considered. This distinction corresponds roughly to Goldman's distinction between testimony and argumentation as epistemic practices. I do not, however, mean to restrict the pooling of presumptive facts to cases of testimony, which typically involves the reporting of firsthand observations. The pooling of facts that I have in mind is simply a matter of suggesting that something might be the case. Then collective reasoning – argumentation, in Goldman's scheme – is employed to determine whether there is any justification for accepting that it is the case, and to determine what it implies.

13 Collective judgment must, then, not be confused with the collective beliefs described by Margaret Gilbert in *On Social Facts* (London: Routledge,

1989), chap. 5. Collective belief, in Gilbert's sense, is really a form of collective action, the action of adopting a certain view as the view of the group. Gilbert is explicit that this need not be any member's personal view (pp. 298–299). Collective judgment must also be distinguished from an individual's accepting a belief (making a judgment) for – on behalf of – a group, as discussed by Harman in *Change in View*, pp. 50–52. Harman notes that there are special constraints governing such judgments. One must be able coherently to suppose that no other members of the group possess relevant facts that one has not considered. But a judgment of this sort would still be an individual judgment.

14 Of course, we must use reasons to provide such an account. There is no getting beyond the sphere of reasons. (Cf. T. M. Scanlon, *What We Owe to Each Other* [Cambridge, MA: Harvard University Press, 1998], chap. 1, and Thomas Nagel, *The Last Word* [New York, Oxford University Press, 1997].) But the question of what reasons are can be addressed by reason, and I believe it must be addressed if we are to determine whether a collective judgment can get a better grip on the force of a body of reasons.

15 This latter claim is made by Scanlon in *What We Owe to Each Other*, chap. 1, esp. pp. 37–55. It seems that it must be restricted to human desires, however. We can speak of the desires of animals without bringing in the notion of a reason. Presumably, those who wish to ground reason in desire mean to employ the same notion of desire that is employed in talking about animals. For a theory that seeks to explain all the features of moral normativity, including the criticism of desires, on the basis of desire and aversion, see Simon Blackburn, *Ruling Passions* (Oxford: Clarendon Press, 1998). For a theory that argues that there must be more to the normativity of reason than facts about motivation, see Jean Hampton, *The Authority of Reason* (Cambridge: Cambridge University Press, 1998).

16 "Wittgenstein's views about what it is to follow a rule apply . . . both to the understanding of reasons and to the understanding of the relationships among reasons." Hurley, *Natural Reasons*, p. 49.

17 For Kripke's view, see *Wittgenstein on Rules and Private Language* (Cambridge, MA: Harvard University Press, 1982). For McDowell's, see "Wittgenstein on Following a Rule." *Synthese* 58 (1984), pp. 325–363. The reference to "bedrock" is from Wittgenstein, *Philosophical Investigations*, G. Anscombe, trans. (New York, Macmillan, 1971), sect. 217.

18 We need not suppose that the practices grounding reasons involve explicit linguistic formulations of the associated rules. See Robert Brandom, *Making It Explicit: Reason, Representation, and Discursive Commitment* (Cambridge, MA: Harvard University Press, 1994), chap 1.

19 My argument has proceeded on the assumption that there are two basic ways of understanding the normativity associated with reasons. In *The Sources of Normativity* (Cambridge: Cambridge University Press, 1996), Christine Korsgaard distinguishes four hypotheses regarding the sources of normativity in the moral case, ultimately defending the view that moral normativity is grounded in a capacity to reflect on our particular actions, and on the motives underlying them. She says: "The reflective structure of consciousness gives us authority over ourselves. Reflection gives us a

kind of distance from our impulses that both forces us, and enables us, to make laws for ourselves, and it makes those laws normative" (pp. 128–129). I believe, however, that she is best regarded as defending a version of the practice-based view. Reflective endorsement must be on some basis, and if this is not provided by inherently normative entities (the realist alternative, which Korsgaard rejects), it must be provided by practices. Reflective endorsement would then involve the extrapolation of a preexisting reason-constituting practice (possibly associated with a practical identity) to the particular motives with which one finds oneself. It can be said to create normativity because on the practice-based view, there are no reasons without reasoners, no rules without rule-following decisions. But if there is to be a basis for endorsement, there must be an ongoing – and thus preexisting – practice. We create normativity, but we do not create it ex nihilo.

20 Michael Smith, *The Moral Problem* (Oxford: Blackwell, 1994), p. 176.

21 It should be noted that my argument has concerned the judgments that other people make about what is supported by the reasons relevant to some question. When others are simply reporting observations they have made in their capacity as normal human observers – the case of testimony – their reports may justify changing one's mind even if one does not have any independent reason to suppose that what they say is correct. Goldman discusses the question of whether one needs a substantive justification for accepting ordinary testimony in *Knowledge in a Social World*, pp. 126–130.

Writers seeking to provide a naturalistic account of normativity sometimes posit a basic desire to be in agreement with others, which leads the members of a group who initially agree to converge on a single view. Thus, Philip Pettit says, "whenever we form discrepant beliefs in response to apparently the same situation . . . we tend to look for a resolution of the divergence" (*The Common Mind*, p. 98). Similarly, in developing an expressivist account of rational appraisal in *Wise Choices, Apt Feelings* (Cambridge, MA: Harvard University Press, 1990), Allan Gibbard argues that a virtually inescapable stance toward oneself pressures one to regard the fact that someone else accepts something as a reason to accept it oneself (see chap. 9). So described, it appears that these mechanisms could lead an individual to exchange a view that he regarded as well supported by the evidence for one that he regarded as having little, if any, support. But in places, Gibbard, at least, speaks as if he might be sympathetic to the points about independence and reconsideration that I have been making. He grounds the fundamental authority of others in the fact that their influence can improve one's own judgment, and he seems to view the improvement as taking place, ultimately, through discussion – that is, through presentation of convincing reasons. Pettit's view will be discussed in Section V.

22 Another example would be cooperation between joint authors to produce a book. To produce a certain cooperative product, they must reason to agreement on what statements are justified by the evidence they are considering.

23 It does not seem that fairness would always play a role in cases of this

sort. When jurors disagree, for example, their giving considerations of fairness (within the group of jurors) a role in determining the verdict seems at least as questionable as compromising their convictions in the way that bargaining power dictates.

24 Ian Hacking, *The Social Construction of What?* (Cambridge, MA: Harvard University Press, 1999), p. 117.

25 For one view of the connection, see Robert Brandom's *Making It Explicit*. He grounds the content of concepts in social practices of reasoning (of offering and accepting reasons).

26 For a discussion of these problems, see Paul Boghossian, "The Rule-Following Considerations," *Mind* 98 (1989), pp. 507–549.

27 See Hurley, *Natural Reasons*, chap. 3.

28 Hurley also distinguishes an intermediate possibility, but it is different from the one I consider.

29 "The responsibility of essentially contested concepts to structured sets of conflicting criteria thus makes deliberation, argument, and criticism not only intelligible but inevitable." Hurley, *Natural Reasons*, p. 51.

30 McDowell speaks of "the resemblances between individuals on which, in this vision, the possibility of meaning seems to depend," and goes on to say that "a certain disorderliness below 'bedrock' would undermine the applicability of the notion of rule following" ("Wittgenstein on Following a Rule," pp. 348–349.

31 For a view of this sort that focuses on reasons for valuing, see Mark Johnston, "Dispositional Theories of Value," *Proceedings of the Aristotelian Society*, Suppl. Vol. 63 (1989), pp. 164–165.

32 In the essays in Parts I and II of *The Interpretation of Cultures* (New York: Basic Books, 1973), Clifford Geertz presents a view according to which humans have evolved to possess a culture. That is, the behavioral repertoire necessary for a successful life as a human being does not take the form of a set of genetically programmed instincts. Instead, we are genetically programmed to learn the particular repertoire of the culture into which we are born.

33 In discussing the inescapability of reason (normativity) in *The Last Word*, Thomas Nagel resists a characterization of it in terms of foundational propositions or rules of inference. He describes reason, rather, as "a framework of methods and forms of thought that reappear whenever we call any specific proposition into question" (pp. 68–69). This suggests that a kind of proper functioning may be involved.

The central notion in the account of normative judgment that Allan Gibbard offers in *Wise Choices, Apt Feelings* is "makes sense." He presents an expressivist (noncognitivist) interpretation of the use of this phrase. In some respects, my talk of the proper functioning of a being who has been socialized to certain practices of judgment provides the basis for a cognitivist reading of the notion of what it makes sense to do. Proper functioning is, however, in the first instance an attribute of persons, not actions. What it makes sense to do in a particular situation is whatever constitutes proper functioning (on the part of a person who has been socialized to certain practices).

34 Alvin Plantinga, *Warrant: The Current Debate* (New York: Oxford University Press, 1993), and *Warrant and Proper Function* (New York: Oxford University Press, 1993). Knowledge has a normative element. One aspect of this is provided by the fact that what is known must be true. Truth itself is a normative notion; true beliefs are epistemically good. Plantinga evidently feels that an acceptable account of knowledge must supplement the normativity of truth with normativity of a further sort, which must be something more than instrumental rationality. There is more to warrant than the reliable production of true beliefs.

35 See *Warrant and Proper Function,* chaps. 11 and 12.

36 See Johnston's "Dispositional Theories of Value," p. 155.

37 The idea that normativity can be understood in terms of proper functioning goes back to Aristotle. For a somewhat different attempt to find a biological home for genuine normativity, which also draws inspiration for Aristotle, see John McDowell's account of second nature and *Bildung,* in *Mind and World* (Cambridge, MA: Harvard University Press, 1994), esp. pp. 78–86.

38 Pettit, *The Common Mind,* pp. 76–108.

39 Boghossian discusses the possibility of defending a dispositional account of normativity by making use of the notion of optimal conditions for the exercise of a disposition in "The Rule-Following Considerations," pp. 537–540.

40 "Commonability is a property of rules.... [I]t requires them to be such that if there are others, and if they try to identify the rules [one] follows as rules they can follow themselves, then it is possible they will succeed: it is possible that they will knowledgeably identify the rules in that way." Pettit, *The Common Mind,* p. 181. There is a clear summary of the view on p. 115. For a related idea, see Hilary Putnam's discussion of what he calls the "universal intercommunicability of human cultures" in *Meaning and the Moral Sciences* (London: Routledge and Kegan Paul, 1978), p. 56.

41 In *The Common Mind,* Pettit argues that the capacity for thought depends noncausally (constitutively) on certain social relations. The hybrid view that I have proposed does not have this consequence, but it does imply that social relations are important for thinking *well.*

42 For an accessible account, see Charles Taylor, *Hegel* (Cambridge: Cambridge University Press, 1975). In turning Hegel on his head, Marx viewed normative ideas as epiphenomena, with the result that normative change has external causes but no internal rationale.

43 Richard Rorty has championed the view that the process through which our repertoire of concepts changes, or established concepts change their sense, is just a sequence of contingencies. Thus, he says, "Europe did not *decide* to accept the idiom of Romantic poetry, or of socialist politics, or of Galilean mechanics. That sort of shift was no more an act of will than it was a result of argument. Rather Europe gradually lost the habit of using certain words and gradually acquired the habit of using others." *Contingency, Irony, and Solidarity* (Cambridge: Cambridge University Press, 1989), p. 6. This statement is related to his view that there are no criteria, pro-

vided by the intrinsic nature of the world or the human self, by reference to which we can justify the transition from one vocabulary to another. But if the claims I make in the text are correct, some changes in our linguistic practices can be regarded as guided by reason, even in the absence of such criteria.

44 An example of an episode that can be understood in this way is the change in attitudes toward the natural world that has taken place in the West in the past 500 years. This has involved a transition from the traditional Christian idea that the natural world exists for the benefit of humans to the idea that it has a kind of intrinsic value. See Keith Thomas, *Man and the Natural World* (Oxford: Oxford University Press, 1983). We can explain this transition by saying that what seems to be an appropriate use of the concepts we employ in making value judgments about the natural world – or what seem to be the appropriate concepts – has changed as humans have gained greater control over the world, thus altering the circumstances in which they live.

45 The stability of a judgmental practice, too, can have an internal rationale. In *The Social Construction of What?*, chap. 3, Ian Hacking raises the question of whether the stability exhibited by the natural sciences is to be provided with an external explanation (the social power exercised in the scientific community by leading scientists) or an internal explanation (the fact that as new members join the scientific community, they are shown the reasons that support the conclusions that have been reached, and see that these reasons are decisive).

CHAPTER 6. OVERCOMING MALFUNCTION

1 Crispin Wright, *Truth and Objectivity* (Cambridge, MA: Harvard University Press, 1992), chap. 3.

2 On the view presented in Chapter 5, it is not possible to ground normativity in practices viewed simply as social facts. We need to combine practices with something inherently normative – I suggested the notion of proper functioning – that enables us to distinguish appropriate from inappropriate participation in them.

3 "The opinion which is fated to be ultimately agreed to by all who investigate, is what we mean by the truth, and the object represented in this opinion is the real." Charles S. Peirce, "How to Make Our Ideas Clear," in *Philosophical Writings of Peirce*, J. Buchler ed. (New York: Dover, 1955), p. 38. Constructivist views regard facts or truths of a certain kind as constituted by the evidence for them. On the usual interpretation of Peirce, he is offering a view of this kind.

4 I am assuming that each benefits from collective reasoning in the moral case by coming to form a better-justified judgment regarding what the relevant moral reasons are and what they support. There may be other benefits as well, however. In his discussion of freedom of speech in *On Liberty* (C. Shields, ed., [New York: Macmillan, 1956]), chap. 2, John Stuart Mill mentions several virtues of free speech, by which he seems to mean what I have called collective reasoning. He says, for example, that unless

a received opinion is contested, its "meaning" may be lost, so that it proves unable to influence conduct even if it is true.

5 For an account of the objective "phenomenology" of moral thinking, see David Brink, *Moral Realism and the Foundations of Ethics* (Cambridge: Cambridge University Press, 1989), pp. 23–31. See also Michael Smith, *The Moral Problem* (Oxford: Blackwell, 1994), Sects. 1.3 and 2.8.

6 See J. L. Mackie, *Ethics: Inventing Right and Wrong* (Harmondsworth, Eng.: Penguin, 1997), pp. 42–46

7 Philip Pettit has made a similar point about contractualist political theories that view the parties as reasoning their way to agreement. See *The Common Mind: An Essay on Psychology, Society, and Politics* (New York: Oxford University Press, 1993), pp. 297–302.

8 J. L. Mackie, *Ethics: Inventing Right and Wrong*, chap. 4.

9 For a general account of bias, see Robert Nozick, *The Nature of Rationality* (Princeton, NJ: Princeton University Press, 1993), pp. 100–106.

10 "Discourse Ethics: Notes on a Program of Philosophical Justification," in *Moral Consciousness and Communicative Action*, C. Lenhardt and S. W. Nicholsen, trans. (Cambridge, MA: MIT Press, 1990), p. 65 (Habermas's emphasis). In addition to (U), Habermas has formulated a principle that he says "contains the distinctive idea of an ethics of discourse":

> (D). Only those norms can claim to be valid that meet (or could meet) with the approval of all affected in their capacity as participants in a practical discourse. ("Discourse Ethics," p. 66)

(U) states a reason on the basis of which all must accept a principle or norm – namely, that it is in the interests of all – while (D) leaves this open. The points that I shall make about (U) apply to (D) as well.

11 See Jürgen Habermas, *Justification and Application*, Ciaran Cronin, trans. (Cambridge, MA: MIT Press, 1993), esp. pp. 36–38 and 128–130.

12 In "Reconciliation through the Public Use of Reason: Remarks on John Rawls's *Political Liberalism*" (*Journal of Philosophy* 92 [1995]), Habermas says, "Discourse ethics rests on the intuition that the application of the principle of universalization, properly understood, calls for a joint process of 'ideal role taking'" (p. 117). The interpretation I have just presented assumes that this ideal role taking is to be understood constitutively – that is, as constituting morally required impartiality. An epistemic construal, of the sort described in the previous section, is also a possibility, but this leads us in the direction of the remarks that follow.

13 "Remarks on Discourse Ethics," in *Justification and Application*, Ciaran P. Cronin, trans. (Cambridge, MA: MIT Press, 1993) p. 32 (Habermas's emphasis).

14 This way of reading Habermas is suggested by Jon Elster in "The Market and the Forum: Three Varieties of Political Theory," in J. Elster and A. Aanund, eds., *The Foundations of Social Choice Theory* (Cambridge: Cambridge University Press, 1986), pp. 103–132. Reprinted in James Bohman and William Rehg, eds. *Deliberative Democracy: Essays on Reason and Politics* (Cambridge, MA: MIT Press, 1997), pp. 3–33.

15 See Jürgen Habermas, *The Theory of Communicative Action*, Vol. 2, Thomas McCarthy, trans. (Boston: Beacon Press, 1987), p. 113–152.

16 As we saw in Section IV of Chapter 5, when the members of a group have an independent reason to reach agreement because they can then attain some further cooperative benefit, they may keep trying to convince each other of their respective views until a piecemeal consensus is attained.

17 An interpretation of Habermas that seems to proceed in this way has been provided by William Rehg. See his "Discourse and the Moral Point of View: Deriving a Dialogical Principle of Universalization," *Inquiry* 34, (1991), 27–48.

18 See the discussion of negotiation in Section V of Chapter 5.

19 In "Discourse and Morality" (*Ethics* 110 [April 2000], pp. 514–536), I make a further argument against interpreting Habermas's (U) as requiring a collective judgment. Let us say that a *maximal* collective judgment is a collective judgment that involves everyone capable of appreciating an answer to the question being considered. Habermas's discourse ethics, in speaking of the agreement of all affected by the acceptance of a moral principle, appears to posit maximal collective judgments concerning what would be in the interests of all. The thrust of the argument is that the Wittgensteinian considerations that are normally thought to show that rule following cannot be too atomic also tell against maximal collective judgments. In particular, we cannot say that an individual can attain rational conviction only by participating in a maximal collective judgment. The imposition of such a requirement actually creates a situation in which none of the participating individuals can be regarded as following a rule (and thus grasping a reason). It should be mentioned, however, that a weaker result suffices to establish the conclusion that there is no cognitive requirement to suspend judgment so long as anyone disagrees. This is that if a maximal collective judgment can genuinely grasp the force of a certain body of reasons, so can a judgment made by an independent individual. The hybrid view I presented in Chapter 5 works this way. Like the realist view of reasons, it has the consequence that maximal collective judgments can be fully in order, but so can judgments made by independent individuals.

20 "I shall speak of 'discourse' only when the meaning of the problematic validity claim conceptually forces participants to suppose that a rationally motivated agreement could in principle be achieved, whereby the phrase 'in principle' expresses the idealizing proviso: if only the argument could be conducted openly enough and continued long enough." Habermas, *The Theory of Communicative Action*, Vol. 1, Thomas McCarthy, trans. (Boston: Beacon Press, 1984), p. 42. See also Habermas's "Discourse Ethics," p. 105.

21 Habermas's theory could be interpreted as contractarian. But it is different enough from standard contractarian moral theories that I have given it separate treatment.

22 Margaret Urban Walker, *Moral Understandings: A Feminist Study in Ethics* (New York: Routledge, 1998). As we saw in Chapter 5, any such view

faces the question of whether the negotiation at issue is to be understood as a causal process or one that involves the marshaling of reasons. But although Walker occasionally nods in the direction of postmodernism, she seems to envisage a large supply of common reasons. Walker gives the concept of responsibility a central role; the negotiation she describes takes place within the framework of practices of responsibility. The hybrid view sketched in the previous chapter may be useful in explicating this idea. Practices of responsibility give our moral lives a particular content, but there is still the question of what constitutes appropriate participation in them. And the notion of proper functioning as a being that has been socialized in a certain way can provide an interpretation of this that allows us to say that someone who disagrees with others sharing the same socialization is nevertheless participating appropriately.

23 See Gauthier's *Morals by Agreement* (Oxford: Clarendon Press, 1986), esp. chap. 5.

24 I have in mind, in particular, the view Rawls developed in *A Theory of Justice* (Cambridge, MA: Harvard University Press, 1971)

25 T. M. Scanlon, "Contractualism and Utilitarianism," in Amartya Sen and Bernard Williams, eds., *Utilitarianism and Beyond* (Cambridge: Cambridge University Press, 1982), p, 110. See also *What We Owe to Each Other* (Cambridge, MA: Harvard University Press, 1998), p. 153.

26 For further discussion of this point, see Philip Pettit, "Two Construals of Scanlon's Contractualism," *Journal of Philosophy* (March 2000), pp. 148–164.

27 Scanlon, *What We Owe to Each Other*, pp. 168–71.

28 In *Equality and Partiality* (Oxford: Oxford University Press, 1991), Thomas Nagel uses the notion of reasonable rejection this way. In addition to reasons of egalitarian impartiality, Nagel posits agent-relative reasons deriving from sources of value that can compete with impartiality. The notion of the reasonable does the work of determining what can legitimately be asked of people who accept values of these kinds. Since Nagel thinks that arrangements can be reasonably rejected as demanding too great a sacrifice of what one values, especially relative to what others will be giving up, he presumably has something like reasonableness-as-fairness in mind. In some places, however, he seems to fall back on reasonableness-as-competence. Thus he says, "Reasonable persons may fail, however, to converge on a solution that is reasonable *tout court*, without finding one another unreasonable" (p. 172). The point here appears to be that people can fail to agree on what would be reasonable-as-fair without manifesting intellectual incompetence, or being regarded by one another as manifesting intellectual incompetence.

In *Justice as Impartiality* ([Oxford: Clarendon Press, 1995], chap. 7), Brian Barry presents an argument for liberal neutrality that invokes what he calls "the Scanlonian original position." But it is, I believe, marred by a confusion between the two senses of "reasonable" that I have distinguished. Barry posits a desire to reach agreement with others on a basis that no one could reasonably reject, and argues that no particular conception of the good could provide such a basis. This is because each person must acknowledge that his conception of the good could be reasonably rejected. But the sense of reasonable rejection involved here is the "competence" sense. Since disagreement about conceptions of the good does not involve cognitive malfunction, each can reject the others without displaying intellectual incompetence. This does not, however, by itself vindicate neutrality. As Barry acknowledges (p. 172), one can remain committed to policies favoring one's own view. The ground of liberal neutrality is, rather, the value of reasonableness-as-fairness. Making a particular conception of the good, not shared by all, the basis of a group's common life would be unfair.

29 Scanlon, *What We Owe to Each Other*, pp. 206–208.
30 Ibid., p. 162.
31 Ibid., p. 195.
32 Ibid., pp. 202–206
33 Ibid., p. 221.
34 Ibid., p. 157.

CHAPTER 7. REASONING TO AGREEMENT

1 Some implications of finite human capacities for what constitutes successful reasoning are discussed by Gilbert Harman in *Change in View* (Cambridge, MA: MIT Press, 1986).

2 In *Ruling Passions* (Oxford: Clarendon Press, 1998), which presents a sophisticated theory of this sort, Simon Blackburn seems to hold that the striving and avoidance associated with the formation of belief is also to be reduced to facts about motivation. See pp. 92–94. In *The Authority of Reason* (Cambridge: Cambridge University Press, 1998), chaps. 5 and 6, Jean Hampton argues that even instrumental reasoning presupposes "objective" reasons (over and above those justifying belief).

3 It is interesting that views that reduce value to desire, and thus provide for disagreement without cognitive malfunction, typically employ very simple, instrumental accounts of practical rationality, which afford less opportunity for error. By contrast, the theories of practical reasoning defended by those who hold that practical disagreement means malfunction are often quite complicated, so that it is easy to see how people might make mistakes and thus fall into disagreement.

4 I do not mean to suggest here an act of commitment. Such acts may sometimes occur, but normally agents will have reasons for making them – for example, that the resulting complex of values will be more coherent. The fact of pluralism arises, rather, from the fact that agents find themselves with certain values when they start to reason practically, and there are limits to the new ones they can rationally add.

5 See Bernard Williams, *Ethics and the Limits of Philosophy* (Cambridge, MA: Harvard University Press, 1985), p. 129, and chap. 8.

6 This need not involve recognizing a state of affairs characterizable in nonevaluative terms. It may be that our only route to the feature of the world associated with a particular evaluative concept is through that concept. This does not necessarily mean that one must accept that value oneself, in the sense of regarding it as providing one with a reason for

action, to know when judgments employing it will be appropriate. For discussion of these points, see John McDowell, "Non-Cognitivism and Rule Following," in S. Holtzman and S. Leich, eds., *Wittgenstein: To Follow a Rule* (London: Routledge, 1981), pp. 141–162.

7 Thomas Nagel, *The Possibility of Altruism* (Oxford: Clarendon Press, 1970). The view of reasons that Nagel presents there is not, however, practice based.

8 In Section IV of Chapter 5, I suggested that it might be possible, when disagreement is taken to indicate malfunction, to regard its existence as a reason to suppose that everyone is wrong, so that concessions seem more acceptable. But this alternative is not available when disagreement stems from the holding of different values by the parties.

9 The discussion by Shaun P. Hargreaves Heap and Yanis Varoufakis, *Game Theory: A Critical Introduction* (London: Routledge, 1995), chap. 4, was mentioned in Chapter 2, note 1. For a proposal by a philosopher, see David Gauthier, *Morals by Agreement* (Oxford: Clarendon Press, 1986), chap. 5.

10 The fact that it can be rational, in light of one's values, to acquiesce in the actual distribution of bargaining power can make it difficult to see the difference between reasoning and bargaining in a given case. What looks like reasoning to an agreement, because the parties officially accept that the force of the relevant reasons should determine the outcome, and consequently proceed by presenting arguments, may actually be bargaining to a compromise. Various pressures to reach agreement, especially the threat of losing the benefits of cooperation, may lead the parties to alter their positions in ways that they would not regard as justified if they were considering the issue in a disinterested way – for example, in a discussion group.

11 See Section II of Chapter 2 and Section III of Chapter 4.

12 This process must be distinguished from the mere combining of presumptive reasons into an all-things-considered judgment. We can imagine this being done by collective reasoning as well. Deliberation results in the construction of a pool of presumptive reasons, and then each makes an all-things-considered judgment regarding what they require. If everyone has the same appreciation of the force of the reasons, the result will be a piecemeal consensus. But this is a process that takes place within an evaluative point of view. All the values invoked are regarded by each member of the group as providing genuine reasons for action. And disagreement can be seen as arising from cognitive malfunction. In the process we are now considering, by contrast, the parties occupy different evaluative points of view and, thus, their initial disagreement does not involve malfunction. The idea is that collective reasoning may be able to integrate these different perspectives into a more complete picture of the value of the candidate cooperative schemes.

13 For one example of this way of thinking about perspectives, see Iris Marion Young, "Difference as a Resource for Democratic Communication," in James Bohman and William Rehg, eds., *Deliberative Democracy: Essays on Reason and Politics* (Cambridge, MA: MIT Press, 1997), pp. 383–

406, and "Communication and the Other: Beyond Deliberative Democracy," in Seyla Benhabib, ed., *Democracy and Difference* (Princeton, NJ: Princeton University Press, 1996), pp. 120–135. In the latter article, Young makes it clear that she sees the communication of socially situated knowledge as serving the goal of securing a just solution of collective action problems. So the argument I present in the text regarding the role of the value of fairness in postmodern theory applies to her view.

14 I leave aside the question of whether coming to understand a concept associated with a conceptual scheme different from one's own means incorporating it into one's own.

15 The idea can, perhaps, be traced to Friederich Nietzsche. See *Beyond Good and Evil* (Walter Kaufmann, trans., [New York: Vintage Books, 1989]), Sect. 22. It may be, however, that Nietzschean perspectivism is best understood as the sort considered earlier, where our interests determine our concepts, but judgments employing them are made true or false by a single world, common, at least, to all humans. An interpretation of this kind is defended by Brian Leiter in "Nietzsche's Respect for Natural Science" (*The Times Literary Supplement*, no. 4983 [October 2, 1998], pp. 30–31).

16 In *Contingency, Irony, and Solidarity* (Cambridge: Cambridge University Press, 1989), Richard Rorty says, in discussing the idea that there might be criteria by reference to which we can justify the transition from one vocabulary to another, "[t]he temptation to look for criteria is a species of the more general temptation to think of the world, or the human self, as possessing an intrinsic nature, an essence. That is, it is the result of the temptation to privilege some one among the many languages in which we habitually describe the world to ourselves" (p. 6). He then goes on to say that "[t]he difficulty . . . is to avoid hinting that . . . my sort of philosophy corresponds to the way things really are" (pp. 7–8). "To say that we should drop the idea of truth as out there waiting to be discovered is not to say that we have discovered that, out there, there is no truth" (p. 8). He recommends a strategy of evasion.

17 As was mentioned in note 8, when people who regard disagreement as attributable to malfunction must agree on a cooperative scheme, they may feel justified in compromising their convictions on the ground that disagreement shows that everyone is wrong. But in Chapter 5, where this point was initially made, I also said that proceeding in this way is not fully in order from the epistemic point of view. Opponents of postmodernism can be understood as people who are unwilling to sacrifice epistemic integrity when they regard disagreement as attributable to cognitive malfunction.

18 See Richardson's *Practical Reasoning About Final Ends* (Cambridge: Cambridge University Press, 1994), esp. Part 5.

19 Richardson says, "A 'norm' I think of simply as a principle – an item with propositional content – which has at least potential normative significance." (*Practical Reasoning about Final Ends*, p. 50.) This is the same interpretation I placed on Habermas's use of the word in Chapter 6.

20 Ibid., Sect. 38. This point was considered above, in Chapter 5.

21 Ibid., pp. 245–247.

22 "Since the holistic conception of practical reflection . . . allows that deliberation may work from the more specific to the more general and vice
versa, revising in either direction, it may accept an agreed starting point
at any level of generality." Richardson, *Practical Reasoning about Final Ends*,
p. 277.

23 Ibid., Sect. 44.

24 See John Rawls, *Political Liberalism* (New York: Columbia University Press,
1993), pp. 144–150.

25 Richardson, *Practical Reasoning*, chap. 13.

26 Ibid., p. 288.

27 This is Rorty's view. See note 43 to Chapter 5.

28 Charles Larmore, *Patterns of Moral Complexity* (Cambridge: Cambridge
University Press, 1987), chap. 1.

29 Ibid., p. 7.

30 Ibid., pp. 7–9.

31 See Rawls, *Political Liberalism*, Lecture IV.

32 It is sometimes suggested that democratic deliberation has intrinsic value.
From the standpoint of the present account, democratic deliberation is (1)
collective reasoning that is (2) undertaken to answer the question of which
cooperative scheme to adopt (where the ultimate decision may be made
by a vote). In the first aspect, it has the same intrinsic value as the
collective reasoning found in a discussion group. The members get to
exercise their intellectual muscles, they receive the satisfactions of a
shared activity, and by giving each other a respectful hearing, they may
realize some moral values. If the second aspect adds anything to this, it is
just that when deliberation concerns how the benefits and burdens of
some further cooperative enterprise are to be distributed, the moral reason for giving the others a respectful hearing is stronger, and thus the
moral value of the associated behavior greater.

33 This same problem arises in connection with the "retreat to common
ground" described by Larmore in *Patterns of Moral Complexity*, chap. 3. It
is not enough that the members of a group can find common ground. It
must also be the case that this common ground, together with the value
of respect for others that leads us to seek it, is regarded by each as having
a moral status sufficient to defeat the remaining moral reasons acknowledged by each party (which could support using bargaining power to
subvert what the common values require).

CHAPTER 8. THE RATIONALITY OF COLLECTIVE
REASONING

1 Here I am speaking only of the internal dynamic of discussion. External
features, such as the fact that a majority has been convinced by what has
already been said, and will regard any continuation of the discussion as
an imposition, may inhibit people from making contributions they regard
as apposite, with the result that the order in which people speak becomes
important. The claim that the order and termination point of discussion
affect the outcome is made by James Johnson in "Arguing for Deliberation:

Some Skeptical Considerations," in Jon Elster, ed., *Deliberative Democracy* (Cambridge: Cambridge University Press, 1998):, p. 176. Johnson credits David Austen-Smith for the point.

2 As was noted in Chapter 5, some rules that discussants should follow if they are to achieve the cognitive goal of true belief are described by Alvin Goldman in *Knowledge in a Social World* (Oxford: Clarendon Press, 1999), pp. 139–144. These rules are equally germane to the project of constructing a shared pool of reasons on the basis of which individuals can make justified judgments.

3 With the growth of the Internet, talk of a single large pool becomes less metaphorical.

4 A bit more should be said about how the case would look if the PCR provided the only reason for contributing. As was noted earlier, the PCR will not operate in conjunction with a common choice mechanism that assigns contributions. The situation is one in which each decides independently what to contribute. This does not mean, however, that everyone who benefits from the evolving pool is required by the PCR to make some sort of contribution. An action counts as a contribution only if it increases the benefit provided to all by the pool. So an individual who can think of nothing cogent to say and therefore contributes nothing is not failing to act as the PCR requires. The point has general applicability. The PCR establishes a condition under which those who can contribute to the production of a public good must do so. It does not require those who cannot contribute to take steps to deny themselves the benefit of the good. Still, in ordinary cases, there will often be a common choice mechanism assigning contributions, and it will assign each a contribution that he or she could make. The question whether it is permissible under the PCR to enjoy a public good without contributing will then take the form of the question whether the relation of the benefit received to the cost of one's assigned contribution is such that the PCR gives one sufficient reason to make this contribution.

5 We might think of this as her accepting at some level that the disagreement of others constitutes an interpersonal reason to reconsider, but feeling that she has already reconsidered enough, so that she responds by trying to make the reason to reconsider disappear.

6 For an account of invisible-hand processes, see Robert Nozick, *Anarchy, State, and Utopia* (New York: Basic Books, 1974), pp. 18–22.

7 For an interesting account of a cultural trait that has similar consequences, see Diego Gambetta, " 'Claro!': An Essay on Discursive Machismo," in Elster, ed., *Deliberative Democracy*, pp. 19–43.

8 Presumably the consensus sought will be, in particular, an integral consensus. A piecemeal consensus consists in agreement among people who regard it as legitimate to make up their own minds. In Chapter 5 we saw that there is no basis for supposing that the cognitive goal of better justified judgment would be more successfully attained by a collective judgment of the kind associated with integral consensus. But here we are assuming that the parties have reasons of some other sort for making up their minds collectively, yet want the resulting judgment to be as well

justified as possible. The goal of justified consensus might also be re-garded as a step good, so that the contributions create no value until they crystalize into a consensus. As was noted in Chapter 1, it is sometimes possible for cooperation to produce a step good to proceed on the basis of the PIR alone. But the case would still be very different from collective reasoning when the participants have personal cognitive goals.

9 The situation thus resembles a chicken game, as described in Chapter 1.

Works Cited

Anderson, Elizabeth. *Value in Ethics and Economics*. Cambridge, MA: Harvard University Press, 1993.

Baier, Kurt. *The Rational and the Moral Order*. Chicago: Open Court, 1995.

Barry, Brian. "Is Democracy Special?" In P. Laslett and J. Fishkin, eds., *Philosophy, Politics, and Society*, 5th series. New Haven: Yale University Press, 1979, pp. 155–196.

Justice as Impartiality. Oxford: Clarendon Press, 1995.

Benhabib, Seyla, "Toward a Deliberative Model of Democratic Legitimacy," in Seyla Benhabib, ed., *Democracy and Difference*. Princeton, NJ: Princeton University Press, 1996, pp. 67–94.

Benhabib, Seyla, ed. *Democracy and Difference*. Princeton, NJ:Princeton University Press, 1996.

Berlin, Isaiah. "Two Concepts of Liberty." In *Four Essays on Liberty*. New York: Oxford University Press, 1970.

Blackburn, Simon. *Ruling Passions*. Oxford: Clarendon Press, 1998.

Boghossian, Paul. "The Rule-Following Considerations." *Mind* 98 (1989), pp. 507–549.

Bohman, James. "Deliberative Democracy and Effective Social Freedom: Capabilities, Resources, and Opportunities." In James Bohman and William Rehg, eds., *Deliberative Democracy:Essays on Reason and Politics*. Cambridge, MA: MIT Press, 1997, pp. 321–348.

Bohman, James, and William Rehg, eds. *Deliberative Democracy: Essays on Reason and Politics*, Cambridge, MA: MIT Press, 1997.

Bonjour, Laurence. *The Structure of Empirical Knowledge*. Cambridge, MA: Harvard University Press, 1985.

Brandom, Robert. *Making It Explicit: Reason, Representation, and Discursive Commitment*. Cambridge, MA: Harvard University Press, 1994.

Bratman, Michael. *Intention, Plans, and Practical Reason*. Cambridge, MA: Harvard University Press, 1987.

"Shared Cooperative Activity." *Philosophical Review*, 101 (1992), pp. 327–341.

"Shared Intention." *Ethics*, 104 (1993), pp. 97–113.

Brink, David. *Moral Realism and the Foundations of Ethics*. Cambridge: Cambridge University Press, 1989.

Works Cited

Broome, John. *Weighing Goods.* Oxford: Blackwell, 1991.

Buchanan, Allen. *Secession: The Morality of Political Divorce from Fort Sumter to Lithuania and Quebec.* Boulder, CO: Westview, 1991.

Christiano, Thomas. *The Rule of the Many.* Boulder, CO: Westview Press, 1996.

Cohen, Joshua. "Deliberation and Democratic Legitimacy." In A. Hamlin and P. Pettit, eds., *The Good Polity.* Oxford: Blackwell, 1989, pp. 17–34.

"Procedure and Substance in Deliberative Democracy." In Seyla Benhabib, ed., *Democracy and Difference.* Princeton, NJ: Princeton University Press, 1996, pp. 95–119.

Copp, David. *Morality, Normativity and Society.* New York: Oxford University Press, 1995.

"The Idea of a Legitimate State." *Philosophy and Public Affairs* 28 (Winter 1999), pp. 3–45.

Cullity, Garrett. "Moral Free Riding." *Philosophy and Public Affairs* 24 (Winter, 1995), pp. 3–34.

Daniels, Norman. *Justice and Justification: Reflective Equilibrium in Theory and Practice.* Cambridge and New York: Cambridge University Press, 1996.

Elster, Jon. "The Market and the Forum: Three Varieties of Political Theory." In J. Elster and A. Aanund, eds., *The Foundations of Social Choice Theory.* Cambridge: Cambridge University Press, 1986, p. 103–132. Reprinted in James Bohman and William Rehg, eds., *Deliberative Democracy:Essays on Reason and Politics.* Cambridge, MA: MIT Press, 1997, pp. 3–33

The Cement of Society. Cambridge: Cambridge University Press, 1989.

"Introduction." In Jon Elster, ed., *Deliberative Democracy.* Cambridge: Cambridge University Press, 1998, pp. 1–18.

Elster, Jon, ed., *Deliberative Democracy.* Cambridge: Cambridge University Press, 1998.

Estlund, David. "Making Truth Safe for Democracy." In D. Copp, J. Hampton, and J. Roemer, eds., *The Idea of Democracy.* Cambridge: Cambridge University Press, 1993.

"Beyond Fairness and Deliberation: The Epistemic Dimension of Democratic Authority." In James Bohman and William Rehg, eds., *Deliberative Democracy:Essays on Reason and Politics.* Cambridge, MA: MIT Press, 1997, pp. 173–204.

Gambetta, Diego. " 'Claro!': An Essay on Discursive Machismo." In Jon Elster, ed., *Deliberative Democracy.* Cambridge: Cambridge University Press, 1998, pp. 19–43.

Gaus, Gerald. *Justificatory Liberalism.* Oxford: Oxford University Press, 1996.

Gauthier, David. *Morals by Agreement.* Oxford: Clarendon Press, 1986.

Geertz, Clifford. *The Interpretation of Cultures.* New York: Basic Books, 1973.

Gibbard, Allan. *Wise Choices, Apt Feelings.* Cambridge, MA: Harvard University Press, 1990.

Gilbert, Margaret. *On Social Facts.* London: Routledge, 1989.

"What Is It for *Us* to Intend?" In G. Holmstrom-Hintikka and R. Toumela, eds., *Contemporary Action Theory.* Dordrecht: Kluwer, 1997, pp. 65–85.

Goldman, Alvin. *Knowledge in a Social World.* Oxford: Clarendon Press, 1999.

Green, Leslie. *The Authority of the State.* Oxford: Clarendon Press, 1998.

Works Cited

Gutmann, Amy, and Dennis Thompson. *Democracy and Disagreement.* Cambridge, MA: Harvard University Press, 1996.

Habermas, Jürgen. *The Theory of Communicative Action.* Vols. 1 and 2, Thomas McCarthy, trans. Boston: Beacon Press, 1984 and 1987.

"Discourse Ethics: Notes on a Program of Philosophical Justification." In *Moral Consciousness and Communicative Action,* C. Lenhardt and S. W. Nicholsen, trans. Cambridge, MA: MIT Press, 1990, pp. 43–115.

"Remarks on Discourse Ethics," In *Justification and Application,* Ciaran P. Cronin, trans. Cambridge, MA:MIT Press, 1993, pp. 19–111.

Justification and Application, Ciaran P. Cronin, trans. Cambridge, MA: MIT Press, 1993.

"Reconciliation through the Public Use of Reason: Remarks on John Rawls's Political Liberalism." *Journal of Philosophy* 92 (1995), pp. 109–131.

"Popular Sovereignty as Procedure." In *Between Facts and Norms,* W. Rehg, trans. Cambridge, MA: MIT Press, 1996, pp. 463–490.

"Three Normative Models of Democracy." In Seyla Benhabib, ed., *Democracy and Difference.* Princeton, NJ: Princeton University Press, 1996, pp. 21–30.

Hacking, Ian. *The Social Construction of What?* Cambridge, MA: Harvard University Press, 1999.

Hampton, Jean. *Hobbes and the Social Contract Tradition.* Cambridge: Cambridge University Press, 1986.

"Free-Rider Problems in the Production of Public Goods." *Economics and Philosophy.* 3 (1987), pp. 245–273.

The Authority of Reason. Cambridge: Cambridge University Press, 1998.

Hardin, Russell, "Collective Action as an Agreeable n-Prisoner's Dilemma." *Behavioral Science.* 16 (1971), pp. 472–481.

Collective Action. Baltimore: Johns Hopkins University Press, 1982.

Hargreaves Heap, Shaun P., and Yanis Varoufakis. *Game Theory: A Critical Introduction.* London: Routledge, 1995.

Harman, Gilbert. *Change in View.* Cambridge, MA: MIT Press, 1986.

Hart, H. L. A. "Are There Any Natural Rights." *Philosophical Review.* 64 (1955), 175–191.

Hume, David. *A Treatise of Human Nature,* L. A. Selby-Bigge, ed. 2d ed. Oxford: Clarendon Press, 1978.

Hurley, S. L. *Natural Reasons.* Oxford: Oxford University Press, 1989.

Johnson, James. "Arguing for Deliberation: Some Skeptical Considerations." In Jon Elster, ed., *Deliberative Democracy.* Cambridge: Cambridge University Press, 1998, pp. 161–184.

Johnston, Mark. "Dispositional Theories of Value." *Proceedings of the Aristotelian Society,* Suppl. Vol. 63 (1989), pp. 139–174.

Knight, Jack, and James Johnson. "What Sort of Democracy Does Deliberative Democracy Require?" In James Bohman and William Rehg, eds., *Deliberative Democracy: Essays on Reason and Politics.* Cambridge, HA: MIT Press, 1997, pp. 279–319.

Korsgaard, Christine. "Kant's Formula of Universal Law." In *Creating the Kingdom of Ends.* Cambridge: Cambridge University Press, 1996, pp. 77–105.

The Sources of Normativity. Cambridge: Cambridge University Press, 1996.

Works Cited

Kripke, Saul. *Wittgenstein on Rules and Private Language*. Cambridge, MA: Harvard University Press, 1982.

Larmore, Charles. *Patterns of Moral Complexity*. Cambridge: Cambridge University Press, 1987.

Leiter, Brian. "Nietzsche's Respect for Natural Science." *The Times Literary Supplement*, no. 4983 (October 2, 1998), pp. 30–31.

Mackie, J. L. *Ethics: Inventing Right and Wrong*. Harmondsworth, Eng. Penguin, 1977.

Mansbridge, Jane. "Using Power/Fighting Power: The Polity." in Seyla Benhabib ed., *Democracy and Difference*. Princeton, NJ: Princeton University Press, 1996, pp. 46–66.

McDowell, John. "Non-Cognitivism and Rule Following." In S. Holtzman and S. Leich, eds., *Wittgenstein: To Follow a Rule*. London: Routledge, 1981, pp. 141–162.

"Wittgenstein on Following a Rule." *Synthese* 58 (1984), pp. 325–363.

Mind and World. Cambridge, MA: Harvard University Press, 1994.

McMahon, Christopher. "Promising and Coordination." *American Philosophical Quarterly* 26 (1989), 239–247.

Authority and Democracy:A General Theory of Government and Management. Princeton, NJ: Princeton University Press, 1994.

"Discourse and Morality." *Ethics* 110 (April 2000), pp. 514–536.

Mill, John Stuart. *On Liberty*, C. Shields, ed. New York: Macmillan, 1956.

Morris, Christopher. *An Essay on the Modern State*. Cambridge: Cambridge University Press, 1998.

Morrow, James D. *Game Theory for Political Scientists*. Princeton, NJ:Princeton University Press, 1994.

Nagel, Thomas. *The Possibility of Altruism*. Oxford: Clarendon Press, 1970.

Equality and Partiality. Oxford: Oxford University Press, 1991.

The Last Word. New York, Oxford University Press, 1997.

Nell, Onora [Onora O'Neill]. *Acting on Principle*. (New York: Columbia University Press, 1976)

Nietzsche, Friederich. *Beyond Good and Evil*, Walter Kaufmann, trans. New York: Vintage Books, 1989.

Nozick, Robert. *Anarchy, State, and Utopia*. New York: Basic Books, 1974.

The Nature of Rationality. Princeton, NJ: Princeton University Press, 1993.

Otsuka, Michael. "The Paradox of Group Beneficence." *Philosophy and Public Affairs* 20 (1991), pp. 132–149.

Parfit, Derek. *Reasons and Persons*. Oxford: Clarendon Press, 1986.

Peirce, Charles S. "How to Make Our Ideas Clear." In *Philosophical Writings of Peirce*, J. Buchler ed. New York: Dover, 1955, pp. 23–41.

Pettit, Philip. "Free Riding and Foul Dealing." *Journal of Philosophy* 83 (1986), pp. 361–379.

The Common Mind: An Essay on Psychology, Society, and Politics. New York: Oxford University Press, 1993.

"Two Construals of Scanlon's Contractualism." *Journal of Philosophy*. 97 (March 2000), pp. 148–164.

Plantinga, Alvin. *Warrant: The Current Debate*. New York: Oxford University Press, 1993.

Works Cited

Warrant and Proper Function. New York: Oxford University Press, 1993.

Przeworski, Adam. "Deliberation and Ideological Domination." In Jon Elster, ed., *Deliberative Democracy.* Cambridge: Cambridge University Press, 1998, pp. 140–160.

Putnam, Hilary. *Meaning and the Moral Sciences.* London: Routledge and Kegan Paul, 1978.

Rawls, John. *A Theory of Justice.* Cambridge, MA: Harvard University Press, 1971.

Political Liberalism. New York: Columbia University Press, 1993.

Raz, Joseph. "Reasons for Action, Decisions and Norms." In Joseph Raz, ed., *Practical Reasoning.* Oxford: Oxford University Press, 1978, pp. 128–143.

The Morality of Freedom. Oxford, Clarendon Press, 1986.

Rehg, William, "Discourse and the Moral Point of View: Deriving a Dialogical Principle of Universalization." *Inquiry.* 34 (1991), 27–48.

Richardson, Henry. "Specifying Norms as a Way to Resolve Concrete Ethical Problems. *Philosophy and Public Affairs* 19 (1990), 279–310.

Practical Reasoning about Final Ends. Cambridge: Cambridge University Press, 1994.

Rorty, Richard. *Contingency, Irony, and Solidarity.* Cambridge: Cambridge University Press, 1989.

Rousseau, Jean-Jacques. *Discourse on the Origin of Inequality.* In D. Cress, trans., *The Basic Writings Political Writings.* Indianapolis, IN: Hackett, 1987.

Scanlon, T. M., "Contractualism and Utilitarianism," In Amartya Sen and Bernard Williams, eds., *Utilitarianism and Beyond.* Cambridge: Cambridge University Press, 1982, pp. 103–128.

What We Owe to Each Other. Cambridge, MA: Harvard University Press, 1998.

Schmidtz, David. *The Limits of Government.* Boulder, CO: Westview Press, 1991.

Sen, Amartya, "Isolation, Assurance and the Social Rate of Discount." *Quarterly Journal of Economics.* 80 (1967), pp. 112–124.

"Rational Fools." In F. Hahn and M. Hollis, eds., *Philosophy and Economic Theory.* Oxford: Oxford University Press, 1979, pp. 87–109.

Simmons, A. John. *Moral Principles and Political Obligations.* Princeton, NJ: Princeton University Press, 1979.

"Justification and Legitimacy." *Ethics* 109 (1999), pp. 739–771.

Skinner, Quentin. *Liberty Before Liberalism.* Cambridge: Cambridge University Press, 1998.

Smith, Michael. *The Moral Problem.* Oxford: Blackwell, 1994.

Sugden, Robert. "Reciprocity: The Supply of Public Goods Through Voluntary Contributions." *Economic Journal* 94 (1984), pp. 772–787.

Taylor, Charles. *Hegel.* Cambridge: Cambridge University Press, 1975.

Taylor, Michael. *The Possibility of Cooperation.* Cambridge: Cambridge University Press, 1987.

Thomas, Keith. *Man and the Natural World.* Oxford: Oxford University Press, 1983.

Toumela, Raimo. "We Will Do It: An Analysis of Group-Intentions." *Philosophy and Phenomenological Research.* 51 (1991), pp. 249–77.

Works Cited

Velleman, J. David. "How to Share an Intention." *Philosophy and Phenomenological Research* 57 (1997), pp. 29–50.

Walker, Margaret Urban. *Moral Understandings: A Feminist Study in Ethics.* New York: Routledge, 1998.

Williams, Bernard. "Internal and External Reasons." In *Moral Luck,* Cambridge: Cambridge University Press, 1981, pp. 102–113.

"The Truth in Relativism." In *Moral Luck.* Cambridge: Cambridge University Press, 1981, pp. 132–43.

Moral Luck. Cambridge: Cambridge University Press, 1981.

Ethics and the Limits of Philosophy. Cambridge, MA:Harvard University Press, 1985.

Wittgenstein, Ludwig. *Philosophical Investigations,* G. Anscombe, trans. New York, Macmillan, 1971.

Wright, Crispin. *Truth and Objectivity.* Cambridge, MA: Harvard University Press. 1992.

Young, Iris Marion. "Communication and the Other: Beyond Deliberative Democracy." In Seyla Benhabib, ed., *Democracy and Difference.* Princeton, NJ: Princeton University Press, 1996, pp. 120–135.

"Difference as a Resource for Democratic Communication." In James Bohman and William Rehg, eds., *Deliberative Democracy: Essays on Reason and Politics.* Cambridge, MA:MIT Press, 1997, pp. 383–406.

Index

Index

collective, as resolving conflict, 136–139

conducted as if there is a right answer, 137

and conflicts of interest, 136

first order, 138

second order, 138

Morris, Christopher, 71, 215 n2

motivational content, 161

multiperson games, 12–13

Nagel, Thomas, 161, 217 n15, 227 n33, 232 n28

Nash equilibrium, 9

negotiation, 122, 127–129, 177–178, 179

as intranormative, 129

as mutual reconsideration, 129

not a two-stage process, 129

Nell, Onora, 209 n28

Nietzsche, Friederich, 235 n15

noncooperative outcome, 23, 45, 81

normativity, 159–160, 225 n19, 226 n21

as having a history, 129–131, 176

and practices, 114

realist view of, 113

norms, 53, 61, 214 n23

Nozick, Robert, 206 n15, 222 n1

objectivity, as interpersonality, 135

outcomes

causal production of, 32

constitutive promotion of, 32

overlapping consensus, 220 n19

Pareto optimality, 17, 205 n7

Parfit, Derek, 47

PCR, *see* Principle of Collective Rationality

Peirce, Charles S., 135–136

perspectives, evaluative, 165

Pettit, Philip, 127, 148–149, 226 n21, 228 n42, 230 n7

philosophical anarchism, 65

PIR, *see* Principle of Individual Rationality

Plantinga, Alvin, 126, 228 n34

pluralism

of Isaiah Berlin, 108, 160, 164

moral, 19

reasonable, 107–108

political cooperation

and enforcement of the law, 72

holistic versus piecemeal, 69–70

and moral disagreement, 70

and the PCR, 64

pooling, of reasons, 109

and the elimination of malfunction, 134

and the flow of discussion, 185

and interpersonal reasons, 110

postmodernism, 166, 168

and fairness, 169

rejection of, 170

Principle of Collective Rationality, 6, 7–8, 21–22

and assurance, 22

and authority, 52

and constrained maximization, 38

and contractarian political theory, 64

and contribution to unfair schemes, 26

as a form of reasonableness, 220 n16

as a formal moral principle, 28

and incommensurable values, 31–32

and individualism, 24

and Kant's Categorical Imperative, 209 n28

and noncooperative outcome, 23

and philosophical anarchism, 66

and the possibility of contributing, 237 n4

as preferable to principle of fairness, 25

as preserving evaluative commitments, 181

as a principle of rationality, 27–29

and promising, 59–61

and the reason to reason, 237 n4

and reciprocity, 28–29

249